The Armand Hammer Collection

Five Centuries of Masterpieces

Edited by John Walker

Director Emeritus, National
Gallery of Art, Washington, D.C.

Photography by Seth Joel

Harry N. Abrams, Inc.,
Publishers, New York

EDITORS: ELLYN CHILDS ALLISON, MARGARET DONOVAN
DESIGNER: ULRICH RUCHTI

Library of Congress Cataloging in Publication Data
Main entry under title:
The Armand Hammer collection.
Includes index.
1. Hammer, Armand, 1898-   —Art collections
—Catalogs. I. Walker, John, Dec. 24, 1906-
N5220.H26A73   750′.74′013   78-12867
ISBN 0-8109-1069-1
Library of Congress Catalogue Card Number: 78-12867

Colorplates printed in Japan
Text printed and bound in Korea
Portrait of Dr. Hammer (p. 10) by Joseph Wallace King

CONTENTS

LIST OF PLATES

1 Peter Paul Rubens, *Adoration of the Shepherds*
2 Peter Paul Rubens, *Venus Wounded by a Thorn*
3 Peter Paul Rubens, *Young Woman with Curly Hair*
4 Peter Paul Rubens, *The Israelites Gathering Manna in the Desert*
5 Rembrandt van Rijn, *Portrait of a Man of the Raman Family*
6 Rembrandt van Rijn, *Portrait of a Man Holding a Black Hat*
7 Rembrandt van Rijn, *Juno*
8 Jean-Honoré Fragonard, *The Education of the Virgin*
9 Francisco de Goya y Lucientes, *El Pelele*
10 Francisco de Goya y Lucientes, *Portrait of Doña Antonia Zárate*
11 Théodore Géricault, *Portrait of a Gentleman*
12 Jean Baptiste Camille Corot, *Medieval Ruins*
13 Jean Baptiste Camille Corot, *Harvester Under Trees*
14 Jean Baptiste Camille Corot, *Distant View of Mantes Cathedral*
15 Jean Baptiste Camille Corot, *Portrait of a Girl*
16 Jean Baptiste Camille Corot, *Morning*
17 Jean Baptiste Camille Corot, *Pleasures of Evening*
18 Honoré Daumier, *The Lawyers (The Bar)*
19 Eugène Boudin, *Sailing Ships in Port*
20 Eugène Boudin, *Quay at Camaret*
21 Eugène Boudin, *Beach at Trouville*
22 Gustave Caillebotte, *Square in Argenteuil*
23 Alfred Sisley, *Timber Yard at St.-Mammès*
24 Claude Monet, *View of Bordighera*
25 Camille Pissarro, *Boulevard Montmartre, Mardi Gras*
26 Pierre-Auguste Renoir, *Grape Pickers at Lunch*
27 Pierre-Auguste Renoir, *Antibes*
28 Pierre-Auguste Renoir, *Two Girls Reading*
29 Berthe Morisot, *Paule Gobillard — Niece of Berthe Morisot*

30 Paul Cézanne, *Boy Resting*
31 Henri Fantin-Latour, *Peonies in a Blue and White Vase*
32 Henri Fantin-Latour, *Portrait of Miss Edith Crowe*
33 Henri Fantin-Latour, *Roses*
34 Edgar Degas, *Three Dancers in Yellow Skirts*
35 Henri Marie Raymond de Toulouse-Lautrec, *In the Salon*
36 Gustave Moreau, *Salome*
37 Gustave Moreau, *King David*
38 Sir John Everett Millais, *Caller Herrin'*
39 Paul Gauguin, *Bonjour M. Gauguin*
40 Emile Bernard, *Wheat Harvest*
41 Vincent van Gogh, *Garden of the Rectory at Nuenen*
42 Vincent van Gogh, *Lilacs*
43 Vincent van Gogh, *The Sower*
44 Vincent van Gogh, *Hospital at St.-Rémy*
45 Pierre Bonnard, *Street Scene*
46 Pierre Bonnard, *Nude Against the Light*
47 Edouard Vuillard, *In the Bus*
48 Edouard Vuillard, *At the Seashore*
49 Edouard Vuillard, *Rue Lepic, Paris*
50 Edouard Vuillard, *Interior*
51 André Derain, *Still Life with Basket, Jug, and Fruit*
52 Amedeo Modigliani, *Woman of the People*
53 Chaim Soutine, *The Valet*
54 Georges Rouault, *Circus Girl*
55 Maurice de Vlaminck, *Summer Bouquet*
56 Marie Laurencin, *Women in the Forest*
57 Marc Chagall, *Blue Angel*
58 Gilbert Stuart, *Portrait of George Washington*
59 William Michael Harnett, *Still Life*
60 William Michael Harnett, *Cincinnati Enquirer*
61 John Singer Sargent, *Dr. Pozzi at Home*
62 John Singer Sargent, *Portrait of Mrs. Edward L. Davis and Her Son, Livingston Davis*

CONTRIBUTORS

J. Fred Cain, Jr., former Curator, National Gallery of Art, Washington, D.C.
Larry J. Curry, former Fellow, National Gallery of Art, Washington, D.C.
Kenneth Donahue, Director Emeritus, Los Angeles County Museum of Art
Marcia Early, former Fellow, National Gallery of Art, Washington, D.C.
Ebria Feinblatt, Senior Curator, Prints and Drawings, Los Angeles County Museum of Art
Charles Millard, Chief Curator, Hirshhorn Museum and Sculpture Garden, Washington, D.C.
Konrad Oberhuber, Curator of Drawings, Professor of Fine Arts, Fogg Art Museum, Harvard University
Seymour Slive, Director, Fogg Art Museum, Harvard University
John Walker, Director Emeritus, National Gallery of Art, Washington, D.C.
Christopher White, Director of the Paul Mellon Centre for Studies in British Art, London

ACKNOWLEDGMENTS

When Dr. Hammer asked me to catalogue his collection, I pointed out that he had published a series of excellent catalogues for the many exhibitions of his pictures held all over the world. Nevertheless, he said he wanted a new version that would include recently purchased paintings and drawings and bring the previous editions up to date. I thought at first that I would write new notes on all the pictures myself; but when I had studied carefully what had been written by Kenneth Donahue, Ebria Feinblatt, Charles Millard, Larry J. Curry, Lorenz Eitner, and J. Fred Cain, Jr., all specialists in the fields covered by the collection, it was evident to me that I could only rewrite and plagiarize what they had done so admirably. I decided to ask each scholar whether he wished to make any changes in his text, and to concentrate myself on those paintings and drawings for which the notes were incomplete or inadequate, and on the new acquisitions.

I also persuaded two other distinguished experts, Konrad Oberhuber and Christopher White, who had had a lesser role in the original Hammer catalogues, to make a much greater contribution, and I prevailed upon Seymour Slive to write the notes on the three superb Rembrandt paintings. For editorial assistance and also for a number of new notes, I turned to Marcia Early, a Fellow of the National Gallery of Art, Washington, D.C., from 1963 to 1965. Without her help I could never have completed the text in time to fulfill Dr. Hammer's wish to have the catalogue published with dispatch. I am grateful to Maria Vilaincour, who has checked the bibliography and brought it up to date. I have been the thankful recipient of a wealth of biographical material from Victor Hammer, who has been most generous with his time over the months it has taken to complete this book. All the people I have mentioned have important and demanding jobs, and I cannot adequately express my gratitude to them for the time they have taken to help me. I should like to add that the checking of all data in the text by Ellyn Childs Allison surpassed anything of this kind I have experienced in many years of writing.

London, where much of the work has been done, is a paradise for scholars doing research in the history of art. I must once more declare my appreciation of the London Library and the Victoria and Albert Museum, as I have in other books I have written. For anyone engaged in art-historical writing, these two institutions are uniquely helpful.

To Carter Brown I would like to express my gratitude for permission to reprint some material that originally appeared in a catalogue of the National Gallery of Art, Washington, D.C., of which he is the director.

To this I must add how much I benefited from the assistance I received from Dennis Gould, Director of The Armand Hammer Foundation, and Quinton Hallett, Assistant Director. My thanks also to Martha Wade Kaufman, Consultant and former Director of Art/Curator of the Foundation.

And lastly I wish to express my appreciation to Dr. Hammer for his painstaking editing of my Introduction. It has never been my good fortune to have the text of any of the books I have written so carefully scrutinized, nor have I ever received so many useful emendations. I am most grateful to him for his helpfulness throughout the preparation of this catalogue.

Without the help of those I have mentioned, the Hammer Collection catalogue would never have been prepared in time, and with unlimited time it would never have been prepared as well. It is a joint enterprise, the result of the collaboration of a number of outstanding scholars, to whom I shall always be grateful.

JOHN WALKER

Collecting art is a challenge — one I have pursued throughout my life, traveling the world over and learning that art has a universal way of speaking to each of us. A work of art requires no spokesman, for it visually communicates the quality and meaning of life, taking us beyond our everyday selves and providing us with a chance to share a unique bond of wonder and delight.

What you see in this catalogue is my attempt to assemble some of the visions of man's realities, delights, and dreams. I feel a deep commitment to share with others the vision, excitement, and joy that these works of art have given me.

Armand Hammer

ARMAND HAMMER: COLLECTOR AND ENTREPRENEUR

I have spent my life with collectors—Wideners, Mellons, Dales, Kresses, Calouste Gulbenkian, and others — and among these the most astounding I have come to know is Dr. Armand Hammer, a medical doctor who never practiced medicine, yet who has become probably the richest doctor in the world. Part of my astonishment derives from the fact that what he has said on the preceding page is literally true. Every work of art in this catalogue almost from the moment of its acquisition has been on public view. Unlike other collectors, he has acquired nothing for his private enjoyment. When he dies, his major paintings, those here catalogued, will go to the Los Angeles County Museum of Art, his drawings to the National Gallery of Art. None of them has he hung in his several houses. In his home in Los Angeles, apart from some secondary Impressionist and modern pictures, the best painting is a copy by his wife of a Modigliani portrait he has given to the Los Angeles County Museum.

This does not mean, however, that he has not enjoyed his pictures, as much perhaps in the pursuit as in the possession. Collecting, he once told me, is fun. "It's a hunt," he said. "I get a certain joy out of finding rare works, out of learning the stories connected with them. I've always liked to collect. I used to collect stamps. My father had a great stamp collection. But pictures are something more than just collecting. You are connecting yourself with something that really is immortal, something that has survived all these centuries. When you form a collection with the purpose of donating it ultimately to a public institution, you are preserving something for posterity."

To be a great collector of old masters in these days requires an immense amount of money. Armand Hammer's career shows half-a-dozen ways to gather a fortune and just as many ways to disperse one's riches. For giving away money has been an avocation to which he has devoted the same zeal he has shown in his many vocations: his pharmaceutical company, his Russian import-and-export business, his manufactory of pencils, his art trading, his cattle breeding, and his final achievement, the creation of one of the world's largest multinational companies, Occidental Petroleum Corporation. His art collection not only was made possible by the success of these enterprises but was in a way the product of several of them. Thus, the extraordinary and unexpected events of his life throw light on his becoming a collector. To understand how and why the paintings and drawings in this catalogue

came to be assembled one must know something of Armand Hammer's affairs.

Few rich men are the sons of socialists; socialists are more apt to be the sons of rich men. Armand Hammer's father, also a doctor, joined the Socialist Labor Party at an early age. He was descended from a wealthy Jewish family who had made their money in Russia building warships for Nicholas I (1796 – 1855). In the days of Armand's grandfather Jacob, the Hammer fortune, invested in salt, was washed away one night by unprecedented high water in the Caspian Sea. Jacob Hammer, his wealth liquidated, migrated to America with his one-year-old son, Julius. After a year of disillusionment, Jacob moved to Paris, where he engaged in several businesses, including, prophetically, an art business. When these proved unsuccessful, Jacob brought his family back to America and settled in Connecticut. Julius began life in a foundry doing such strenuous manual work that in the end he could bend a railroad spike with his bare hands. But while his muscles developed, his bank account atrophied. He was determined to escape long hours of grueling work for wages that kept him close to poverty. Urged on by this ambitious youngster, Armand's grandfather moved his family again, this time to New York City.

To help his family survive, Julius needed an immediate job. He came across an advertisement for a drug clerk in an Italian neighborhood on the Bowery. He applied at once, only to find that an ability to speak Italian was required, for the druggist himself did not speak the language after living for twenty years in the same Italian community. Julius assured the druggist that he would master the language in two weeks or ask for no pay. The Hammers, like so many Russians, have a remarkable gift for languages, and in a fortnight Julius knew enough Italian to handle his customers. His delighted employer accepted him as an apprentice, and the rise of the Hammer family from near destitution to immense wealth had begun.

Julius became a registered pharmacist, bought out his employer, and opened two more drugstores. He was amazed at the high prices charged for standard remedies. Realizing that there was an opportunity for cut-rate drugs, he bought an empty loft and set up his own pharmaceutical company. He was then in his early twenties.

With prosperity came a desire to marry. He chose a young Russian widow, Rose Robinson, whom he had met at a Socialist picnic. In 1898 their first child, Armand, was born. Four months later, Julius was admitted to the Columbia College of Physicians and Surgeons. His physical strength, built up hammering in the foundry, must have stood him in good stead, for while studying medicine he had at the same time to run his pharmaceutical company, his chain of drugstores, and to provide for a growing family. When he graduated, although he was doing well as a druggist, his socialistic ideals were more in accord with the practice of medicine than the making of money. He sold his business and became a much-loved doctor in the Bronx, an altruist who would often treat a poor patient and leave behind enough money to buy the medicine he had prescribed. He is said to have delivered more than five thousand babies before his death in 1948 at seventy-four.

Armand was determined from an early age to follow in his father's footsteps. In 1917, when he was nineteen, having completed a two-year premedical course, he enrolled at Columbia, in the same school of medicine that years before had trained his father. Then came a sudden devastating stroke of adversity. Two generations earlier, the Hammer fortune had been dissolved by a Caspian tidal wave; now Dr. Julius told his son that they were facing a second disastrous liquidation. He had invested all his savings in a pharmaceutical company. Due to mismanagement, the company was facing bankruptcy. Realizing his partner's incapacity, Dr. Julius had no choice but to buy him out. Worse news was to follow. Dr. Julius had had a heart attack and for a time was unable to practice medicine. Unless Armand could make the drug company pay, the Hammers were once more facing indigence.

It was obvious to Armand that he must try to salvage something from the family business. He decided he would do what his father had done — work in the daytime and study at night. By the time he had graduated from medical school, the pharmaceutical company had grown so successfully under his management that at twenty-three he was a millionaire. Combining socialistic altruism with a keen sense of the value of money, he then sold his business to his employees for two million dollars. At last able to concentrate on medicine, he accepted an appointment as an intern in the Bellevue Hospital. He had received the highest recommendation of the faculty of the College of Physicians and Surgeons at Columbia, who judged him the most promising member of the graduating class. He was elected to the honorary scholastic fraternity Alpha Omega Alpha, the medical equivalent of Phi Beta Kappa. Dr. Hans Zinsser, one of the great bacteriologists of his time, prophesied for Armand a brilliant future in bacteriology and immunology.

With these accolades, he was ready in June, 1921, to begin his hospital training. His internship, however, did not start until the following January, seven months after his graduation. Armand Hammer has never been one to waste time. Typhus, he learned, had broken out in Russia, and he decided to spend his enforced leisure there. Work in the plague-stricken Urals would offer an opportunity to be useful as a physician and to learn more about immunology. At the same time, he could collect some payments that were owing his pharmaceutical company for much-needed drug shipments sent to Russia immediately after the Revolution in spite of Clemenceau's attempted blockade. The Russians, he was told, did not welcome foreigners, and he decided to tempt the commissars with a desirable gift — a fully equipped hospital, surplus war property purchased from the United States government at considerable expense.

Russian visas in 1921 were reluctantly issued by a suspicious Foreign Office. Perhaps because his father was a well-known socialist, perhaps because Armand himself was a potential benefactor, his cables to Moscow, to everyone's surprise, were effective; after waiting in Berlin for ten days, Armand received an answer, in what was considered to be record time, saying: "Visa granted, Litvinov."

Armand was less fortunate in Moscow, where there were endless delays. He became seriously ill in a horribly squalid hotel, and when he had almost decided to go home, as it seemed impossible to operate his field hospital, an official in the Foreign Office offered him a place on a special train that was leaving for the Urals on an inspection trip. The chance to go along provided an opportunity to learn about conditions in the area of famine while his own plans materialized. He left Moscow expecting to be back in America within six months. He was to stay in Russia for nine years.

When he arrived at his destination, what he saw sickened him. As he wrote years later in an enthralling autobiography (now unfortunately out of print), "I had imagined that my professional training as a physician had steeled me against human suffering, but the first vision in Ekaterinburg . . . struck me cold with horror." Unburied dead were everywhere. A train that had started out carrying a thousand passengers arrived with only two hundred still alive. Disease and famine were ubiquitous; yet, ironically, so were tremendous factories and mines, stocks of platinum, mineral products, Ural emeralds, and semi-precious stones. Vast resources were everywhere, yet human beings were dying of starvation. Production had ceased, and there seemed no way to provide food to keep the population alive until new crops could be harvested.

Young Dr. Hammer decided something must be done. He asked the commissar in charge of the inspection trip to assemble the local Soviet, and he addressed the leaders in Russian, which he had been studying during his few weeks in Russia. He told his audience that he was prepared to buy a million bushels of American wheat, which would feed the people until next year's crop could be harvested. He proposed that each boat, which he would load with grain, should, on its return trip, take back goods for the American market. Through this barter system, there would be a continual replenishment of supplies. When he finished his address, the applause was deafening, but in the babble of voices he could make out one word he did not understand. He asked what it meant. The commissar said everyone was yelling, "Translate!" His audience thought he was speaking English. When his speech was translated he became, at twenty-three, the hero of the Urals.

Word got back to Moscow, and when the special train returned he was requested to see Lenin at once. He found the ruler of the Soviet Union a man much smaller than he expected, with a large domed head and warm brown eyes. They spoke in English. Armand said he was still learning Russian, trying to memorize a hundred words a day. Lenin, who had studied English in London in a similar fashion, sympathized. They became immediate friends and their friendship lasted until Lenin's death. Armand treasures a photograph dedicated to "Comrade Armand Hammer from V. I. Ulyanov (Lenin)."

It was Lenin's belief that America and Russia were complementary — that Russia was a backward land with immense resources in need of American capital and technology and that the United States was an industrial country in a position to develop these Russian resources, which would some day be necessary to American industry. Lenin said to Hammer, "We don't need doctors as much as we need businessmen, people who can do such things as you have done." He was eager to grant concessions to foreigners under a new economic policy, and he urged the young doctor to be the first concessionaire. He offered every

cooperation, and all the promises he made were fulfilled. When he was dying, he said to Professor Foerster, his doctor brought from Germany, "Tell young Hammer I have not forgotten him and wish him well. If he has any difficulties, tell him to be sure and let me know."

Armand asked for two concessions. On his trip to the Urals he had seen an asbestos mine, which an engineer on the train had said could easily be put into operation and would prove profitable. Although Armand knew nothing about mining, he decided to ask for the asbestos concession. It was one of his few miscalculations, for after World War I the price of asbestos slumped badly, and it was several years before his concession showed even a small profit.

But if he was ignorant of mining, he was an instinctive trader. The second concession, one for foreign trade, was a bonanza. He realized that Russia needed machinery, especially to mechanize agriculture. The newly developed Ford tractor was the answer. Armand has always gone to the top with his proposals. To get Ford tractors for Russia he decided he had to see Henry Ford himself. From an uncle who had once been an agent for Ford in czarist Russia, he got a letter of introduction. Making friends easily is a characteristic of Armand's that has always been a great asset; Henry Ford immediately became a friend of the young doctor-turned-businessman. In spite of Ford's disapproval of Communism, he granted Armand the Ford agency for cars as well as tractors for the whole of Russia.

During November, 1922, the first Fordson tractors arrived, and Armand and Mikoyan met them in Novorossisk and drove the whole fleet to Rostov, a distance of about one hundred miles. Everywhere along the route there were crowds of shouting, applauding Communists. The only limitation on sales was the availability of foreign currency; hence, the concession agreement provided that Armand must export goods equivalent in value to his imports. Armand became the representative of thirty-seven American companies: Allis-Chalmers, U.S. Rubber, Underwood Typewriters, and Parker Pen among others. Victor Hammer, Armand's younger brother, once said that in those days for a Russian to wear a large Parker pen in his jacket pocket was the equivalent of the Legion of Honor. When Armand finally began purchasing works of art from the Russian government, he distributed his "Legions of Honor" lavishly.

For a time, the Hammer Trading Company enjoyed a virtual monopoly of trade between the Soviet Union and the United States. Branches were opened all over Russia, especially in fur-trading stations. Armand even shipped the first caviar sent from Russia since the Revolution. The business grew so big that he opened offices in London, Paris, Berlin, and New York.

He rented a palatial house in Moscow. It was unfurnished, and decorating his new residence gave him his first interest in art. Victor, who had come to Russia to help him, had studied the history of art at Princeton. Together they bought, for virtually nothing, everything that made the life of a Russian noble the most luxurious in Europe. At that time, furniture, tapestries, silver, porcelains, and jewels were sold in commission stores in Moscow, where they were brought by the impoverished aristocracy and by the government, which was disposing of some of the contents of the czarist palaces. There were so few foreigners in the Soviet Union that, except for some competition from the French and German ambassadors, the Hammer brothers had the field to themselves.

Armand had been infected with the virus of collecting, against which his knowledge of immunology was powerless. He recognized the splendor beautiful objects had brought into the lives of the Russian nobility. He had rented a palace and he, too, wanted it adorned palatially. Later, his purchases of works of art had other motives, as we shall see: first, the conversion of these treasures into dollars; and then, the pleasure his collection might give the public. It was only during the first phase of his collecting that he assembled treasures primarily for himself, for the decoration of his palace. His instinctive taste, except for this early splurge, has been simple. Although far richer today than when he was in Russia, he lives in a modest home in a Los Angeles suburb, has a converted carriage house in the Greenwich Village section of New York City, and a comfortable apartment in Moscow. His only period of ostentation was in his twenties, when he was living in the Soviet Union and doing business with Communists.

This brings us to the formation of the first of the three Hammer collections, the third and last of which is illustrated in this catalogue. In 1928 Armand and Victor had begun to deal in works of art. Their stock consisted of eighteenth-century furniture, tapestries, rugs, silver, service after service of Sèvres and Meissen porcelain, jewels (especially the Easter eggs of precious stones made by Fabergé and exchanged by the aristocracy at Easter), icons, and church vestments. At about this time, they met a New York art dealer who had come to Moscow on a visit.

He was amazed at the bargains the Hammers had found. For example, Victor on one occasion had heard that all the priestly vestments from the royal chapels in Leningrad were being disposed of. Checking on this rumor, he found a pile of chasubles, stoles, and dalmatics filling an entire room of a palace from floor to ceiling. As most were woven with threads of gold and silver, the officials in charge were about to burn them for the metal that would remain, just as so many of the tapestries in France were burnt at the time of the French Revolution, for the same reason. Victor informed Armand, who asked the value of the gold and silver they expected would remain, and found it was a comparatively small amount. He offered double and bought the whole lot.

As their friend the New York dealer had not succeeded in doing business with the Soviet functionaries, he was anxious to enter into partnership with the Hammer brothers, who were permitted to export works of art. A tax, of course, was imposed and a release from the Russian museums required, but the opportunities were staggering. A company was formed, and Armand bought a partnership for Victor, but the firm existed for only a year. The stock market crash of 1929 bankrupted their partner, and Armand had to buy him out. This was the beginning of the Hammer Galleries, with Victor in charge. Stocking the new gallery was no problem. All the furnishings of Russian palaces were available for a song and in New York could be sold for the equivalent of an oratorio. It was a very profitable enterprise.

About 1928 the greatest of all art deals began — the sale of paintings from the Hermitage Museum. The Hammer brothers, however, were not active participants. They had had an unfortunate experience and were wary of old masters. They had purchased a painting attributed to Rembrandt for the modest sum of twenty-five thousand dollars. It had been brought to their attention by the best-known Russian restorer, who worked for the Hermitage. Armand has generally tried to subject his own judgment to the critical opinion of the best authorities, and something about the Rembrandt aroused his suspicions. He sent Victor with the painting to Max J. Friedländer, an expert on Dutch art and then the director of the Kaiser Friedrich Museum in Berlin. According to Victor, Friedländer was at first favorably impressed, but he asked his restorer to test the picture with a weak solution of acetone. The paint came away at once, which proved that it had been recently applied. The Rembrandt was a forgery.

When the Hammer brothers confronted the man from the Hermitage who had recommended the picture, he confessed at once. The director of an important museum in Moscow, he admitted, had painted the Rembrandt. Many well-known collectors and museums had been swindled by the same forger. Armand threatened to denounce him and the director to the Soviet authorities unless his money was returned, and, facing a cold Siberian future, they readily agreed to pay back all they could. It turned out, however, that the forger's wife was a concert pianist, a career Armand's piano teacher had predicted for him when he was a child, and her husband had used part of the money to buy her a piano. This had caused a shortage of rubles. Armand was touched and gladly donated the piano to the musical wife, expressing the hope that concerts instead of forgeries would provide the family income.

After their unsatisfactory experience with Rembrandt, the Hammers restricted their purchases to less important works by seventeenth-century Dutch painters and to Russian icons. These were the staple of the Russian private collections. Victor took particular delight in watching these blackened panels cleaned. They were never sold, and Armand eventually gave them away.

Although the Hammers did not buy paintings from the Hermitage, they were among the first to know of these sales. In 1928 they received a cable from their brother Harry in New York, saying that a syndicate of American dealers knew the Soviet Union needed money and that they were interested in buying pictures from the Hermitage. They offered a 10 percent commission on whatever they bought. They wished the Hammers to find out whether anything could be acquired.

With this cable in hand, which they felt sure the Russian officials had already read, they went to see the head of Antiquariat, the organization in charge of the sale of all works of art. The director was enraged at the mere thought of such a proposal. But after a well-timed pause, he said, "If your friends in America want to make reasonable offers we are obligated to submit them to the proper authorities."

The Hammers cabled America and two days later received a reply listing forty of the greatest paintings in the Hermitage, a list that included work by Leonardo da Vinci, Raphael, Jan van Eyck, Rubens, and other masters. For the entire lot of these fantastic masterpieces they offered five million dollars. In Victor's graphic language, "This was like offering ten dollars for a Rembrandt." Nevertheless, the Hammers went back to their friend the commissar with the cable. He reacted furiously. He banged his hand on the table and pointed to the reproduction of the *Benois Madonna* by Leonardo in the Hermitage catalogue. "This picture alone is worth five million gold rubles [$2.6 million]," he said.

As soon as they heard this, Armand and Victor knew the Hermitage paintings, in spite of the commissar's protests, were really for sale. They cabled New York and received a reply signed by Max Steuer, a New York lawyer, saying, "Concrete offer on Leonardo da Vinci two million dollars. If offer accepted will arrange irrevocable letter of credit and ask Bernard Berenson to go to Leningrad to seal up picture."

Now the Hammers had a definite offer within range of the asking price, and, as Victor told me, he and his brother were beginning to spend their 10 percent. Armand went at once to see his close friend Mikoyan, who said, "We are serious. We do need money." And then jokingly added, "Of course, one day you will have a revolution in your country and we'll take the picture back, so we are really only lending it to you." But as regards the price, he did not joke. He repeated five million gold rubles. In 1913 the Czar had paid $1.5 million for the picture, and so a price of $2.6 million twenty-five years later was not out of line. The Hammers spent lavishly, cabling back and forth to New York, but the syndicate would not come up and the Soviets would not come down. Shortly thereafter, Calouste Gulbenkian and then Andrew Mellon began buying works of art from the Soviets, but they never acquired the *Benois Madonna,* which remained at twice the price of the most expensive painting either bought.

Armand realized that his capital in foreign currency was not great enough to compete with these two collectors. Moreover, he was having trouble with his own trading company. The success of private enterprise in a socialistic state is precarious. One day the commissar in charge of foreign trade explained cordially but firmly that the Soviets had their own organizations for trade abroad, ARCOS and AMTORG, and that henceforth they would not share with foreigners an export-import monopoly. He added, however, that his government was not ungrateful for the contribution Armand Hammer had made at a critical time in the history of the Soviet Union and that he hoped the American doctor would find another and not less profitable enterprise in Russia. He suggested choosing a manufacturing concession.

Armand Hammer pondered awhile. The new concession must show more immediate profits than asbestos. He asked the commissar whether the government did not intend to teach every Russian to read and write. The answer was a strong affirmative. "Then," said Armand Hammer, "I would like the lead pencil concession." This, he felt, was an industry with a guaranteed future! He knew nothing about lead pencils, but, after trying to buy one himself, he had made some enquiries and found there was a great shortage and that every pencil in the Soviet Union was being imported from Germany. He went to the Central Concessions Committee and offered to pledge fifty thousand dollars that he could set up a pencil factory within twelve months of signing the concession and that he would do at least a million dollars' worth of business in the first year. The Soviets had been trying, unsuccessfully, to manufacture pencils for some time, and they thought him mad. Nevertheless, in October, 1925, the concession was signed.

Armand was committed to making pencils. All that remained was to learn how to make them. The process was a closely guarded secret, known only to a few manufacturers, among whom the most important was the Faber family in Nuremberg. Armand immediately traveled to Germany and, not unexpectedly, received no cooperation from the Fabers; but worst of all, he was unable to penetrate their factory. When he was most despondent, aware that he could not abandon the concession much as he wished to, he met a young, disgruntled engineer, an employee of Eberhard Faber, who was eager to help him enter the pencil fortress. Once inside, he found many of its closely guarded inmates encouragingly disloyal. Promising them homes with gardens, schools for their children, all the amenities of German life including beer, he enticed a number of the more ambitious to come with him to Russia. In England, in Birmingham, the center of the pen industry, he found much the same situation, and again induced many of the younger men to join him in the Soviet Union.

Once back in Moscow, he began to build his factory, install machinery, and construct the village he had promised his recruits. Within six months, he was producing pencils every bit as good as the German imported ones,

half a year earlier than his agreement, and instead of the million-dollar gross he had predicted for the first year, he did two and a half million dollars' worth of business. Instead of importing, the Russians were exporting, and the price of pencils in the Soviet Union fell from fifty cents to five cents apiece. By the end of 1929, the first factory had become five factories, producing — besides pencils — various metal objects, celluloid, and allied products.

This was one of the most profitable business ventures of Armand's career — except that rubles were not dollars! It was also evident that Stalin, who had become head of the Soviet Union, was hostile to foreign concessions, unlike Lenin. In America the Depression had begun, and in 1930 foreign financing had grown difficult, which made expansion virtually impossible. For these and other reasons, although the concession still had five years to run, Armand decided to sell out to the Russian government. A committee of four was chosen to evaluate the property and a fair price decided on, payable in dollars and in notes spread over several years. But one of the most important conditions of the contract was the right to take out of Russia all personal belongings, which included the treasures Victor had been buying.

After nine years in the Soviet Union, Armand departed and settled down in Paris as a private banker. His principal business was discounting Russian notes, which could be bought at less than 30 percent of their face value, one of the few ways of making money in the Depression. Like his own bills, at the end of three years the notes were fully paid. Skepticism about Soviet finances caused several well-known American businessmen to present him with handsome profits.

He enjoyed Paris, but one day he received a cable from his brothers in New York begging him to return. With the collapse of the stock market, the art market had fallen apart. It had become impossible to sell Russian art. With much of his capital tied up in the Hammer Galleries, Armand's assets were frozen. As his brothers in New York pointed out, they couldn't eat Fabergé Easter eggs. People were selling apples on street corners. Victor expected to be selling art objects the same way. They needed Armand's genius to prevent a third family disaster.

Undismayed, the doctor-turned-banker decided that something spectacular was required to liquidate his stock. He returned to New York from Paris and immediately wrote the chief executives of a dozen of the leading department stores in various cities asking for an entire floor to exhibit his unique collection of what he did not hesitate to call "the greatest works of art ever to leave Russia." He offered a share of the profits. Only one favorable reply was received, a wire saying, "Come immediately," from the Scruggs Vandervoort department store in St. Louis.

Armand moves swiftly, which is another reason for his success. On receipt of the telegram, he and Victor walked over to Sixth Avenue and found a number of trunks belonging to a bankrupt theatrical troupe. Into these huge receptacles they packed their works of art and took a train for St. Louis, checking the trunks in the baggage compartment.

Photographs of all the treasures were available, and Armand asked the head of the department store to arrange for him to call on the editors of the local newspapers the next day. He gave each editor his photographs, told about his adventures in Russia, recounted the history of the works of art, and stressed that everything for sale was closely associated with the Romanoffs, the pathetically slain royal family. This made the Hammer Collection "news."

Armand and Victor beautifully installed the works of art, working day and night, and next morning all the St. Louis newspapers carried photographs with variations of the headline "Million-dollar art collection from the Russian royal palaces goes on sale today." When the exhibition opened, there were a thousand people waiting to get in, and the police had to be called to keep the queue in line. Before the day was over, Armand had to phone Harry, who had remained in New York, to come to St. Louis with more trunks loaded with art treasures.

Marshall Field sent a vice-president to beg Armand to have the next exhibition in their store in Chicago, where the Hammer Collection had an even greater success. Armand was asked to lecture, and every afternoon he told how he had managed to assemble his collection and miraculously to export it. These talks were the basis of his book published in 1932 and reprinted in 1952, *The Quest of the Romanoff Treasure.* The exhibition in Chicago was supposed to last three weeks. It lasted three years.

The Hammers soon organized a second exhibition, which traveled all over the country. Their routine was to stay two weeks in one place and on Saturday evening to pack what was unsold. Then their trucks would travel all night; Sunday they would unpack; Monday they would have a preview; and Tuesday they were in business again. After exhibitions in the principal cities in the United States, they wound up at Lord & Taylor in New York, where they had the greatest triumph of all.

In the midst of the Depression, Armand Hammer had sold art worth many millions of dollars. Liquidity proceeded so rapidly that Victor had to return to Russia for more stock. Armand had created a market that was exhausted only when he ran out of material to sell. These works of art, the first Hammer Collection, have been entirely dispersed. They were acquired primarily to decorate Armand's palace and to convert rubles into dollars.

Charles McCabe, the publisher of the New York *Daily Mirror,* a friend of the Hammers, was so impressed by what they had done with their own collection that he asked them to help his employer, William Randolph Hearst. McCabe said the banks were about to foreclose on all the Hearst newspapers, whose only liquid assets were the Hearst works of art. But in two years the company set up to sell these assets had grossed less than the corporate expenses. Would the Hammer brothers help out, on a basis of a 10 percent commission on the retail sales? Armand agreed and, never one to undervalue his projects, wrote immediately to his friend Beardsley Ruml, chairman of Macy's, saying, "I think I have the greatest merchandising promotion any department store ever had—the sale of a fifty-million-dollar art collection in a department store. Nothing like this has ever been attempted before."

The statement was no exaggeration. The printed catalogue of the Hearst collection ran to 334 pages. There were tapestries, sculptures, paintings, furniture, stained glass, gold and silver services, pottery, china, and glassware—even light fixtures, and wearing apparel from the Middle Ages. There were also such mysterious objects as two "Chopes," several "Schnelles," and one "Krug" (words not defined in the *Oxford English Dictionary*), of the sixteenth and seventeenth centuries. There were whole rooms, such as a Venetian frescoed council chamber of the sixteenth century, French paneling dating from the fifteenth to the eighteenth centuries, and Gothic, Jacobean, and Georgian interiors. There was the famous twelfth-century Cistercian monastery from Spain in 10,500 packing cases, each stone wrapped in straw, which the United States Customs insisted had to be unpacked and rewrapped because of the possibility that the straw might carry hoof-and-mouth disease. (A supreme example of the Hammer salesmanship was Armand's and Victor's placement of the monastery with an undertaker for use as a funeral parlor. Hearst refused to accept the sale, however, and eventually, I am glad to say, the building was reconstructed as a monastery.)

The officials of Macy's were staggered by the magnitude of what Armand was offering but they insisted that they should control the pricing of all the items. When their evaluations proved ridiculously low, Armand decided to go to Gimbel's instead. Fred Gimbel was delighted, agreed to let Victor evaluate the Hearst works of art, and offered a whole floor of his store for the exhibition. But Armand wanted at the same time a more prestigious marketplace in order to appease Mr. Hearst, who was aghast at having his art treasures sold in Gimbel's basement. As Gimbel's owned Saks Fifth Avenue, he proposed that part of the collection be shown there. The only room available at Saks, however, was on the floor where dresses were shown, and Armand had to settle for a small space beside the elevator where he could install a small group of the finest objects with a sign saying that the rest of the collection could be seen on the fifth floor of Gimbel's. One hundred thousand customers with charge accounts at Saks were asked to black-tie openings held on three days to accommodate everyone who accepted. The first day, the Hammers sold five hundred thousand dollars' worth of works of art. Within a few months, they had sold enough to pay off eleven million dollars in Hearst bank loans, and they would have liquidated the whole collection had Hearst not decided to stop the sale after half the collection was dispersed. From then on, the Hammers were besieged by executors of estates (Clarence Mackay, J. P. Morgan, and others) asking for their help.

The most profitable result of their association with Gimbel's, however, came from a suggestion by Fred Gimbel that Armand buy stock in The American Distilling Company, listed on the New York Stock Exchange. The war was on and whiskey was very scarce. It was difficult for Gimbel's to supply their own retail department. But American Distilling had voted to give each shareholder as a dividend a barrel of whiskey for each share of stock. Fred Gimbel explained that his store could not purchase the stock because under the law a retailer cannot own part of a wholesaler. He told Armand, however, that Gimbel's would be his distributor.

Armand quickly bought 5,500 shares of American Distilling, and, to his surprise and, in some ways, to his consternation, in a few months he had disposed of 2,500 of his 5,500 barrels—almost half his stock dividend. This meant his company would soon be out of whiskey. What he had bought was all too liquid. But in Armand's life the right person has always turned up at the right time. One day a chemist whom he had befriended in Russia came to see him and they discussed the liquor business. Armand explained his predicament: rapidly diminished supply and, because of the embargo on grain, no foreseeable replenishment. The chemist offered an easy solution: stretch the whiskey fivefold with alcohol made from potatoes. He told Armand he knew exactly what to do.

They left at once for Maine, where surplus potatoes purchased by the government to aid farmers were rotting in warehouses. They found an abandoned rum distillery in New Hampshire, which they bought for next to nothing. The War Production Board was delighted since the issue of disposing of the rotting potatoes was becoming a political scandal. The law this time was helpful, for it provided that only 20 percent of four-year-old whiskey had to be derived from grain in order for the brew to be called "blended whiskey." Thus, overnight, instead of three thousand barrels of straight whiskey, Armand had fifteen thousand barrels of blended whiskey. It was at least potable; and in those days blended bourbon, made from grain or not, was welcome to parched throats.

There was, however, a hitch. The government made Armand put on his label what went into the whiskey, and people had an inexplicable aversion to anything called "potato alcohol." Armand asked the appropriate officials for a dispensation from using the word "potato." The government was adamant. He pointed out that "grain alcohol" did not specify what grains a liquor was made from. Why couldn't his alcohol be called "vegetable alcohol," which would seem less unpalatable? The government's position was that, as he used only potatoes, the designation "potato alcohol" would have to stand. Supposing, Armand said, that his alcohol was made of several vegetables, would the term "vegetable alcohol" be permitted? The answer was in the affirmative. Armand was delighted, and thereafter a bushel of carrots was added to every carload of potatoes.

In the thirsty days of the war, his whiskey sold magnificently. He had a surplus of potato alcohol, and he would offer to trade with other distillers three barrels of his brew for one barrel of aged whiskey. Thus, by bartering his potato alcohol for whiskey aged four years, he was able to keep replenishing his stock. All went well until one day the government declared a grain holiday and gave the distillers the right to go back and produce grain alcohol. Armand had a warehouse piled to the roof with potatoes, and no one would touch potato alcohol. He gambled the grain holiday would not last and he went ahead building up inventory. Luckily, at the end of a month he was proved right: the ban was reimposed and his former customers were back. But he had learned his lesson. To stay in business he needed some grain distilleries. He then bought J. W. Dant and several other grain distilleries in Kentucky and elsewhere. But manufacturing whiskey was not a business he enjoyed. He was delighted to sell the J. W. Dant Company to Schenley, just ten years after he had bought his first distillery in New Hampshire, and eventually he liquidated his other distilleries as well.

Many cattle breeders and feeders had found the residue of Armand's distilleries — the mash from which the whiskey had been extracted — a nutritious feed. This led Armand to take some interest in beef, but his real incentive was to get better steaks for his kitchen. Persuaded by a neighbor that the best steaks came from Black Angus, he went to a cattle sale. At auction Armand is a compulsive bidder, and he found to his surprise that he had bought a cow for a thousand dollars. It belonged, coincidentally, to Seymour Knox of Buffalo, an important collector. Knox's chief stockman congratulated Armand on purchasing a champion and asked about his nonexistent herd. Armand explained that he was a beginner in cattle breeding; then he heard himself say that his mash was marvelous nutriment for cattle and that he would like to show how good it was by raising the best purebred herd in America. He offered a job to the stockman, who accepted on the spot, delighted to come to Armand, for, as he explained, his present employer was more interested in acquiring modern art than in buying bulls.

The virus of collecting, to which Armand has always been vulnerable, had attacked him in a new way. The outbreak of his latest infection caused him to say that he wanted to be the top breeder at once; his new manager told him, in that case, he would have to buy immediately the best bull in the country. The manager knew the animal, a bull called Prince Eric of Sunbeam, shortly to be put up for auction. Armand went to the sale, but for once in his life he was the underbidder. He stopped at $35,000 and the bull went to a hosiery manufacturer for $35,100. Armand had to be satisfied with the second-best bull, for which he paid $27,500. His herd increased and his cattle-feed business boomed. Nevertheless, he was disgruntled.

He did not own the supreme champion. When bidding on works of art, he never likes to take second place, and the same was true of cattle. For a few hundred dollars more, he thought, he might have owned Prince Eric. This exasperated him. One day a veterinarian told him the champion had become impotent at the surprisingly young age of eight. His owner had bred him so often that he had grown disgusted with the opposite sex. Yet, the veterinarian said, although he admitted it was a gamble, he believed he could get semen from Prince Eric and artificially impregnate cows. Armand decided to take a chance; and after long haggling with the owner bought the bull, in spite of his impotency, for one hundred thousand dollars, about three times what he might have had to pay at auction three years earlier. But, miraculously, Prince Eric then produced a thousand calves, among them six international champions, and earned Armand two million dollars.

When the bull was eleven, to everyone's surprise, sex came back into his life. It was a fatal change, for it was a heifer in heat that destroyed him. She was separated from her suitor by a high barbed-wire fence. In spite of being slashed by the barbs, Prince Eric tried to knock down the fence or to climb it. He almost got to his loved one, but the exertion was too great. He had an internal hemorrhage, as the autopsy proved, caused by an increase of blood pressure from undue excitement. He was found dead in his paddock, lying beside the fence that had frustrated his restored virility. Armand within the year sold his entire herd. His greatest work of living art was gone, and he had no heart for further breeding. Although taxes played their part in his decision, he was above all a collector deprived of his major masterpiece. Without Prince Eric, his herd of Black Angus cattle, so quickly yet painstakingly assembled, seemed meaningless.

Armand moved west in 1956 and settled in a suburb of Los Angeles, determined to retire. He was now happily married, and he thought at the age of fifty-eight he could relax and do nothing for the rest of his life. But this was not to be.

A friend brought to his attention a rundown oil company called Occidental Petroleum, the shares of which, at eighteen cents apiece, were worth roughly one hundred thousand dollars in all. Armand and his new wife, Frances, agreed to loan the company fifty thousand dollars to make it possible to drill two unpromising holes; to everyone's surprise (and to the consternation of the Hammers, who had expected to take a tax deduction on dry holes), both wells proved to be productive. The stock jumped to a dollar a share. Armand's collecting virus attacked again: he became a collector of oil wells. He had the prerequisite, boundless optimism, and he also had the right approach, "find and hire the best expert." Gene Reid, looked upon as the outstanding driller in California, had the necessary rigs, and he agreed to accept Occidental stock in lieu of cash. He entered the venture, telling Armand he hoped to make a million dollars before he died. At his death, twelve years later, his estate was valued at thirty million dollars.

But in the oil business success can be elusive. In 1961, after Occidental had drilled a series of dry holes, the company was again almost out of money. A young geologist brought in by Reid felt sure that in the Sacramento Valley, at a site abandoned by Texaco, there was gas. Armand persuaded the directors of his company to put the last few dollars of their exploration fund into one more gamble. Texaco had given up, after drilling a dry hole at 5,600 feet. "Oxy," as it came to be known on the New York Stock Exchange, drilled close by and went to 8,600 feet. At this depth, the bit punctured the second largest gas field in California, a find worth around two hundred million dollars. Nearby, Oxy hit the Brentwood field, another bonanza. The stock rose to fifteen dollars a share.

Gas and the fertilizer business are closely linked. Oxy bought the Best Fertilizer Company. Armand's wells supplied the necessary gas, and he had the ammonia, but he needed phosphate, potash, and sulphur. Again to everyone's amazement, he discovered phosphate in northern Florida. He then bought at bargain price a sulphur company that was doing badly. His scientists at the same time discovered a way of combining phosphate and sulphuric acid so that it could be shipped as superphosphoric acid with the bulk reduced by three fourths. The Russians were so impressed by this technical breakthrough that they contracted with Oxy for the purchase of this acid, to be paid for by the sale to Oxy of ammonia made from Russian natural gas, a deal of such magnitude that it is said to be worth a billion dollars a year for twenty years.

The greatest coup of all for Oxy seemed, for a time, to be in Libya. Near the Egyptian border, Esso had brought in a vast field, and the other oil giants started to bid for concessions. By comparison, Oxy was very small indeed. But Armand, the perpetual optimist, decided to compete. He had his bidding documents impressively written on sheepskin; but, more important, he offered 5 percent of pretax profits to the government of King Idris, at that time

the Libyan ruler, and also to drill for water in the desert at a place called Kufra, where the king's family came from. To the astonishment of the big companies, but not to Armand's surprise, he was offered two concessions. They looked good on paper; nevertheless, Oxy drilled three dry holes. Some members of the board of Oxy referred to the concessions as "Armand's folly," but he did not agree. He hung on, and finally his drills hit the Aguila field. The oil was unusually high grade and the potential was one hundred thousand barrels a day. Esso offered to buy the site for one hundred million dollars profit to Oxy, but the deal fell through. Then more wells were drilled and eventually Oxy was producing eight hundred thousand barrels a day.

Armand did not forget his promise to look for water at Kufra. His drilling team found an underground water reserve as big as the flow of the Nile for 200 years. With Oxy's fertilizers, the desert bloomed. The discovery of water in the desert may in the long run prove more important than the discovery of oil.

These successes pushed the value of Oxy stock to $55 a share, or $165 before it was split three-to-one, a breathtaking rise for shares that had been worth eighteen cents when Armand took over the company. But the oil business is unfortunately tied into politics. King Idris, by this time Armand's friend, was overthrown in 1969 by Colonel Qaddafi and his revolutionary council. Libyan oil was threatened with nationalization. But Armand, unlike most of his competitors, was convinced he could live with the new regime. Whereas the other concessionaires were recalcitrant, Oxy agreed to the Libyan terms of 51 percent for the government and 49 percent for the oil companies. Armand's competitors looked on this as a surrender and a betrayal, but the arrangement was favorable for Oxy, which was all Armand wanted. Moreover, as a payment, his company received $136 million compensation for equipment. Oxy is still making money in Libya.

While Oxy stock was at its peak, Armand collected a number of companies: Signal Oil's marketing resources, Island Creek Coal Company, third largest in the United States, the Hooker Chemical Company, worth eight hundred million dollars, and other smaller businesses. Most of these purchases were made with Oxy stock, common and preferred. Armand has also made large deals on behalf of Oxy with France, Rumania, Peru, Bolivia, and other countries. His company, as major participant and operator for a small group of companies, produces 35 percent of all the oil from the North Sea now flowing into the United Kingdom. At eighty-two, he spends most of his time flying in his private plane from one to another of these far-flung enterprises.

His ceaseless activity, his endless travels, are the result of a deep sense of obligation to the shareholders of Oxy, but he is also, it must be said, interested in making money himself. Since he already has such wealth, why more? The answer is, the delight he experiences giving his money away. A great part of his fortune has been spent on his collection, which has been on constant public exhibition all over the world. But he and his wife also founded the Frances and Armand Hammer Wing of the Los Angeles County Museum of Art, and he has endowed the Armand Hammer Center for Cancer Research at the Jonas Salk Institute, in La Jolla, California, with a gift of five million dollars and the Julius and Armand Hammer Health Sciences Center at his alma mater, Columbia University, with a like amount.

Since its inception in 1968, The Armand Hammer Foundation, personally endowed by Armand with gifts of several million dollars annually, has supported such organizations and institutions as: the California Institute for Cancer Research, the University of California, Los Angeles; The Friendship Force, Atlanta; the Harvard-Columbia Russian Studies Fund; the Lyndon B. Johnson School of Public Affairs, Austin; the International Institute of the Rights of Man, Strasbourg, France; the Royal Academy of Arts, London; and the Center for International Studies, the University of Chicago. Recently, H.R.H. Prince Charles officiated at the opening of the Armand Hammer Collection exhibition at the National Gallery of Scotland and the Royal Scottish Academy in Edinburgh. In a speech before the opening ceremony, Armand pledged contributions totaling £75,000 to the National Arts Collection Foundation of Scotland, the United World Colleges International, Ltd., the Chair of Maritime Archaeology at the University of St. Andrews, and the Royal Scottish Academy. Prince Charles later remarked to Armand, "This was certainly a pretty expensive luncheon for you!"

Armand's biography, *Larger Than Life,* has been written by the well-known columnist and author Bob Considine. He is also the subject of a chapter in Louis Nizer's book *Reflections Without Mirrors,* as well as one in my own book *Self-Portrait with Donors: Confessions of an Art Collector.* He has received numerous decorations and awards, among which are: the Humanitarian Award from The Eleanor Roosevelt Cancer Foundation; the Com-

mander of the Order of the Crown, presented by King Baudouin of Belgium; the Commander of the Order of Andres Bellos, presented by the president of Venezuela; the Mexican Order of the Aztec Eagle, presented by the president of Mexico; the Officier of the National Order of the Legion of Honor, from France; the Order of Friendship Among Peoples, from the Soviet Union; the National Art Association's Distinguished Honoree Award of the Year; and honorary Doctor of Laws degrees from Pepperdine College, Southeastern University, Washington, D.C., and, most recently, from Columbia University.

Active as Armand Hammer's life as a businessman has been he has always found time to search out and collect works of art. It was his collecting that first brought us together. I have described his original collection, which was sold so successfully by the Hammer Galleries. A second collection, bought partly in Russia and partly acquired in the United States, was given to the University of Southern California. This group of old masters, well suited to a university museum where the history of art is taught, has proved itself invaluable to professors and students. The third collection, which is shown in the present catalogue, consists of his more important acquisitions. In this case, as I mentioned earlier, the paintings are destined for the Los Angeles County Museum of Art and the drawings for the National Gallery of Art, in Washington, D.C.

Whether as a breeder of cattle or as a collector of art, Armand Hammer has always wanted to reach the top quickly. But in 1970 he received a setback. He showed a number of his paintings and drawings at the Smithsonian Institution, but unfortunately the galleries assigned to the exhibition were inadequate and obsolete. The principal review of the show was so scathing as to be, in my opinion, unfair. Armand was surprised and disturbed. He wondered whether there was any basis for this criticism, which seemed to him biased.

A mutual friend advised him to consult me. As fellow trustees of the Los Angeles County Museum of Art, we had met once or twice, but quite casually. To my surprise, he telephoned me from New York and asked me to make a study of his collection and give him my advice. I told him I had just retired as director of the National Gallery and that I was determined to spend my time enjoying myself and doing the writing I had been too busy to do before. We said goodbye in a friendly spirit, and I went back to the book I was working on. Three hours later, my secretary said Dr. Hammer had arrived in Washington and was waiting in the office to see me. He was unwilling, as he has always been, to take "no" for an answer; and, as he is accustomed to do, he got his way. I agreed to go to work for him, and for many months, with the help of a most able research assistant, made a thorough survey of his collection.

I divided his pictures into two categories: those I would welcome as gifts to the National Gallery, which were considerable in number, and those I thought more suitable for regional museums, or for disposing of by trade or sale, a relatively small group. Even when I was disparaging about a work of art, there was no criticism of my findings. Of all the collectors I have known, none has received adverse judgments with the goodwill Armand has shown. He did not object when I eliminated, for reasons of quality, some of the paintings and drawings from the group shown at the Smithsonian. The works of art that remain from that exhibition are what he insisted they should be—up to the standards maintained at the National Gallery. Since the Smithsonian exhibition, Armand has added many paintings and drawings to his collection. These have all been outstanding and represent some of his greatest acquisitions.

Although the focus of the collection has continued to be on the nineteenth century, there were in the original Smithsonian show important earlier masters. For example the Los Angeles County Museum of Art was enabled by gifts from the Armand and Frances Hammer Purchase Fund to acquire two splendid seventeenth-century panels: Rembrandt's *Portrait of a Man of the Raman Family,* a superb example of the master's early style, and Rubens's *The Israelites Gathering Manna in the Desert,* a brilliant study for the tapestries ordered by Archduchess Isabella, ruler of the Spanish Netherlands (Plates 4 and 5). The earliest two paintings by Rubens in the collection, an *Adoration of the Shepherds* and *Venus Wounded by a Thorn* (Plates 1 and 2), are brilliant examples of Rubens's virtuosity when, as a young man of thirty-one, he was traveling in Italy. The third work, *Young Woman with Curly Hair* (Plate 3), I place among the most enchanting portraits I know. The flesh tones are luminous and the transitions from light to shadow are done with a subtlety that is breathtaking.

There were only two eighteenth-century paintings in the Smithsonian exhibition. The first, Fragonard's *The Education of the Virgin* (Plate 8), owes its chiaroscuro and sepia tones to Rembrandt and its fluent brushwork and vir-

tuosity to Rubens. The second, a sketch by Goya (Plate 9), an early work preliminary to the cartoons for tapestries preserved in the Pardo Palace, was selected by the Sociedad Española de Amigos del Arte for the 1949 exhibition in Madrid of Goya's work, a fact worth noting, since only the finest Spanish pictures meet the society's exacting standards.

The nineteenth century opens with two masterpieces, portraits of an actress, Doña Antonia Zárate, by Goya and of an unidentified man by Géricault (Plates 10 and 11). Dr. Hammer has given the Goya portrait to the Hermitage Museum in Leningrad, the only work by that master in the great Russian collection. The painting by Géricault is of an individual who stands for the very essence of his period. Every line of the sitter's face shows that self-confident and ruthless determination we associate with Stendhal's heroes. Here we see the new man of the Napoleonic era — self-made and boundlessly ambitious.

But the artist of this period Armand Hammer has always loved best was a gentler painter, Corot. At one time, there were twenty-four of his canvases in the collection. Of these, only the six finest are included in this catalogue. Historically the most interesting is a landscape known as *Pleasures of Evening* (Plate 17), an appropriate title for one of the painter's very last efforts. Writing about it in 1892, Jules-Antoine Castagnary touchingly said, "When the imagination is still so fresh, and sensitivity still so alive, death should take pity and not interrupt." The painting, unhappily, has darkened with time, as often occurs in Corot's late work. By contrast, for those who prefer his more colorful style—and I am among them—there are the fresh, springlike tones of *Distant View of Mantes Cathedral* (Plate 14) and the hot sunshine of the dramatic *Medieval Ruins* (Plate 12). And here I confess to a weakness: I often fall in love with the painted likenesses of women, and, given this failing, I admit that of all the Corots in the collection I am most enamored of a portrait of a young minx, whose half smile and appraising glance enthrall me, as they must have captivated Corot (Plate 15).

One of the most touching friendships in the history of art was that of Corot and Daumier. *The Lawyers* (Plate 18) is a painting Daumier gave Corot in return for a most generous gesture, described in the notes on the picture. Of Daumier's numerous oils connected with the courts of justice, this ranks among his greatest masterpieces.

With Corot as the leader, the greatest school of landscape painting the West has known flourished in and around Paris. To realize this, one need only think of Boudin, Pissarro, Monet, Sisley, and the other Impressionists, as well as the Barbizon painters; and though one misses the names of Turner and Constable, these French landscapists painted nature in a way unrivaled in art history. Not even Constable, for example, outdid Boudin in his rendering of clouds, as we can see in *Sailing Ships in Port* (Plate 19). But such pictures were not the ones that earned Boudin his living. He depended on his beach scenes, paintings like the sparkling *Beach at Trouville* (Plate 21). These were popular and always salable; the others were not. Nevertheless, he himself admired more his studies of working people, as we see them plying their trades on the *Quay at Camaret* (Plate 20), a typical example of his sketches of everyday life.

Boudin was admired by Pissarro, Sisley, and Monet, a triumvirate who revolutionized the painting of nature. Their struggles for recognition, even survival, are well known. One of the few contemporary collectors to appreciate them was himself a painter, Gustave Caillebotte. He bought many of their pictures, which he bequeathed to the Louvre, and he took part in their exhibitions. His own work, however, was rarely as fresh and broadly painted as *Square in Argenteuil* (Plate 22), which is a remarkable masterpiece by a minor painter.

The triumph of Impressionistic landscape rests largely on the work of the triumvirate I have mentioned: Pissarro, Sisley, and Monet. Pissarro's *Boulevard Montmartre, Mardi Gras* (Plate 25), which moved from one Californian collector to another, from Norton Simon to Armand Hammer, shows the quintessence of their technique. It vibrates with light and color, an effect only possible through the use of those short, quick brushstrokes that are the hallmark of Impressionism. It seems as though Mardi Gras in this painting were being celebrated with a shower of streamers and confetti, and that this downpour, rendered by flecks of pigment, has taken on the configuration of trees, crowds of people, and marching men. Sisley's landscape, although it is less original, is characteristic. It represents the *Timber Yard at St.-Mammès* (Plate 23), the town where he eventually retired. Monet touches a peak of Impressionism with a masterpiece of light and air, *View of Bordighera* (Plate 24), which seems painted with ground jewels, to become a mist of color pierced by sunbeams.

There was, of course, a reaction to the insubstantiality of such paintings. The figures in Renoir's *Grape Pickers at Lunch* (Plate 26), for instance, are more tangible, and one

feels volume again exists in painting. What happiness is exuded by these robust peasant girls enjoying their picnic! Here is a new and enchanting paganism that Renoir introduces into art. The world and all that is in it is lovely, as entrancing as that quintessence of youthful beauty, the *Two Girls Reading* (Plate 28), and as joyous as the landscape of *Antibes* (Plate 27), where everything seems made for love and sensuality. It is Watteau's *A Pilgrimage to Cythera* in modern dress.

The sensuality of Renoir, however, vanishes with Cézanne. Of this change, *Boy Resting* (Plate 30), which has been widely exhibited, is typical. Who could look more uncomfortable and less seductive than this youth leaning on his arm? Cézanne cared little for the delights of this world. With passionate intensity, he sought to render, instead, planes receding to the distant hills and the plasticity of the human figure.

In the next movement, Post-Impressionism, volume and solidity again lost their significance for painters. *Bonjour M. Gauguin* (Plate 39) is a flat pattern of trees and fields, totally unlike the Cézanne. In spite of the bright, intense colors, there is an ominous quality, at least in the figure of the artist. The picture was painted for an innkeeper, Madame Marie Henry, who one imagines may well have asked, when she saw a brooding, menacing figure approaching, her payment in advance. This curiously sinister example of the change to Post-Impressionism leads us to the four great paintings by Gauguin's friend and occasional antagonist Van Gogh.

The earliest of Van Gogh's works in the collection, an almost monochromatic winter scene, was done before he left his native land (Plate 41). The next three canvases are separated each by a year, 1887, 1888, and 1889. Having departed from Holland and come to Paris, Van Gogh had seen the work of the Impressionists and learned to appreciate its entrancing chromatic beauty, as he demonstrated when painting *Lilacs* (Plate 42). *The Sower* (Plate 43), the next in date, obviously influenced by Millet, marks Van Gogh's removal from Paris to Arles. Here his color has become strident, compulsive, almost like a physical blow. The last and most impressive of the series shows the asylum of St.-Rémy, the site of his tragic struggle to regain his sanity (Plate 44). He wrote of this, one of his greatest achievements, "I tried to reconstruct the thing as it might have been, simplifying and accentuating the haughty, unchanging character of the pines and cedar clumps against the blue." Although the words in Van Gogh's letter are calmly descriptive, the trees are more like flames reaching to the sky in a windblown conflagration. They reflect the fire that was burning in the artist's brain.

American collecting has been focused on the Impressionists. Consequently, the availability of important work by these artists has been so reduced that it is only by the rarest chance that an outstanding canvas like *Paule Gobillard* by Berthe Morisot (Plate 29) now comes on the market. In this case, the opportunity arose when the artist's descendants decided to part with a family treasure, a picture obviously painted with love both for the artist's niece and for her dog.

The vogue for Impressionism and Post-Impressionism has meant less enthusiasm for other artists working in Paris at the same time. Two important painters who stand apart from these movements seem to me undervalued, Fantin-Latour and Moreau, both brilliantly represented in the Hammer Collection. Fantin-Latour's flower pictures are often to be met with in America, although few equal in quality the two belonging to Armand Hammer (Plates 31 and 33), especially *Peonies in a Blue and White Vase;* but the painter's superb portraits are less frequently to be seen in this country. His likeness of *Miss Edith Crowe* (Plate 32) is one of the most poetic examples of nineteenth-century portraiture. The strongly accentuated light and shadow create a mood of pensive brooding, the essence of the romantic image.

After Delacroix and Géricault, the greatest of all French romantic painters is Gustave Moreau. If I were speculating in the monetary value of works of art, I would buy as many of his paintings as possible. The difficulty is that so much of his entire output is in the Musée National Gustave Moreau, in Paris. Dr. Hammer is fortunate enough, however, to possess two of his finest canvases, *King David* and *Salome* (Plates 36 and 37). The latter had a deep effect on J. K. Huysmans, and in *A Rebours* he wrote a long description of the painting in prose as glittering as the picture itself. In 1876 P. de Saint-Victor said of it: "M. Gustave Moreau's entry in the Salon far exceeds any of his previous exhibits. . . . If an opium fiend could translate his visions into reality with a goldsmith's skill, it would give some idea of this artist."

The momentum of the great French artistic movements of the nineteenth century carried creativity well into the first half of the twentieth century. The artists who made Paris in our time the mecca for painters, especially Vuillard and Bonnard, are beautifully represented. It is difficult to choose among the Vuillards; they are all of such high quality. But my favorite remains *At the Seashore* (Plate 48). Jacques Salomon in a recent book perfectly expresses my response to this exquisite canvas when he says it "is like a cry from the heart, the echo of which ravished me . . . the touch is so alive, so alert, so completely submissive to the rhythm of Vuillard's feeling." Bonnard's early *Street Scene* (Plate 45) evokes the loveliness of the simplest happenings of Parisian life, and the *Nude Against the Light* (Plate 46), suggesting the artist's unique combination of sensitivity and sensuality, reminds one of the nudes Titian painted at the end of his life.

The next generation that lends such luster to the School of Paris is represented by a great portrait by Modigliani (Plate 52), already a part of the collection of the Los Angeles County Museum of Art; by Soutine's famous study of a young man (Plate 53), painted with such scintillating brushwork and mastery of pigmentation that the other artists who frequented the Café de la Rotonde must have been astounded; by Vlaminck's *Summer Bouquet,* equaling De Staël in its display of palette-knife virtuosity (Plate 55); and by Derain's *Still Life with Basket, Jug, and Fruit* (Plate 51), which is distinguished by its simplicity of composition, its elimination of all but essential forms, and its restricted palette.

Two other School of Paris pictures must also be mentioned. Both are as insubstantial as a dream: Marie Laurencin's *Women in the Forest* (Plate 56), which once belonged to John Quinn, the pioneer among American collectors in his appreciation of the school; and Chagall's *Blue Angel* (Plate 57), which was once in the collection of Frank Crowninshield, the able editor of *Vanity Fair,* a publication largely responsible for the American vogue of these Parisian artists.

In recent years, Dr. Hammer has added to his collection several American paintings. His earliest picture is the most famous of American icons, Gilbert Stuart's *Portrait of George Washington* (Plate 58). Known as the *Lewis Washington,* it is more interesting than many other versions, showing the first president seated at a table, with his sword resting on his arm and a glimpse of sky in the distance.

A great portrait painted just eighty years later is Thomas Eakins's *Portrait of Sebastiano Cardinal Martinelli* (Plate 63). For its psychological penetration, its simplicity and dignity, its noble humanity, this may well be considered an American Rembrandt. Sylvan Schendler, writing in 1967 referred to it as "the most powerful portrait of its kind ever painted by an American."

Slightly earlier is a fine still life by Harnett (Plate 59), which has the distinction of being among the few American pictures of the late nineteenth century ever exhibited at the Royal Academy in London, where it was shown in 1885 and bought by an English painter, George Richmond. A second Harnett still life has been lent to President and Mrs. Carter, who chose it for the adornment of their main sitting room (Plate 60). The President admired it so greatly that Dr. Hammer decided it should remain there and recently has made a gift to The White House collection of this masterwork.

American Impressionism is represented by *On the Beach* (Plate 66), painted in 1916 by Maurice Prendergast. Owned until recently by Mrs. Charles Prendergast, it is a picture she parted with reluctantly, as it was always considered in the family one of her brother-in-law's two greatest masterpieces.

Two Americans who lived abroad, Mary Cassatt and John Singer Sargent, are superbly represented, each by two pictures, one of the Sargents having been bought by the Los Angeles County Museum of Art with funds provided by Dr. and Mrs. Hammer. Mary Cassatt's double portrait *Reine Lefebvre and Margot* (Plate 65) is, in my opinion, her finest pastel done after 1900, and the idyllic *Summertime* (Plate 64), the most important of her rare landscapes.

The two portraits by Sargent, though both were painted relatively early, are totally different from each other. *Dr. Pozzi at Home* (Plate 61), dated 1881, is highly dramatic, as though the doctor were an actor about to go on stage. It is a masterpiece of Salon painting, sophisticated and cosmopolitan. The double portrait *Mrs. Edward L. Davis and Her Son, Livingston Davis* (Plate 62), is much more sober, more American in a straightforward, realistic way. Sargent has here recorded the essence of upper-class America, which has learned to be fashionable without learning to be chic.

Originally the Hammer Collection contained only a few drawings and the famous Gauguin sketchbook. But when the Mrs. Jesse I. Straus sale took place in 1970, Dr. Hammer acquired from that fastidiously chosen collection eight masterpieces of French draftsmanship, ranging in date from Watteau to Degas. In the years following, he has assembled the finest private collection of drawings in

America, an extraordinary achievement in these days of scarcity.

Among the earliest works is a study of cowslips by Albrecht Dürer (Plate 67). There are, so far as we know, only six such studies, four of which are in the Albertina in Vienna. Dürer observed his subject with painstaking fidelity, delineating not only the plant itself but the entwined weeds and grasses. These beautiful and delicate botanical studies, done in gouache on vellum, disclose that new interest in nature and its scientific investigation that comes into art with the Renaissance.

The greatest of the Italian artists of the High Renaissance —Leonardo da Vinci, Michelangelo, Raphael, Andrea del Sarto, and Correggio—are each represented in the Hammer Collection. The sketches by Leonardo (Plate 68) are on the fragment of a large sheet, which must have been the size of the drawing of the Virgin and Child and Saint John at Windsor Castle, generally dated 1478 – 80. The ink and paper are the same, and, for the following reason, it seems to have been done at about the same time. At the bottom of the sheet there is a bust of a young girl who looks at the spectator. She closely resembles a drawing at Oxford of a maiden with a unicorn. Some years ago, in an article on Leonardo's *Ginevra de' Benci,* now in the National Gallery in Washington, I pointed out the similarity between the Oxford sketch and the portrait, which I date about 1480, or in exactly the same period as the Windsor sheet. Fortunately, Dr. Hammer has indicated that his drawing will go to Washington: thus, the National Gallery of Art will have not only Ginevra's actual portrait but what might be called a memory-image of her face, a tracing of that strange beauty that haunted the master's mind in his youth, in the days just after he had gained his independence from his apprenticeship with Verrocchio.

Michelangelo's drawing in black chalk (Plate 69) is related to his concept of a sculptured group in which Christ's body would be shown supported by two men. The central idea is echoed in the unfinished *Pietà* that once belonged to the Rondanini family, now in the Castello Sforzesco in Milan. All the contours of the figures in the Hammer drawing, especially the outlines of each side of the torsos and limbs, are so sensitively related one to the other that they suggest three-dimensional form as weighty and solid as the marble from which the Rondanini *Pietà* was to be carved.

These studies rank with the finest examples of the

graphic arts ever brought to America. The other three Renaissance drawings, though somewhat less important, are all of the highest quality. The sketches by Raphael and Correggio are for well-known murals. The Raphael drawings of prophets (Plate 70) show the original conception of the figures now heavily overpainted in the Chigi Chapel in Sta. Maria della Pace in Rome; and the verso of the sheet by Correggio with its shorthand delineation of Saints Matthew and Jerome (Plate 72) is the first idea for the pendentives in S. Giovanni Evangelista at Parma. The recto of the same sheet shows one of the two known studies for the *Madonna della Scodella,* the celebrated altarpiece now to be seen in the Pinacoteca of Parma.

The last of the Renaissance drawings, the study of the head of a young woman (Plate 71), reveals how carefully Andrea del Sarto has scrutinized a tired, wistful face. He was one of the few artists of his time to draw carefully from the model. Thus, his searching observation and brilliant rendering of his subject's mood are rarely found in Renaissance art.

To copy a Rembrandt drawing is to discover the meaning of economy of line. In the early study in the Hammer Collection of a *Beggar Man and Woman in the Street* (Plate 73), each stroke of the pen models the figures and describes posture and gesture. There is not an unnecessary touch. In the late sketch of a biblical subject (Plate 74), the lines are still fewer and empty space predominates.

With Giovanni Battista Tiepolo, this warm, human sympathy has vanished (Plates 75 and 76). The figures are now cold and distant. Even the angel who points to Saint Jerome's Bible is supercilious. But for the sheer delight to be found in brilliantly handled sepia washes one must look to such incomparable sketches. These two drawings in the Hammer Collection, one once owned by Pietro Monaco, the Venetian engraver, the other from the famous Orloff album, are supreme examples of Tiepolo's virtuosity.

Turning from a wash drawing by Tiepolo to a sketch in chalk by Watteau means to refocus one's eyes. In place of dazzling bravura, there is delicacy of accent; instead of that wizardry of the brush, there is the precision of the pencil's touch. What modesty and restraint, one feels, are in the study of a young girl with downcast eyes (Plate 77)!

There is a second Watteau drawing in the Hammer Collection that is still more exquisite (Plate 78). The hands of the man leaning on his elbow are as beautifully articulated as any in art; his slender fingers seem tremulous with nervous energy. His companion, who supports her straight little back with one arm, is the entrancing girl to be seen constantly in Watteau's *fêtes galantes.* Such drawings as these are the raw material of Watteau's paintings, but, alas, with the transfer from paper to canvas something of their spontaneity and precision often vanishes. Wonderful as are his oils, one must admit he was, on the whole, a poor craftsman, and many of his paintings have cracked and faded. His drawings, on the other hand, have retained their pristine clarity, and every touch has remained delicately and precisely modulated.

Compared to Watteau, Boucher seems a little coarse. His *Venus Reclining Against a Dolphin* (Plate 80) is plumper and more sensuous than Watteau's *Young Girl.* Nevertheless, the drawing is delightfully conceived, especially the dolphin against which the goddess leans. Was it a touch of satire that the look in his angry eyes and the expression of his drooping mouth suggest a disgruntled and aging roué, who is literally supporting a voluptuous mistress?

Boucher executed at least fifty drawings on the theme of Venus, but his landscape sketches are much rarer. *Landscape with a Rustic Bridge* (Plate 79) is outstanding among them and was chosen by Agnes Mongan for her book *Great Drawings of All Time.* Like all his pastoral scenes, it is romanticized and self-consciously picturesque; yet there is at its basis the tradition of Dutch landscape, the work of artists like Van Goyen, Hobbema, and Ruisdael.

The five wash drawings by Fragonard in the Hammer Collection (Plates 82 – 86) are difficult to surpass anywhere. The earliest is a study for a painting, *The Education of the Virgin.* The others, though similar to some of Fragonard's paintings, were done as works of art in themselves. Each is so beautiful that it is hard to choose a favorite, but I have a slight preference for the thunderous grandfather who scowls at his erring grandchild.

Grandparents and their offspring appealed to the eighteenth century. The contrast of age and youth attracted a society that looked upon itself as still young but which was growing old more rapidly than it realized. *A Tired Woman with Two Children* by Greuze (Plate 81) might well serve as an allegory of the *ancien régime,* worn out by its own excesses and surrounded by the children whose rebellion was only beginning.

Ingres belongs to the new age, to the postrevolutionary

period with its return to classical restraint. In his drawing of *Mrs. Charles Badham,* who was portrayed in Rome in 1816 (Plate 87), no trace of the eighteenth century remains. Lightly drawn in the background is the Villa Medici, then as now the French Academy, and also visible is the obelisk at the top of the Spanish Steps, near the Via Gregoriana, where Ingres was living. His perfect control of line, his remarkable conjunction of eye and hand, set a standard for French draftsmanship throughout the nineteenth century.

Two artists totally different in temperament have particularly appealed to Armand Hammer: Daumier and Degas. A drawing by Daumier in watercolor, ink, and gouache of a lawyer pleading for his client (Plate 88) ranks among the artist's finest achievements. The old bespectacled advocate is vibrant with passion, and the whole court seems caught up in the intensity of the drama. One is almost overwhelmed by the concentrated endeavor of the unknown lawyer. A second drawing is a preliminary sketch for the *Third-Class Carriage* (Plate 89). Here the use of red chalk on a blue paper gives the strange effect of a photographic negative. A third sketch in ink, white chalk, and brown-and-black wash represents *The Virgin Holding the Infant Christ, with Saint Anne* (Plate 90).

Dr. Hammer has also acquired the Daumier lithographs formerly owned by George Longstreet, comprising more than four thousand different examples. These were collected over a period of forty years and represent one of the finest groups of Daumier lithographs ever brought together. Dr. Hammer has said that he hopes "the collection will serve as a nucleus for what I intend to become the most complete Daumier collection it is possible to assemble." It will be located at the Los Angeles County Museum of Art. To this end, he has already added a number of Daumier bronzes, the only poster ever created by Daumier, and one of the actual stones used for his lithographic prints, as well as many additional and rare examples of Daumier's lithographs.

There are five works by Degas in the Hammer Collection. One is an oil, one is drawn in charcoal, and three are pastels. But though different media are used, stylistically they have much in common. *Three Dancers in Yellow Skirts,* the oil (Plate 34), is an arabesque of ballerinas, as is *Theater Box,* a pastel (Plate 99), which adds to the pattern of the ballet dancers on the stage a further complexity — the silhouettes of foreground figures seated in a loge. Both are masterpieces of movement, and both have that extraordinary sense of immediacy that Degas was able to seize and hold in the visual kaleidoscope he saw.

The laundresses, drawn in charcoal and pastel, are, by contrast, motionless, caught in a timeless and unchanging equilibrium (Plates 96 and 97). They show Degas's mastery of volume and of balanced tensions.

Degas was also probably the greatest portraitist of the nineteenth century. His likeness of a man, whose staring eyes are so strangely hypnotic, is thought to be of his framemaker, *Jacquet* (Plate 98). The identity of the sitter, however, is unimportant; the significance of the painting is the mysterious personality of a human being caught in a few strokes of colored chalk.

The chromatic intensity attainable with pastel is clearly shown in the vase of flowers by Redon (Plate 103). A painter active when Impressionism and Post-Impressionism were the important movements in art, Redon was, like Gustave Moreau, *sui generis,* an individualist content to exploit his own particular vein of beauty.

Another artist in whom Armand Hammer is deeply interested is Gauguin. He owns several of his most beautiful drawings, but the *chef d'oeuvre* of his Gauguin collection, apart from *Bonjour M. Gauguin,* is a sketchbook containing 268 drawings on 105 pages (Plates 107A – 107J). Dr. Hammer has always been interested in sketches that enable one to appreciate the artist's first moments of creation, when, in his own words, "he sets down his concept in the most personal and spontaneous manner." Raymond Cogniat, in the introduction to John Rewald's book describing these sketches, has pointed out the invaluable insight these rapid notes give us into Gauguin's mental processes: "Perhaps we experience the deepest emotion when we are confronted by a rough draft, when a few strokes, at first illegible, suddenly become comprehensible as they reappear in a finished painting. Poring over the pages of this sketchbook, we have felt pleasure, the same joy the researcher experiences when he discovers the key to a problem." Gauguin himself helps us to solve these problems, for there are also in this same sketchbook eleven pages of his *Notes Synthétiques* — his first written statement on art theory.

Van Gogh, Gauguin's frequent companion, was not a theorist, nor had he Gauguin's facility. Integrity and intensity instead are his qualifications for immortality. The four drawings and the watercolor, *The Weaver,* in the Hammer Collection are all from the artist's early days in Holland before he saw Paris and met the Impressionists. He doggedly depicted the shabby little cottages he knew and the old men worn out with work who inhabited them (Plates 108 – 111). *The Weaver* (Plate 112) is now in the permanent collection of the Louvre, a gift from Armand Hammer.

To realize most vividly the nature of Van Gogh's plodding sincerity, contrast the fluency and the sophistication of three other drawings in the Hammer Collection done more or less at the same time. They are Renoir's pencil study entitled *Girlhood* (Plate 100) and the charcoal sketches by Manet of two tall young men — one on the recto, wearing a cloak, the other, on the verso, a cape (Plate 95). The Renoir drawing is fairly late, showing the same two girls as in Plate 28, where they are seen reading together; the Manet youths, who look down so disdainfully at the spectator, were sketched when the artist was a young man fresh from the studio of Thomas Couture. Their insolent expressions seem to anticipate the self-protective contempt that was to be assumed by many of the Impressionists after their public rejection.

The scorn of the public was one of several reasons why Cézanne, a close friend of all the Impressionists, returned from Paris to his native Aix-en-Provence. There he painted a monumental likeness of his father, which is now in the National Gallery in Washington. The study on the verso of the Hammer drawing (Plate 101) is his preliminary sketch for this.

When not engaged in portraiture or figure composition, Cézanne spent his days tramping around the familiar countryside, pitching his easel constantly before its principal feature, Mont Ste. Victoire. His late oils became more and more abstract; but it was in his watercolors that he reduced landscape to the limits of abstraction while still retaining recognizable features. The great escarpment of Mont Ste. Victoire is rendered in the Hammer sketch (Plate 102) with half-a-dozen sweeping brushstrokes, and the trees, over which it looms, with a few blots of colored wash.

Seurat, the next in chronological order among the draftsmen in the Hammer Collection, was much younger than Cézanne, but he died fifteen years earlier. He was only thirty-two. Had he lived longer, the revolution he introduced in painting might have been carried further by artists more able than his devoted follower, Henri-Edmond Cross, whose nocturne entitled *Cypresses* (Plate 114) is a charming work, somehow suggestive of the

nostalgic poetry of Verlaine. It is typical of *fin de siècle* sentimentality. Seurat himself, on the other hand, was the least sentimental of artists. He was a strong believer in scientific method, and his paintings were designed with mathematical precision. This is true also of his drawing *Study After "The Models"* in the Hammer Collection (Plate 113), which is as stark and uncompromising as a drawing by Pollaiuolo.

How different is the lithe, captivating girl pulling on her stocking by Bonnard (Plate 115)! Balanced on one leg, she seems to be dancing, and the rhythm of her movement is perfectly realized. This quick pencil drawing evokes an enticing femininity, a refined and delightful sensuality. Given the apparent direction of modern painting, Bonnard may have presented us with the last echo of voluptuousness in art, attenuated as it has become in his work.

The nude women and the young man drawn by Picasso (Plate 116), on the other hand, are powerful, savage beings, far from attractive. Although they are without a trace of charm, they, not Bonnard's dancing girl, are the prophets of contemporary art. They foretell a bleak world, charmless and neurotic.

It would be unsuitable to end this brief survey of the paintings and drawings in the Hammer Collection on this depressing note, and I have saved for the last the climax of Dr. Hammer's collecting, which is not a drawing but an oil.

The *Juno* by Rembrandt (Plate 7), recently acquired from Mr. and Mrs. J. William Middendorf, II, is, in my opinion, the finest single work of art that has remained in an American private collection. I well remember that this supremely beautiful painting struck me as unsurpassed when I first saw it exhibited. Like the drawing by Leonardo it, too, is a memory-image—a loving tribute to Hendrickje Stoffels, Rembrandt's mistress, who died in 1663, probably the year after the canvas was begun. When it finally goes to the Los Angeles County Museum, in the rapidly growing collection of that remarkable gallery, the Rembrandt *Juno* will long remain its outstanding treasure and also a magnet for visitors to the museum.

As a collector Armand Hammer is like a fisherman who throws back everything he catches. The lucky recipients are museums. Besides the National Gallery and the Los Angeles County Museum of Art, he has enriched the Hermitage Museum in Leningrad with a beautiful Goya (Plate

ARMAND HAMMER: COLLECTOR AND ENTREPRENEUR

10) and given to the Pushkin Museum in Moscow an important Raoul Dufy. He has contributed to the Queen's Silver Jubilee *At the Seashore* by Winston Churchill; to the National Museum of Poland, Slewinski's painting *Young Woman Seated;* to the San Carlos Museum in Mexico City a painting by Fragonard; and to the Louvre in Paris, Van Gogh's *The Weaver* (Plate 112). Beneficiaries in the United States include the Isaac Delgado Museum of Art, the Fine Arts Gallery of San Diego, the Brooks Memorial Art Gallery, the Fogg Art Museum, the Tennessee Fine Arts Center, the California Palace of the Legion of Honor, the Buffalo Bill Memorial Association, the White House, the High Museum of Art, and others.

There is a French term *amateur-marchand,* which can be aptly applied to Armand, for, besides collecting, he has never lost interest in the sale of works of art. The Hammer Galleries, of which he is president, continues its profitable business. Now, having sold all its Russian stock, it focuses on Post-Impressionism and modern pictures. In 1971 the oldest art firm in the United States, M. Knoedler & Co., came on the market after a number of unprofitable years. Armand immediately bought it lock, stock, and barrel. Its reputation as the source of a great part of the Mellon, Widener, Frick, and other major American collections had faded with time. It needed publicity, a commodity Armand can always provide. Through his influence in Russia, he arranged to show on its premises two of the most important exhibitions of works of art ever to come to this country. These extraordinary coups he managed by going, as is his custom, to the very top. He flew to Russia in his private plane and talked to Mme. E. A. Furtseva, the Minister of Culture, and asked her to lend forty-one masterpieces of modern art from the Hermitage Museum in Leningrad and from the Pushkin Museum in Moscow. He then had a two-hour conversation with Leonid Brezhnev, who warmly backed the proposed exhibition. The show opened at the National Gallery in Washington, went to New York, where it was shown at Knoedler, and then toured the United States. The attendance was enormous, with queues stretching for several blocks. It was such a success that the Russian authorities offered a second exhibition, this time of old masters and Russian paintings, which again was displayed at the National Gallery and Knoedler, and also drew a myriad of visitors.

Armand Hammer, however, is never satisfied with the profits of any company he owns. He has recently merged Knoedler with Modarco, whose shares are listed on the Geneva stock exchange and which is managed by two Swiss banks.

Although Armand's art dealing has been remarkably successful, more significant is the interest in works of art that he has aroused all over the world. He has sent his own collection on a tour that has brought masterpieces of drawing and painting to more places than have ever been reached by any other private or public collection. In the United States, his pictures have been seen in New York City, Memphis, Washington, D.C., Kansas City, New Orleans, Columbus, Little Rock, San Francisco, Oklahoma City, San Diego, Los Angeles, Nashville, Malibu, Atlanta, Denver, and Buffalo; and abroad, in London, Dublin, Leningrad, Moscow, Kiev, Minsk, Riga, Odessa, Caracas, Lima, Tokyo, Kyoto, Fukuoka, Nagoya, Mexico City, Paris, and Edinburgh.

Everywhere the Hammer Collection has been received with great enthusiasm. I myself saw the crowds on a Sunday afternoon at the Jacquemart-André Museum in Paris. There were so many visitors waiting to buy tickets that we, who were the guests of Armand Hammer, had to stand in a long queue, much, I believe, to his delight, until rescued by an official of the gallery. Similar crowds attended the simultaneous showing of drawings and watercolors at the Louvre. The eagerness of Parisians, the most sophisticated people in the world, to see a private collection underlines the words of René Huyghe, the director of the museum, that "the age of great private collections may soon be a thing of the past.... Perhaps Dr. Hammer's collection signals the end of an era."

JOHN WALKER

Paintings

1. PETER PAUL RUBENS (1577–1640)
ADORATION OF THE SHEPHERDS

Oil on canvas, formerly on panel: 32 x 24½" (81 x 62 cm.)

Collections: Erik W. Bergmann, Monroe, Mich.; Dr. Armand Hammer, Los Angeles; University of Southern California, Los Angeles.

Exhibited: Los Angeles County Museum of Art, *Rubens and Van Dyck,* 1946 (no. 3), repr. in cat.; Hollins, Va., Hollins College, 1954 – 55; Lynchburg, Va., Art Center, 1955; Charlottesville, Va., University of Virginia, 1956; Cologne, Wallraf-Richartz Museum, *Rubens in Italien,* Oct. 15 – Dec. 15, 1977 (no. 12); San José, Costa Rica, Museo de Jade, *Five Centuries of Masterpieces from American Collections Loaned to Costa Rica,* Apr. 12 – July 20, 1978.

Literature: W. R. Valentiner, *Art Quarterly,* vol. 9 (1946), p. 155, no. 7, fig. 1, as Rubens between 1607 and 1608; Leo van Puyvelde, *Rubens,* Paris, 1952, p. 201, note 33; Erik Larsen, *P. P. Rubens,* Antwerp, 1952, p. 215, note 12, as related to the Fermo altarpiece but an independent composition by Rubens of about 1608; W. R. Valentiner and P. Wescher, *The Hammer Collection,* Greenville, S.C., 1957, p. 43; Michael Jaffé, *Proporzioni,* vol. 4 (1963), p. 233, notes 101 and 105, figs. 34 and 35, as Rubens between 1606 and 1607; *The Armand Hammer Collection,* University of Southern California, Los Angeles, 1965, p. 49 (repr. in color on cover); Michael Jaffé, *Rubens and Italy,* Oxford, 1977, p. 98R, plate 337, as Rubens independent of the Fermo altarpiece and about 1607; J. Müller Hofstede, *Rubens in Italien,* catalogue, Wallraf-Richartz Museum, Cologne, 1977, no. 12, plate K-12, as Rubens after the Fermo altarpiece, probably between June 7 and October 28, 1608.

A *Nativity* at S. Filippo in Fermo resembles this *Adoration of the Shepherds,* but the theory that the Hammer painting is a *modello* for the Fermo altarpiece is now discounted by most scholars. Besides being the reverse of the Fermo in composition, the Hammer painting differs in the dis-position of the figures. It appears to be an independent treatment of the subject and, according to Michael Jaffé, may anticipate the Fermo altarpiece by some months. He tentatively suggests the name of Father Flamminio Ricci as the original recipient of this small panel. Ricci was Rubens's patron among the Oratorian Fathers and was responsible for the Fermo commission. J. Müller Hofstede thinks the Hammer painting could have been painted after the Fermo altarpiece, between June 7 and October 28, 1608 (the date of Rubens's return to Flanders). He notes that it was not painted on coarse canvas, as was usual in Italy, but on fine. Therefore, the possibility cannot be excluded that Rubens painted this version in Antwerp after his return to Flanders in 1609. Both Jaffé and Müller Hofstede refute the statement by W. R. Valentiner and P. Wescher that this *Adoration* once belonged to Duke Carlos II of Mantua. Müller Hofstede notes that the *Nativity* at Mantua was listed as being "un braccio e mezzo" (approximately 39¼" or 100 cm.), a figure that rules out the possibility of its being the picture in the Hammer Collection.

According to Leo van Puyvelde, the present *Adoration* could be the little *Nativity* referred to in the inventory of Rubens's studio made at the time of his death. There are at least two drawings related to figures in the Hammer picture, both in reverse: one corresponds to the head of Joseph (Frits Lugt Coll.; first published by Julius S. Held [*Rubens, Selected Drawings,* 1959, repr. vol. 2, plate 154]) and the other to the head of the young peasant woman with a basket who kneels in the center of the Hammer canvas (*Study of a Youth,* Mr. and Mrs. Robert L. Manning Coll., Forest Hills, N.Y.; first published by Jaffé [*Rubens and Italy,* plate 180]). While Rubens was in Italy from 1600 to 1608, he often chose his traveling companion and pupil, Deodato van der Mont, as a model. It may be his face that was used for the adoring shepherdess.

M. E.

2. PETER PAUL RUBENS (1577–1640)
VENUS WOUNDED BY A THORN

Oil on canvas: 32¼ x 24½" (82 x 62 cm.)

Collections: Thélusson Collection, Paris (sold Paris, Dec. 1, 1777 [no. 9], as an oil sketch); Dr. D. Arnon, New York, in 1949; Dr. Armand Hammer, Los Angeles; University of Southern California, Los Angeles, gift of Dr. Armand Hammer, 1966.

Exhibited: Roanoke, Va., Fine Arts Center, Nov. 30, 1954 – Jan. 2, 1955; Lynchburg, Va., Art Center, Jan. 31 – Feb. 21, 1955; Cologne, Wallraf-Richartz Museum, *Rubens in Italien,* Oct. 15 – Dec. 15, 1977 (no. 11).

Literature: *Catalogue of the Thélusson Collection,* Paris, 1777, ms. in the Frick Art Reference Library, New York City; John Smith, *Catalogue Raisonné of the . . . Dutch, Flemish and French Painters,* vol. 2, London, 1830, p. 192, no. 683; A. Hasselt, *Histoire de P. P. Rubens,* Brussels, 1840, p. 306, no. 819; Max Rooses, *L'Oeuvre de Pierre-Paul Rubens,* Antwerp, 1886 – 92, vol. 3, p. 180, no. 697; Erik Larsen, "Un Rubens perdu depuis 1777 et retrouvé," *Revue belge d'archéologie et d'histoire de l'art,* vol. 18 (1949), pp. 169 – 75, repr., as Rubens between 1606 and 1608; Erik Larsen, *P. P. Rubens,* Antwerp, 1952, p. 215, no. 11, as c. 1606 – 8; W. R. Valentiner and P. Wescher, *The Hammer Collection,* Greenville, S.C., 1957, p. 42; *The Armand Hammer Collection,* University of Southern California, Los Angeles, 1965, p. 48, repr.; Michael Jaffé, *Rubens and Italy,* Oxford, 1977, pp. 90R, 98R – 99L, 119 note 38, plate 318, as possibly relating to the painting of the same subject formerly in the collections of William Taverner, London (d. 1772) and James Stuart, London (d. 1788), and in the Richard Cosway sale, Christie's, London, 1791 (no. 31); J. Müller Hofstede, *Rubens in Italien,* catalogue, Wallraf-Richartz Museum, Cologne, 1977, no. 11, plate 339, as an independent work not related to a larger painting.

According to mythology, Venus, distraught over the death of her beloved Adonis, wandered aimlessly in the forest and stepped on a thorn. Her blood, falling upon a white rose, created the red rose, symbol of love. The story of Venus and Adonis fascinated Rubens, and at least two other pictures by him of this subject are known. (Rubens's source for this story is thought to be V. Cartari, *Imagini delli dei degl'antichi,* Venice, 1556.)

J. Müller Hofstede notes that Rubens most certainly modeled his Venus after the small antique bronze of Venus removing a thorn, of which there is a copy in the Bibliothèque Nationale (J. A. Blanchet, *Catalogue des bronzes antiques de la Bibliothèque Nationale,* Paris, 1895, no. 243). With the exception of the hairstyle and the more accentuated twisting of the upper torso, Rubens's Venus is identical to the classical prototype. Both Michael Jaffé and Müller Hofstede call attention to the boldly painted *putti,* whose bodies, contorted in grief and pain, echo the attitude of their mistress.

Müller Hofstede declares the Hammer painting to be an independent work, not a *modello* for a larger painting. Both he and Jaffé point to the influence of the Venetian School, namely, that of Tintoretto and of Titian in his late period. The painting probably dates from Rubens's last years in Italy (1606 – 8), though it is possible that he painted it during the year following his return to Antwerp. Müller Hofstede notes that this small work, characterized by a certain self-confident carelessness in its execution, may be one of Rubens's first attempts at painting a cabinet piece in a free and sketchy manner.

M. E.

3. PETER PAUL RUBENS (1577–1640)
YOUNG WOMAN WITH CURLY HAIR, c. 1618–20

Oil on panel: 17¹/₁₆ x 13³/₁₆″ (43.3 x 33.5 cm.), enlarged to 26 x 20⅝″ (67 x 52.4 cm.)

Collections: M. Schamp d'Aveschoot, Ghent, recorded 1830 (sold Ghent, Sept. 14, 1840); Duc d'Arenberg and descendants, Brussels and later south of France, purchased 1840 at Schamp sale; Edward Speelman, London, purchased 1959 from present duke; Jean Davray, Paris; M. Knoedler & Co., New York, in 1967.

Hammer Collection exhibitions: see catalogue reference page. First exhibited: II; not exhibited: XX.

Literature: John Smith, *Catalogue Raisonné of the Works of the . . . Dutch, Flemish and French Painters,* vol. 2, London, 1830, pp. 260 – 61, no. 881, and vol. 9 (supplement), 1842, p. 330, no. 317; *Catalogue des tableaux . . . composant la galerie de M. Schamp d'Aveschoot, de Gand,* sale catalogue, Sept. 14, 1840, p. 2; Max Rooses, *L'Oeuvre de Pierre-Paul Rubens,* Antwerp, 1886 – 92, vol. 4, pp. 138, 290, no. 1088, as a repetition by Rubens of the Dresden picture, both of c. 1635; J. Nève, "Quelques portraits de la galerie d'Arenberg," *Annales de l'Académie Royale d'Archéologie de Belgique,* Antwerp, vol. 5, ser. 4, tome 10 (1897), pp. 175 – 76; Max Rooses, "Oeuvres de Rubens — addenda," *Bulletin Rubens* (Antwerp), vol. 5 (1909), pp. 83 – 84; Rudolf Oldenbourg, *P. P. Rubens,* Munich and Berlin, 1922, p. 142; Ludwig Burchard, "Portrait of a Young Woman with Curly Hair by Peter Paul Rubens," ms. report on the Arenberg-Hammer painting, c. 1960; Douglas Cooper (ed.), *Great Private Collections,* London, 1963, repr. p. 254, as c. 1635; Michael Jaffé, Cambridge University, to Roland Balay, M. Knoedler & Co., New York, Feb. 3, 1967; Michael Harvard, "Portrait of a Girl with Curly Hair by Rubens," ms. report on the Arenberg-Hammer and Morris paintings, London, Mar., 1969; Michael Jaffé, "The Girl with the Golden Hair," *Apollo,* vol. 90 (Oct., 1969), pp. 310 – 13, repr. in color p. 311, plate IX; Mahonri Sharp Young, "The Hammer Collection Paintings," *Apollo,* vol. 95 (June, 1972), pp. 446, 451, repr. plate II in color, p. 441.

The portrait as Rubens painted it was only the head and shoulders of the young woman. A seventeenth-century copy in the Staatliche Gemäldegalerie in Kassel shows the portrait in its original rectangular shape and size before any of the enlargements. Sometime before the middle of the eighteenth century, the bevelled edge (about one inch all around) was trimmed off and the painting was set into a larger oval panel. Later, this oval was pieced out at the corners to make the present rectangle.

The subject of the Hammer picture must have been extraordinarily popular in the seventeenth and eighteenth centuries, for at least six early repetitions of it are known: the copy in the Staatliche Gemäldegalerie in Kassel of the original before enlargement (canvas, 17¼ x 13¾″, no. 89 in cat. of 1888); four repetitions of the present enlarged image: the oldest version in the Staatliche Kunstsammlungen, Dresden (panel, 25¼ x 19½″, p. 93 in cat. of 1966, repr. in Adolf Rosenberg, *P. P. Rubens, des Meisters Gemälde* [Klassiker der Kunst], 2d ed., Stuttgart and Leipzig, 1906, p. 373); Leningrad, Hermitage Museum (canvas, said to have been transferred from panel, 26 x 21¼″, no. 1692 in cat. of 1958, with additional drapery across the chest and near the shoulder); Althrop, The Earl Spencer Collection (untraceable, but known to Dr. Ludwig Burchard in 1947 and 1960 from a Hanfstaengl photograph, no. 113, showing two jeweled clasps holding the bodice); Kiel, Professor Götz Martius in 1935 (panel, 22⅞ x 16⅞″), similar to the Spencer portrait; and a sixth painting, still further enlarged, in the collection of John C. Morris, Richmond, Surrey. The Morris painting (panel, 28 x 23¼″, repr. in Rudolf Oldenbourg, *P. P. Rubens, des Meisters Gemälde* [Klassiker der Kunst], 4th ed., Berlin and Leipzig, 1921, p. 201) has a slightly lower neckline and extends the torso almost to the hips. Michael Jaffé believes that all these repetitions of the enlarged picture were made after Rubens's death and that only the Hammer picture is an original by Rubens.

The identity of the sitter is not known. Jaffé believes that the painting is a study rather than a formal portrait. According to Burchard, Rubens made a second study of the same girl but in a more frontal pose (Munich, Alte Pinakothek, no. 793 in cat.; exhibited in Bamberg Museum in 1934). The Munich painting measures 18⅞ x 14½″, approximately the same as the Hammer painting originally and, in Burchard's opinion, it was probably painted at the same sitting.

K. D.

4. PETER PAUL RUBENS (1577–1640)
THE ISRAELITES GATHERING MANNA IN THE DESERT, 1625–28

Oil on panel, 25½ x 20¾" (64.8 x 52.7 cm.)

Collections: Isabella Clara Eugenia, archduchess of the Spanish Netherlands, Brussels; Philip IV and Charles II of Spain; Don Francisco Casimiro Pimentel, conde de Benavente, who in 1700, following the death of Charles II, received this and the other paintings from the royal collections kept in the Pieza de las Furias for himself and his successors; duques de Pastrana, Madrid, by inheritance from the condes de Benavente; Emile Pacully, Paris, acquired from the Duque de Pastrana, Madrid, probably at sale of 1888 (sold Hôtel Drouot, Paris, July 5, 1938 [no. 28]); Baron Robert Gendebien, Brussels, acquired from A. Stein, dealer, Paris; Rosenberg & Stiebel, New York; Los Angeles County Museum of Art (Frances and Armand Hammer Purchase Fund, 1969).

Exhibited: Rotterdam, Museum Boymans van Beuningen, *Olieverfschelsen van Rubens,* Dec. 19, 1953 – Feb. 14, 1954 (no. 73), cat. by Egberg Haverkamp-Begemann, pp. 85 – 86, plate 63; Bordeaux, Galerie des Beaux-Arts, *Flandres, Espagne, Portugal du Xve au XVIIe Siècle,* May 19 – July 31, 1954 (no. 80), p. 83 in cat.; Brussels, Musées Royaux des Beaux-Arts de Belgique, *Le Siècle de Rubens,* Oct. 15 – Dec. 12, 1965 (no. 225), pp. 215 – 16 in cat. by Leo van Puyvelde, repr.

Hammer Collection exhibitions: see catalogue reference page. First exhibited: II; not exhibited: IV – X, XX.

Literature: Max Rooses, *L'Oeuvre de Pierre-Paul Rubens,* Antwerp, 1886 – 92, vol. 1, pp. 74, 76, no. 55; Max Rooses, "De Verzameling Pacully te Paris," *Onze Kunst,* 1903, pp. 121– 22; Virgile Josz, "La Collection Emile Pacully," *Les Arts,* 2d year, no. 16 (Apr., 1903), p. 35, repr. p. 36; *Collection Emile Pacully, tableaux anciens et modernes,* sale catalogue, Galerie Georges Petit, Paris, May 4, 1903, pp. 62 – 63, repr. with added garland; N. Sentenac y Cantanas, *La pintura en Madrid desde sus origenes hasta el siglo XIX,* Madrid, 1907, pp. 78 ff. (history and inventory of the Pastrana collection); *Tableaux . . . dépendant de la succession de Monsieur E. Pacully,* sale catalogue, Hôtel Drouot, Paris, 1938, no. 28, repr. with added garland, as by Rubens and Jan Bruegel (this and several other pictures from the 1903 sale were apparently bought back by the owner and kept through his lifetime); Leo van Puyvelde, *Les Esquisses de Rubens,* Basel, 1940, p. 31, no. 7 (Engl. ed.,

London, 1947, p. 29, no. 7); J. A. Goris and J. S. Held, *Rubens in America,* Antwerp, 1947, p. 49; F. Lugt, *Musée du Louvre, inventaire général des dessins des écoles du nord: école flamande,* vol. 2, Paris, 1949, no. 1127; Michael Jaffé, "Rubens' Sketching in Paint," *Art News* (May, 1953), pp. 37, 65, as mostly executed by assistants, with the exception of the woman with outspread skirts, which is by Rubens; Egbert Haverkamp-Begemann, "Rubens Schetsen," *Bulletin Museum Boymans Rotterdam,* vol. 5, no. 1 (Mar., 1954), p. 9., repr. p. 11; Victor H. Elbern, "Die Rubenssteppiche des Kölner Domes, ihre Geschichte und ihre Stellung im Zyklus Triumph der Eucharistie," *Kölner Domblatt,* vol. 10 (1955), pp. 74 – 75, plate 29; Mahonri Sharp Young, "The Hammer Collection: Paintings," *Apollo,* vol. 95 (June, 1972), p. 446, repr. p. 440.

About 1625 Archduchess Isabella Clara Eugenia, daughter of Philip II of Spain and ruler of the Spanish Netherlands, commissioned Rubens to produce eleven huge paintings and several smaller ones to be used as cartoons (full-size patterns) for a series of tapestries glorifying the Eucharist that she wished to present to the convent of the Descalzas Reales (Franciscan Poor Clares) in Madrid. The subjects were: four Old Testament prefigurations of the New Testament Eucharist, one of which was the Israelites gathering manna in the desert; two of the Evangelists and Eucharistic teachers and defenders; and five Eucharistic triumphs. The first series of tapestries made in Brussels was sent to the convent in Madrid in July, 1628. A second series is now in the cathedral of Cologne. Individual cartoons were also woven into tapestries, not as part of a series.

In the preparation of the cartoons, Rubens first painted rough sketches in grisaille, then full-color sketches *(modelli),* which were enlarged by the master and his shop to the desired size of the tapestry. The first sketch for *The Israelites Gathering Manna in the Desert* is a panel (5¾ x 4⅛") in the Musée Bonnat, Bayonne. In it, Moses is in the background of a composition with a strong movement from left to right. In preparing the Los Angeles *modello,* Rubens centralized the composition, confining it between Moses, on the right, and the woman with the child who turns toward center, on the left. The woman is adapted from the woman with a jug in the Raphael *Fire in*

the Borgo in the Vatican; other elements in both the grisaille and the *modello* are related to a Rubens drawing in the Louvre (Lugt, no. 1038, fig. 52; also Victor H. Elbern, "Die Rubensteppiche des Kölner Domes," *Kölner Domblatt,* vols. 14, 15 [1958], fig. 12) after a Giulio Romano *Gathering of the Manna.* Employing Renaissance elements and classic compositional limits, Rubens filled his stage with a dynamic movement and counter-movement of form and light and a subtle implication of psychological relationships that had not been achieved before the seventeenth century.

In 1648 Philip IV asked that the large cartoons and "other small paintings" for the Triumph of the Eucharist series be sent to Madrid. It is assumed by Rubens scholars that the sketches that were in the royal collections of Spain in the late seventeenth century, including the Los Angeles *modello,* were sent at that time. Presumably before 1648, the Los Angeles *modello* was set into a larger panel and surrounded by a garland of flowers and fruits. The garland, originally believed to be by Jan Bruegel, was given by Max Rooses (*Onze Kunst,* 1903) to Pieter Gysels (1621 – 1690). The attribution to Gysels implies a date in the late 1640s. The *modello* with the garland is reproduced in the two Pacully sale catalogues and in *Les Arts,* 1903. The enlargement was removed and the painting restored to its original size after the sale of 1938.

The Los Angeles *modello* was separated from the other Triumph of the Eucharist *modelli* now in the Prado when it was inherited by the conde de Benavente. It was presumably sold to Pacully before the duquesa de Pastrana presented a number of Rubens sketches for the Torre de la Parada from the same Benavente-Pastrana inheritance to the Prado on May 28, 1889 (Prado nos. 2038 – 40).

The large cartoon (canvas, 192 x 163″) made from the Los Angeles *modello* was one of six sent in 1648 to Philip IV. He presented the six to Don Gaspar de Guzmán, conde-duque de Olivares (1587 – 1645), who placed them in his small family church at Loeches, near Madrid. They were removed by French troops during the Napoleonic invasions. Two became the property of the Louvre; four, including *The Israelites Gathering Manna in the Desert,* were sold in 1818 to the duke of Westminster and in 1928 to John Ringling for the Ringling Museum in Sarasota, Fla. (repr. in William E. Suida, *A Catalogue of Paintings in the John and Mable Ringling Museum of Art,* Sarasota, 1949, pp. 178 – 83). A copy of the Los Angeles *modello* is in the Musée des Beaux-Arts, Doornik (Tournai). A School of Rubens drawing of the composition is in the Louvre (Lugt, no. 1127).

The most concise study of the series in English is Julius Held, "Rubens' Triumph of the Eucharist and the *Modello* in Louisville," *J. B. Speed Art Museum Bulletin,* vol. 26, no. 3 (Feb., 1968). The most exhaustive studies are Elias Tormo, "Los tápices: la apoteosis eucarística de Rubens," *En las descalzas reales de Madrid,* vol. 2, fasc. 2, Madrid, 1945; and Victor H. Elbern, "Die Rubensteppiche des Kölner Domes, ihre Geschichte und ihre Stellung im Zyklus Triumph der Eucharistie," *Kölner Domblatt,* vol. 10 (1955), pp. 43 – 88, vols. 14, 15 (1958), pp. 121 ff., vols. 21, 22 (1963), pp. 77 ff.

K. D.

5. REMBRANDT VAN RIJN (1606–1669)
PORTRAIT OF A MAN OF THE RAMAN FAMILY, 1634

Oil on oval panel: 25½ x 19⅞″ (64.8 x 50.5 cm.), enlarged to a rectangle 27⅛ x 20⅞″ (68.8 x 53.2 cm.)
Signed and dated lower right: Rembrandt fe 1634
Inscribed lower left: Ae, 47

Collections: Raman Family, Amsterdam; August de Ridder, Schönberg near Cronberg, before 1909 (sold Galerie Georges Petit, Paris, June 2, 1924 [no. 55]); Ehrich Galleries, New York, 1930 – 36; N. Katz, Basel, by 1948 (sold, Paris, Apr. 25, 1951); Julius Weitzner Galleries, New York, by 1956; P. de Boer, Amsterdam, before 1966; H. Kohn, Wassenaar, the Netherlands, by 1968; H. Shickman Gallery, New York, 1969; Los Angeles County Museum of Art (Frances and Armand Hammer Purchase Fund, 1969).

Exhibited: Frankfurt-am-Main, Städelsches Kunstinstitut, 1911 – 13 (following the death of De Ridder, May 13, 1911); New York, F. Kleinberger Galleries, *The Collection of Pictures of the Late Herr A. de Ridder,* exhibition and private sale, Nov. 24 – Dec. 15, 1913 (no. 1); Detroit Institute of Arts, *Paintings by Rembrandt,* May 2 – 31, 1930 (no. 22), lent by Ehrich Galleries, New York, repr. in cat.; The Hague, Mauritshuis, *Herwonnen Kunstbezit: Tentoonstelling van uit Duitschland Teruggekeerde Nederlandsche Kuntschatten,* Mar. – May, 1946 (no. 49); Basel, Katz Galerie, *Rembrandt Ausstellung,* July 24 – Sept. 30, 1948 (no. 13), lent by Swiss private collector, repr. in cat.; Raleigh, North Carolina Museum of Art, Nov. 16 – Dec. 30, 1956 (no. 9), lent by Julius Weitzner, repr. in cat.

Hammer Collection exhibitions: see catalogue reference page. First exhibited: II; not exhibited: IV – X, XX.

Literature: W. R. Valentiner, *Rembrandt, des Meisters Gemälde* [Klassiker der Kunst], 3d ed., Stuttgart and Berlin, 1909, repr. p. 193, as *Portrait of a Man;* Wilhelm Bode, *Die Gemäldegalerie des Herrn A. de Ridder,* Berlin, 1910, pp. 4, 35, plate 1, as *Portrait of a Man of the Raman Family;* Wilhelm Bode, *The Collection of Pictures of the Late Herr A. de Ridder* (trans. Harry Virgin), Berlin, 1913, no. 1, plate 1; C. Hofstede de Groot, *A Catalogue Raisonné of the Works of the Most Eminent Dutch Painters of the Seventeenth Century,* London, 1916, vol. 6, p. 347, no. 739, as *A Man in a Large Slouch Hat, said to be a member of the Raman family; Catalogue des tableaux anciens . . . composant la galerie de feu M. A. de Ridder,* sale catalogue, Galerie Georges Petit, Paris, 1924, no. 55, repr.; A. Bredius, *Rembrandt Gemälde,* Vienna, 1935, p. 9, no. 194, repr.; A. Bredius, *The Paintings of Rembrandt,* 2d ed., London, 1937, p. 8, no. 194, repr.; Jakob Rosenberg, *Rembrandt,* Cambridge, Mass., 1948, vol. 1, p. 243 (concordance); Kurt Bauch, *Rembrandt Gemälde,* Berlin, 1966, p. 19 (notes), no. 374, repr.; Horst Gerson, *Rembrandt Paintings,* Amsterdam and New York, 1968, p. 495, no. 168, repr. p. 289; Horst Gerson (ed.), *Rembrandt, The Complete Edition of the Paintings of Rembrandt by A. Bredius,* London, 1969, p. 564, no. 194, repr. p. 158; Mahonri Sharp Young, "The Hammer Collection: Paintings," *Apollo,* vol. 95 (June, 1972), pp. 444, 446.

When Rembrandt was seven years old, his father enrolled him in the Latin School at Leiden. His father, a miller, evidently was ambitious for him, since in his time only boys who were expected to study at a university and then go on to the ministry, law, medicine, or another profession were sent to learn Latin and read the classical authors. After spending seven years at the school, Rembrandt matriculated at Leiden University, but he soon dropped out. A contemporary tells us that the fourteen-year-old youth had no appetite for academic studies; his only interest was in painting and drawing.

Rembrandt appears on the scene as an independent artist four or five years later. It is evident from the very beginning that he had high ambitions for himself. Most Dutch artists specialized in portraiture or realistic scenes. Rembrandt was made of different stuff; he was determined to make his mark as a painter of biblical, historical, and mythological subjects. He accepted the idea implicitly or explicitly endorsed by artists and theorists since the early Renaissance that such works were more significant than portraits, genre scenes, landscapes, and still lifes.

From about 1625 to 1630, Rembrandt mainly dedicated his art and volcanic energy to religious and classical subjects. His first commissioned portraits were done in 1631, and from this time until his last years portraiture became his stock-in-trade. However, he did not neglect the themes he considered more consequential. On the contrary, he continued to be preoccupied with them throughout his entire career, and during his last phase they became his principal concern. His *Juno* (Plate 7) is an outstanding late example of this category of his work.

The vast number of commissioned portraits Rembrandt painted during the 1630s indicates that he quickly became the most sought-after painter of likenesses in Holland. His

brilliant *Portrait of a Man of the Raman Family* shows the qualities that made his early reputation: a strong illusionism combined with pictorial effects that no other Dutch artists could match. We sense that Rembrandt provided a speaking likeness of his sitter as well as an accurate description of his clothing, two demands most people continue to make of portraitists. Any suggestion of hardness or overmeticulousness was avoided. Variety of touch and fluid brushwork subtly animate the features of his serious forty-seven-year-old patron, while the strong accent of light on his huge white ruff dissolves the forms of its complicated folds. In the handling of the light and shadow, there is no dramatic spotlight effect. The illuminated areas on the face are soft, the shadows transparent, the convincing roundness of forms is achieved by delicately graded half-tones, and variations in the values of the neutral background provide spaciousness and an atmosphere that envelops the figure.

The portrait belonged to the Raman family of Amsterdam until it was acquired by August de Ridder, before 1909. According to tradition, it had been in their possession since the seventeenth century; hence its title. When it was painted, oval formats for portraits were enjoying a vogue in Holland; at a later date, it was enlarged into a rectangle (the frame now hides the additions). The assumption that the *Portrait of a Woman in a Broad Ruff* of 1636, now in the collection of Lord Kinnaird, Rossie Priory, Perthshire, is its companion piece is supported by technical examinations that revealed that the additions made to alter its shape from oval to rectangular are identical to the enlargements of the Hammer picture.

S. S.

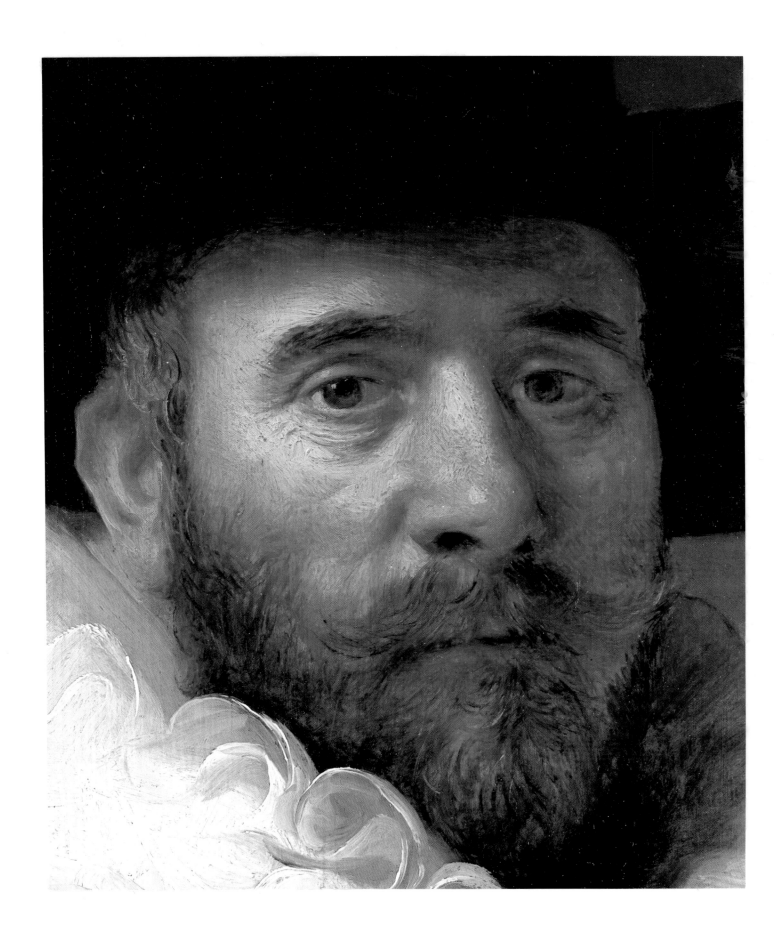

6. REMBRANDT VAN RIJN (1606–1669)
PORTRAIT OF A MAN HOLDING A BLACK HAT, probably 1637

Oil on panel: 32 x 28″ (81.7 x 71 cm.)
Signed lower right: Rembrandt

Collections: In 1836 John Smith catalogued a portrait included in the Proley sale of 1787, which C. Hofstede de Groot (*Catalogue Raisonné of the Works of the Most Eminent Dutch Painters of the Seventeenth Century,* London, 1916, vol. 6, p. 353, no. 751) concluded was identical with this painting; Hofstede de Groot noted that the Proley sale took place in Paris, but efforts to trace a catalogue of the sale have been unsuccessful; Prince Gagarin, Moscow, by 1906; sold by Prince Nicolas Gagarin through Prince Pierre Troubetskoy to Alfred W. Erickson, New York, 1925; Mr. and Mrs. J. W. Middendorf, II, 1961 – 79.

Exhibited: Detroit Institute of Arts, *Paintings by Rembrandt,* May 2 – 31, 1930 (no. 28), lent by A. W. Erickson, New York, repr. in cat., as *Prince Frederick Henry, Governor of the Netherlands,* dated 1637; New York, Metropolitan Museum of Art, 1961 – 79, lent by Mr. and Mrs. J. W. Middendorf, II, as *Prince Frederick of Orange,* dated 1637; Washington, D.C., National Gallery of Art, 1979, lent by Dr. Armand Hammer.

Literature: Possibly identical with no. 263, *A Gentleman, seen in three quarter view, habited in the ancient Dutch costume, and holding his hat in his hand,* in John Smith, *Catalogue Raisonné of the Works of the Most Eminent Dutch, Flemish and French Painters,* vol. 7, London, 1836, p. 99, panel, 2′5″ x 2′2″, collection of M[onsieur]. Proley, 1787; Wilhelm Bode and C. Hofstede de Groot, *The Complete Work of Rembrandt,* Paris, 1906, vol. 8, p. 102, no. 570, repr., as *A Young Man in Profile Holding His Hat in Both Hands,* dated 1637; W. R. Valentiner, *Rembrandt, des Meisters Gemälde* [Klassiker der Kunst], 3d ed., Stuttgart and Berlin, 1909, repr. p. 217, as *Portrait of a Young Man,* dated 1637, described p. 536 as perhaps a portrait of Prince Frederick Henry, Stadholder of the Netherlands; C. Hofstede de Groot, *A Catalogue Raisonné of the Works of the Most Eminent Dutch Painters of the Seventeenth Century,* London, 1916, vol. 6, p. 353, no. 751, as *A Young Man Holding a High Broad Rimmed Hat with Both Hands,* dated 1637; Wilhelm R. Valentiner, *Rembrandt Paintings in America,* New York, 1931 (unpaginated), no. 62, as *Prince Frederick Henry, Governor of the Netherlands,* dated 1637; Jakob Rosenberg, *Rembrandt,* Cambridge, Mass., 1948, vol. 1, p. 248 (reference in his concordance to Klassiker der Kunst, no. 217); A. Staring,

"Vraagstukken der Oranje-Iconographie, III. Conterfeite Rembrandt Frederik Hendrik en Amalia?" *Oud Holland,* vol. 68 (1953), p. 14, not described as being a portrait of Frederick Henry; *Old Master Paintings Collected by the Late Mr. and Mrs. Alfred W. Erickson,* sale catalogue, Parke-Bernet, New York, Nov. 15, 1961, listed as *Prince Frederick Henry of Orange, Governor of the Netherlands,* and as being dated, almost illegibly, 1637; Jakob Rosenberg, *Rembrandt: Life and Work,* London, 1964, p. 371 (reference in his concordance to Klassiker der Kunst, no. 217); Kurt Bauch, *Rembrandt Gemälde,* Berlin, 1966, no. 379, repr., as *Prince Frederick Henry of Orange-Nassau, Stadholder of the Netherlands(?),* dated 1637, described p. 20, no. 379, as *Portrait of a Distinguished Man* (Bauch notes here it is unlikely that the work is a portrait of Frederick Henry).

Since this portrait was first catalogued, in 1906, every published reference to it stated that it was signed and dated 1637. When it was sold in 1961, a qualification regarding its inscription was introduced; the author of the sale catalogue scrupulously noted that the date had become almost illegible. Today it has completely disappeared, but to judge from the painting's style there is little reason to doubt the date earlier specialists recorded. This swagger portrait is characteristic of the fashionable ones Rembrandt painted during the mid-1630s, when his reputation as a painter of likenesses was at its zenith.

Not long after the painting became generally known, it was tentatively identified as a portrait of Frederick Henry, Prince of Orange-Nassau, and soon afterward this suggestion was accepted by some people without reservation. It is not hard to understand why—the reported discovery of a portrait by Holland's greatest artist of a leading hero of his country was a boost to national pride.

As every Dutch schoolchild knows, Frederick Henry was a son of William the Silent, the principal leader of the Dutch struggle for independence from Spain. In 1625 he succeeded his older brother Maurice as hereditary stadholder of the United Provinces of the Netherlands and commander-in-chief of its armies. The prince's military victories and political skills helped end the bitter eighty-year war between Spain and the Netherlands. He died in 1647, a year before the Treaty of Münster finally established peace between the two nations and accorded

the new Dutch Republic *de jure* recognition among the family of nations.

Knowledge that Rembrandt enjoyed the prince's patronage helped lend credibility to the identification of the subject of this portrait as Frederick Henry. As early as 1632, only a year after the artist made his debut as a professional portraitist, he painted a likeness of Frederick Henry's consort, Amalia van Solms. A few years later, the prince acquired Rembrandt's *Raising of the Cross* and *Descent from the Cross,* and by 1636 he had commissioned him to paint three additional scenes from the Passion: an *Entombment,* a *Resurrection,* and an *Ascension of Christ.* The prince not only continued to collect Rembrandt's pictures but was willing to pay top prices for them. In 1646 he instructed his treasurer to send the artist the very substantial sum of 2,400 guilders for two of his paintings, an *Adoration of the Shepherds* and a *Circumcision of Christ.*

In view of the prince's record as a loyal patron of the artist it would almost seem unnatural if he had not commissioned Rembrandt to paint his own portrait. In fact, he may have ordered one — if we can trust the attribution made by the author of an inventory compiled in 1667 of a collection in a palace that belonged to the House of Orange at The Hague. The inventory lists a profile portrait of His Highness Prince Frederick Henry by Rembrandt. There is, however, good reason to believe that the compiler of the inventory muddled matters by wrongly ascribing to Rembrandt a profile portrait of the prince by Gerrit van Honthorst, which is still in the royal collection at The Hague. In any event, that portrait cannot be identical with the Armand Hammer painting; it is specifically described as a portrait done in profile. The man in the Hammer painting is seen almost full face.

Frederick Henry enhanced cultural life at his court in The Hague, but in the prince's time his fame was not founded upon his promotion of the arts. It rested on his brilliance as a military strategist, his gifts as a statesman, and his reputation as a ladies' man. Before his marriage, at the age of forty, to Amalia van Solms, he was reputed to have been too fond of women to tie himself permanently to one of them. Nothing about Rembrandt's portrait appears to contradict this characterization of the prince, but of course it is impossible to determine the degree of a man's fondness for the company of women from an artist's portrayal of him.

Identification of the painting as a portrait of Frederick Henry can neither rest upon the prince's proven patronage of Rembrandt nor on unprovable interpretations of the attitude of the artist's client toward women. It can, however, be tested by checking the resemblance of the man to documented portraits of the prince by Anthony van Dyck and by Honthorst; but comparison of these pictures, which predictably show him in armor accompanied by symbols of his authority, with the Hammer portrait shatters the appealing idea that Rembrandt's painting is a likeness of the prince. As painted by these artists, Rembrandt's sitter resembles Frederick Henry as much as George Washington resembles Paul Revere.

Although the man who commissioned Rembrandt to paint his portrait must join the large ranks of the artist's anonymous patrons, it is possible to deduce a few things about him. Apart from the good taste and judgment he showed when he selected Rembrandt as his portraitist in the 1630s, it is evident that he did not share his contemporaries' taste for sober black clothing. He chose to be painted in a gray moiré jacket. He must have been delighted with Rembrandt's nearly miraculous control of shifts in color and tone that allowed the artist to suggest the way light is variously reflected from the heavily and irregularly ribbed threads of his taffeta jacket, producing watered and rippled effects. The intense realism that characterizes Rembrandt's paintings of this period and the high standard of pictorial richness and execution he maintained are evident in other key passages of this fine portrait, most notably in the artist's characterization of his handsome patron's face. Rembrandt's genius enabled him to accentuate his deep human interest even when giving an unrivaled virtuoso display of his ability to render the color, texture, and weight of stuffs.

S. S.

Oil on canvas: 50 x 48¾″ (127 x 123.8 cm.)

Collections: Harmen Becker, Amsterdam, between 1665 and 1678; possibly Sir John Thomas Stanley, Palmerston House, Turnbridge, England, and his heirs, 1766 – 1850; Otto Friedrich Ludwig Wesendonck, Berlin, 1888 – 96, and his heirs, until 1925; Rheinische Provinzialverband and the City of Bonn, 1925 – 35 (sold Math. Lempertz, Cologne, Nov. 27, 1935); W. Poech and A. J. Schrender, Amsterdam, purchased at Cologne sale, 1935; D. Katz, Dieren, the Netherlands, 1935; C. J. K. van Aalst, K. B. E., Huis te Hoevelaken, the Netherlands, by 1939, and his heirs, until 1966: Hans M. Cramer, The Hague, 1966; Mr. and Mrs. J. William Middendorf, II, 1966.

Exhibited: Bonn, Provinzialmuseum, 1906 – 35, lent by the heirs of Mr. Otto Wesendonck until 1925; Amsterdam, Rijksmuseum, *Internal Art Trade Exhibition,* 1935; New York, Schaeffer Galleries, Inc., *Rembrandt,* Apr. 1 – 15, 1937 (no. 5), lent by D. Katz, repr. in cat.; New York World's Fair, *Masterpieces of European Paintings and Sculpture from 1300 – 1800,* May – Oct., 1939 (no. 312), lent by C. J. K. van Aalst, p. 52 in cat. by G. H. McCall and W. R. Valentiner; Detroit Institute of Arts, *Masterpieces of Art from Foreign Collections* (European paintings from the New York and San Francisco World's Fairs), Nov. 10 – Dec. 10, 1939 (no. 40), lent by C. J. K. van Aalst, repr. in cat.; circulated in 1940 – 41 to Cleveland Museum of Art, Los Angeles County Museum of Art, Minneapolis Institute of Arts, Newark Museum, Springfield Museum, Springfield, Mass., and City Art Museum of St. Louis; Detroit Institute of Arts, *Masterpieces of Art from European and American Collections* (European paintings from the New York and San Francisco World's Fairs), Apr. 1 – May 31, 1941 (no. 49), lent by C. J. K. van Aalst, repr. in cat. p. 18; Detroit Institute of Arts, 1941 – 47, lent by C. J. K. van Aalst; Los Angeles County Museum of Art, *Frans Hals — Rembrandt,* Nov. 18 – Dec. 31, 1947 (no. 30), lent by Estate of C. J. K. van Aalst, pp. 74 – 75, plate XXX in cat. by W. R. Valentiner; Rotterdam, Museum Boymans van Beuningen, Mar. – May, 1966, lent by Mr. and Mrs. J. W. Middendorf, II; New York, Metropolitan Museum of Art, 1966 – 1976, lent by Mr. and Mrs. J. W. Middendorf, II; New York, Wildenstein & Co., Inc., *Gods & Heroes, Baroque Images of Antiquity,* Oct. 30 – Dec. 30, 1968 (no. 34), lent by Mr. and Mrs. J. W. Middendorf, II, color frontispiece in cat.; Kyoto, Municipal Museum, Jan. 3 – Mar. 1, 1969, *The Age of Rembrandt,*

Dutch Paintings and Drawings of the 17th Century (no. 52), lent by Mr. and Mrs. J. W. Middendorf, II; Cambridge, Mass., Fogg Art Museum, Harvard University, Oct. 6 – Dec. 13, 1976; Los Angeles County Museum of Art, New Acquisitions Gallery, Dec. 19, 1976 – Feb. 6, 1977.

Hammer Collection exhibitions: see catalogue reference page. First exhibited: XXX.

Literature: N. De Roever, "Rembrandt, Bijdrogen tot de Geschiedenis van zijn laatste levensjaren," *Oud Holland,* vol. 2 (1884), pp. 90 – 91; O. Wesendonck, *Katalog A. Gemälde Sammlung Wesendonck,* Berlin, 1888, pp. 77 – 78, no. 240; A. Bredius, "Nievwe Rembrandtiana," *Oud Holland,* vol. 17 (1899), p. 4; C. Hofstede de Groot, *Die Urkunden über Rembrandt (1575 – 1721),* The Hague, 1906, pp. 337 – 38, no. 278, pp. 340 – 41, no. 280, pp. 341 – 42, no. 281; W. Cohen, "Die Sammlung Wesendonck," *Zeitschrift für Bildende Kunst,* n.s., vol. 21 (1909), pp. 57 ff.; A. Bredius, "Rembrandtiana II: De Nalatenschap van Harmen Becker," *Oud Holland,* vol. 28 (1910), pp. 195 ff.; W. Cohen, *Katalog der Gemäldegalerie vorwiegend Sammlung Wesendonck,* Provinzialmuseum, Bonn, 1914, p. 156 (2d ed., 1927, p. 154), no. 230; C. Hofstede de Groot, *A Catalogue Raisonné of the Works of the Most Eminent Dutch Painters of the Seventeenth Century,* London, 1916, vol. 6, p. 138, no. 207a; *Westdeutscher Museumbesitz, Sammlung Wesendonck von Bissing,* sale catalogue, Math. Lempertz, Cologne, 1935, p. 26, no. 87, repr.; A. Bredius, "Ein wiedergefundener Rembrandt," *Pantheon,* vol. 18 (1936), p. 277, repr.; A. Bredius, *The Paintings of Rembrandt,* 2d ed., London, 1937, p. 27, no. 639, repr.; A. Heppner, "Eine Rembrandt Entdeckung," *Die Weltkunst,* vol. 8, nos. 31 – 32 (Aug. 9, 1936), p. 1, repr.; G. Isarlo, "La Juno de Rembrandt est retrouvée," *Beaux-arts,* Oct. 9, 1936, p. 2, repr.; J. L. A. A. M. dan Ryckevorsel, "De Teruggevonden Schilderij van Rembrandt: De Juno," *Oud Holland,* vol. 53 (1936), pp. 270 – 74, plate 1; H. G. Fell, "The 'Juno' of Rembrandt," *Connoisseur,* vol. 99 (Jan. – June, 1937), p. 3, repr. in color frontispiece and on cover (includes letters by A. Bredius and W. R. Valentiner); Anon., "Rembrandt's 'Juno,'" *The Art Designer,* vol. 11, no. 13 (Apr. 1, 1937), p. 12, repr.; A. M. Frankfurter, "An Important View of Rembrandt," *The Art News,* vol. 35, no. 27 (Apr. 3, 1937), pp. 9, 24 – 25, repr. p. 8; J. Held, "Two Rembrandts," *Parnassus,* vol. 9, no. 4 (Apr., 1937), pp. 36 – 38, repr.; M. Weinberger, " 'New' Rembrandts," *Magazine*

of Art, vol. 30 (1937), pp. 312 – 14, repr. p. 299; John Rewald, "A l'étranger un Rembrandt vendu par un musée allemand," *Amour de l'art,* vol. 19, no. 9 (Nov., 1938), p. 361, repr.; W. R. Valentiner and A. M. Frankfurter, *Masterpieces of Art, Exhibition at the New York World's Fair 1939 – Guide and Picture Book,* New York, 1939, repr. p. 96; E. Kieser, "Uber Rembrandts Verhältnis zur Antike," *Zeitschrift für Kunstgeschichte,* vol. 10 (1941 – 42), p. 141; Jakob Rosenberg, *Rembrandt,* Cambridge, Mass., 1948, vol. 1, p. 248 (concordance); G. Knuttel, *Rembrandt, De meester en zijn werk,* Amsterdam, 1956, pp. 210, 278; Anon., "Rembrandt's 'Lost' Juno To Be Auctioned at Christie's," *Arts,* vol. 34, no. 5 (Feb., 1960), p. 9; N. Maclaren, *The Dutch School,* catalogue, National Gallery, London, 1960, p. 313; *Highly Important Netherlandish Paintings from the Collection Formed by the Late Dr. C. J. K. van Aalst,* sale catalogue (painting not sold), Christie, Manson, & Woods, London, Apr. 1, 1960, pp. 26 – 27, no. 38, plate 18 and color frontispiece; *Catalogue No. XII 1965 – 66,* G. Cramer Galerie, The Hague, 1965, p. 7, repr.; G.C.V., "Rembrandt 'Juno' in den Haag," *Die Weltkunst,* vol. 35, no. 21 (Nov. 15, 1965), pp. 1091 – 92; Kurt Bauch, *Rembrandt Gemälde,* Berlin, 1966, pp. xv, 15, no. 285, repr.; Anon., "Rembrandt's 'Juno' für das Metropolitan Museum," *Die Weltkunst,* vol. 36, no. 7 (Apr. 1, 1966), p. 291, repr.; Ann Livermore, "Rembrandt and Jansen: A New Interpretation," *Apollo,* vol. 85 (Jan. – June, 1967), p. 245, note 4; Horst Gerson, *Rembrandt's Paintings,* Amsterdam and New York, 1968, pp. 132 – 33, 430 – 31, repr. in color; S. Nodelman, "After the High Roman Fashion," *Art News,* vol. 67, no. 7 (Nov., 1968), pp. 34 ff., repr.; J. T. Butler, "The American Way with Art," *Connoisseur,* vol. 169 (Nov., 1968), p. 200, repr.; M. S. Young, "Letter from U.S.A.," *Apollo,* vol. 87 (July – Dec., 1968), p. 390; J. J. Jacobs, "New York Gallery Notes," *Art in America,* vol. 56, no. 6 (Nov. – Dec., 1968), p. 109, repr. in color; *The Age of Rembrandt, Dutch Paintings and Drawings of the 17th Century,* catalogue, National Museum of Western Art, Tokyo, and Municipal Museum, Kyoto, 1968 – 69, no. 52, repr.; Horst Gerson (ed.), *Rembrandt, The Complete Edition of the Paintings of Rembrandt by A. Bredius,* London, 1969, p. 617, no. 639, repr. p. 396; J. Held, *Rembrandt's Aristotle and Other Rembrandt Studies,* Princeton, N.J., 1969, chap. 3, pp. 85 – 103, repr.; B. Haak, *Rembrandt, His Life, His Work, His Time,* New York, 1969, p. 318, repr. in color p. 318, plate 539; Egbert Haverkamp-Begemann, "The Present State of Rembrandt Studies," *Art Bulletin,* vol. 53 (1971), p. 95.

In Rembrandt's *Juno,* the queen of the gods confronts us squarely, a robust young woman of ample proportions, opulently dressed, with a golden crown on her head and a golden scepter in her hand. Most of the artist's contemporaries would have readily recognized that the peacock at her side is her traditional symbol. The ancient gods were still very much alive in the minds of seventeenth-century Dutchmen. They were introduced to them at an early age —Rembrandt began his study of classical culture when he was a boy of seven—and the numerous references to the gods in the literature of the period show that familiarity with them was taken for granted.

Dutchmen of Rembrandt's epoch knew that the ancients gave Juno many roles. She was venerated as a goddess of the state, a deity of the moon, the goddess of marriage, and the protectress of women—particularly of those in childbirth. They also knew that Boccaccio and later writers and artists popularized her as the goddess of wealth.

Which role did Rembrandt assign to his *Juno,* and for whom did he paint it? Everything that is known about its history and style, as well as what has been learned about it through technical analysis in the laboratory, supports the conclusion that he painted Juno as the goddess of wealth for Harmen Becker, a rich Amsterdam merchant, moneylender, and collector.

Contemporary documents tell us that about 1662 – 63 Becker made two loans to Rembrandt. The artist gave Becker nine of his paintings and two volumes of his prints and drawings as collateral. In 1664 one of Rembrandt's close friends went to Becker on his behalf to repay the principal and interest on the two loans. Becker refused to accept payment. A notarized statement declares that at the time of his refusal Becker said, "Let Rembrandt first finish the *Juno.*" In the following year, the litigation between Rembrandt and Becker was amicably resolved; thus, by 1665 Rembrandt had finished the painting to Becker's satisfaction.

The style of *Juno* strengthens the evidence that it was the picture that was the nub of the controversy between Becker and Rembrandt. The pronounced frontality of the goddess, the even light that plays over her broadly displayed figure, the spontaneous and flexible brushwork

combined with subtle glazing, and the powerful coloristic harmonies are compatible with a date of about 1662 – 65 for the imposing painting.

X-ray radiography has recently revealed some new evidence that may cast light on Becker's displeasure at the delayed delivery of *Juno* (see photograph opposite). The artist made a major alteration in the painting. He originally painted Juno's right arm in a position almost symmetrical to her left, with both of her hands resting on a ledge or a table. Then he had a second thought. He raised her right arm to the present position and gave the goddess her scepter. Possibly Rembrandt began to make this change and then stopped working on the picture; we know that he never won a reputation for finishing his commissions rapidly. Perhaps Becker was irritated by the delay the change caused and so declared, "Let Rembrandt first finish the *Juno.*"

Alternatively, Becker may have insisted that passages of economic brushwork and impasto touches needed a higher degree of finish. If this was the issue, Rembrandt must have finally convinced his patron of the validity of his axiom "A painting is finished when the artist has completed his intention." The summary brushwork and fluctuating impasto passages remain, heightening the pictorial effect.

In any event, Becker received and kept the painting. It is listed in the inventory made of his effects after his death in 1678. His inventory also lists a second, unattributed, life-size painting of Juno, an indication that the rich merchant had a special interest in the goddess of wealth. We also know that Becker had a passion for Rembrandt's work. In addition to *Juno,* his inventory lists fourteen other paintings by the master.

Nothing is known of the whereabouts of *Juno* from 1678 until the eighteenth to mid-nineteenth century, when there is reason to believe that it was in an English private collection. By 1888 it was in the possession of the Berlin merchant Otto Wesendonck. Its subsequent history is worth telling.

After Wesendonck's death, his heirs put *Juno* on loan at the Bonn Provinzialmuseum. When it was catalogued there in 1914, it was not listed as an original Rembrandt but erroneously demoted to the status of a work by one of the artist's anonymous imitators. The Provincial Council of the Rhineland and the City of Bonn acquired the painting in 1925. Not long after the Nazis came to power in 1933, the Bonn museum officials were ordered to concentrate on Rhenish art and sell their holdings unrelated to their new mandate. In compliance with this order, the painting was auctioned at Cologne in 1935 as a work in the "style of Rembrandt," and it fetched 900 marks at the sale. Soon afterward, experts recognized *Juno* not only as an indisputable original but as one of the finest and best-documented late works by Holland's greatest artist.

S. S.

8. JEAN-HONORÉ FRAGONARD (1732–1806)
THE EDUCATION OF THE VIRGIN, 1748–52

Oil on panel: 11¹³⁄₁₆ x 9⅝″ (30.3 x 24.4 cm.)

Collections: J. B. P. Lebrun, Paris; Fontaine, Paris; Charles T—, Paris; Camille Groult, Paris; Wildenstein & Co., Inc., New York; Mr. and Mrs. Henry R. Luce, New York.

Exhibited: New Haven, Yale University Art Gallery, *Pictures Collected by Yale Alumni,* May 8 – June 18, 1956 (no. 19), repr. in cat.

Hammer Collection exhibitions: see catalogue reference page. First exhibited: II; not exhibited: X, XX, XXIII.

Literature: *Catalogue d'objets et curieux, provenant du cabinet et fonds de marchandises de M. Lebrun par cessation de commerce,* sale catalogue, Galerie de M. Lebrun, Paris, Sept. 29, 1806, no. 150; Pierre de Nolhac, *J-H Fragonard,* Paris, 1906, p. 164; Georges Wildenstein, *The Paintings of Fragonard,* London, 1960, p. 195, no. 18, plate 1; Mahonri Sharp Young, "The Hammer Collection: Paintings," *Apollo,* vol. 95 (June, 1972), p. 451.

Fragonard used the subject of Saint Anne teaching her daughter to read in at least three oil paintings. They include an unfinished picture in a private collection in Paris (Wildenstein, *Paintings of Fragonard,* no. 17, 35⅜ x 28⅜″ [90 x 72 cm.], repr. in Louis Réau, *Fragonard,* Brussels, 1956, opp. p. 42), the present oil, which is almost certainly the preparatory sketch for the unfinished picture just mentioned, and a canvas now in the California Palace of the Legion of Honor, San Francisco (Wildenstein, no. 19, 32¼ x 45⅝″ [82 x 116 cm.]), probably cut down between 1793 and 1806. The Hammer oil sketch and a nearly identical black-and-brown wash drawing (15⅜ x 11″ [39 x 28 cm.]) were once the property of M. Camille Groult, Paris. The drawing, probably the original study for the Hammer oil sketch, was sold at the Charpentier sale in Paris, June 9–10, 1953, lot six, but its present whereabouts is not known. The Hammer study and the unfinished painting both show the Virgin looking up at her mother. The Charpentier drawing, in probably the first rendering of this pose, shows the Virgin lifting her face to her mother but with her eyes turned to the viewer. That the Virgin looks up rather than at the book makes an essential difference between this series and Fragonard's other versions of this subject (see Plate 82). The Hammer sketch beautifully reveals the influence of Rembrandt on the young Fragonard, both in the strong handling of light and shadow and in the rich, golden palette.

M. E.

9. FRANCISCO DE GOYA Y LUCIENTES (1746–1828)
EL PELELE, c. 1791

Oil on canvas: 14 x 9⅛″ (35.6 x 23.2 cm.)

Collections: Doña Beatriz Sánchez de la Fuente de Lafora, Madrid; Don Juan de Lafora, Madrid; M. Knoedler & Co., New York; Mr. and Mrs. Henry R. Luce, New York.

Exhibited: Madrid, Sociedad Española de Amigos del Arte, *Bocetos y Estudias para Pinturas y Esculturas,* May – June, 1949 (no. 109), cat. by F. J. Sánchez-Canton; New Haven, Yale University Art Gallery, *Pictures Collected by Yale Alumni,* May 8 – June 18, 1956 (no. 29), repr. in cat.

Hammer Collection exhibitions: see catalogue reference page. First exhibited: II; not exhibited: X, XX.

Literature: August I. Mayer, *Francisco de Goya,* Munich, 1923, p. 210, no. 570a (Engl. ed., London and Toronto, 1924, p. 176, no. 570a); Valentín de Sambricio, *Tápices de Goya,* Patrimonio Nacional, Archivo General del Palacio, Madrid, 1946, p. 273, no. 58a, plate CLXXXIV; Mahonri Sharp Young, "The Hammer Collection: Paintings," *Apollo,* vol. 95 (June, 1972), p. 451.

In 1776 Goya began a series of oil paintings of Spanish popular life to be used as cartoons for forty-six tapestries by the Real Fábrica de Tápices de Santa Bárbara in Madrid. The large cartoons are preserved in the Prado. *El Pelele* (Prado no. 802, 105 x 63″), painted about 1791, was one of the last three cartoons delivered. The tapestry, today in the Palace of El Pardo, was executed in 1793. There are two known *bocetos* for the Prado cartoon, one in the collection of Mrs. R. H. Kress (17½ x 10″), the other in this collection. The Hammer picture is presumably the first concept of the subject, with its freely sketched figures and the *pentimenti* in the straw man. Especially noticeable is the change in the position of the left foreleg. The group stands in an open space before a wall at the left and with the slightest indication of foliage at the right. The figures in the Kress picture are close to those in the Hammer picture; the primary difference is in the development of a more airy and spacious background. The wall has receded and a large shrub has grown between it and the figure group to indicate the extension of space. In the Prado cartoon, the straw man has assumed a new and more limp position, the dresses and features of the four girls have been considerably elaborated, the wall has now become a palace in the far distance, and delicate shrubbery creates a broad and deep landscape so that the straw man can be more effectively silhouetted against the sky.

This may well have been one of the "diez y seis bocetos pequeños de los tápices" listed in the inventory of the personal property of Francisco Goya in Madrid and inherited by his son Javier Goya (inventory published in X. Desparmet Fitz-Gerald, *L'Oeuvre peint de Goya,* Paris, 1928 – 50, text vol. 1, pp. 53 – 54).

K. D.

10. FRANCISCO DE GOYA Y LUCIENTES (1746–1828)
PORTRAIT OF DOÑA ANTONIA ZÁRATE

Oil on canvas: 28 x 23″ (71 x 58.5 cm.)

Collections: Doña Adelaida Gil y Zárate, viuda de Albacete, Madrid; Twelfth Marqués de Villafranca and Sixteenth Duque de Medina-Sidonia, Madrid; Mr. and Mrs. H. O. Havemeyer, New York; Mrs. Evelyn St. George, London; M. Knoedler & Co., New York; Marshall Field, New York; Comtesse de Flers, Paris; Dr. Armand Hammer, Los Angeles; Hermitage Museum, Leningrad, gift of Dr. Armand Hammer, 1972.

Exhibited: Madrid, Ministerio de Instrucción Publica y Bellas Artes, *Goya*, May, 1900 (no. 48); New York, World's Fair, May – Oct., 1940 (no. 131), repr. in cat. p. 93; New York, Wildenstein & Co., Inc., *Loan Exhibition of Goya*, Nov. 9 – Dec. 16, 1950 (no. 22), repr. in cat. p. 48; New York, Metropolitan Museum of Art, *Goya Drawings and Prints*, May 4 – 30, 1955 (no. 176 in cat. suppl.).

Hammer Collection exhibitions: see catalogue reference page. First exhibited: XIV; not exhibited: XX – XXXVIII.

Literature: Zeferino Araujo Sánchez, *Goya*, Madrid, n.d. (1896?), no. 244; A. Schulze-Berge, "Einiges über die Goya-Ausstellung Madrid im Mai 1900," *Zeitschrift für Bildende Kunst*, 11th year (1900), pp. 229, 231; Paul Lafond, *Goya*, Paris, 1902, no. 238; S. L. Bensusan, "Goya: His Times and Portraits," *Connoisseur*, vol. 4 (1902), p. 123, erroneously as "Don Antonio Zárate"; Valerian von Loga, *Francisco de Goya*, Berlin, 1903 and 1921, no. 362; Albert F. Calvert, *Goya*, London and New York, 1908, plate 105; *Retratos de mujeres por Goya*, Madrid, 1909, repr. p. 21; Roger E. Fry and Maurice W. Brockwell, *An Exhibition of Old Masters in Aid of the National Art-Collections*, catalogue, Grafton Galleries, London, Oct. 4 – Dec. 28, 1911, p. 53; Hugh Stokes, *Francisco Goya*, New York and London, 1914, no. 266; A. de Beruete y Moret, *Goya pintor de retratos*, Madrid, 1916, p. 101, plate 37 (Engl. ed., *Goya as Portrait Painter*, London, 1922, p. 123, plate XL); August L. Mayer, *Francisco de Goya*, Munich, 1923, no. 456, p. 80, fig. 184 (Engl. ed., London and Toronto, 1924, p. 62, no. 456, plate 184); *Colección de cuatrocientas cuarenta y nueve reproducciones de cuadros, dibujos y aguafuertes de Don Francisco de Goya . . . publicadas . . . en 1860*, Madrid, 1924, plate 124; Joaquin Ezquerra de Bayo and Luis Pérez Bueno, *Retratos de mujeres españolas del siglo XIX*, Madrid, 1924, p. 44; *Enciclopedia universal ilustrada Europeo-Americana*, vol. 26, Barcelona, 1925, p. 832; X. Desparmet Fitz-Gerald, *Goya*, Paris, 1928 – 50, text vol. 2, no. 365, plate vol. 2, no. 288, repr.; F. J. Sánchez-Canton, *Goya*, Paris, 1930, plate 45; A. C. R. Carter, in *Daily Telegraph* (London), July 4 and July 27, 1939; *Catalogue of the Well-Known Collection of Important Pictures, the Property of Mrs. Evelyn St. George*, sale catalogue, Sotheby & Co., London, July 26, 1939, no. 86, plate XII; *Times* (London), July 27, 1939; *London Illustrated News*, Aug. 5, 1939, repr. p. 245; "Art in the Saleroom," *Apollo*, Sept. 1939, pp. 142 – 43, repr.; "In the Auction Rooms," *Connoisseur*, Sept., 1939, pp. 171 – 72, repr.; Jean Adhémar, *Goya*, Paris, 1941, plate 65; Lionello Venturi, *Modern Painters*, New York, 1947, p. 19, fig. 8; F. J. Sánchez-Canton, *Vida y obras de Goya*, Madrid, 1951, p. 104, plate LVIII; André Malraux, "Goya," *Art News Annual*, vol. 20 (1951), p. 55; E. Bénézit, *Dictionnaire . . . des peintres, sculpteurs . . .*, vol. 4, Paris, 1951, p. 372; Hermann Jedding, *Goya*, Wiesbaden-Berlin, 1955, p. 20, repr.; Juan Antonio Gaya Nuño, *La pintura española fuera de España*, Madrid, 1958, no. 944; Nigel Glendinning, in *Goya and His Times*, catalogue, Royal Academy of Arts, London, Dec. 7, 1963 – Mar. 1, 1964, no. 94 (the other portrait of Doña Antonia Zárate); D. B. Wyndham Lewis, *The World of Goya*, London, 1968, p. 199; Pierre Gassier and Juliet Wilson, *Vie et oeuvre de Francisco Goya*, Fribourg, 1970, no. 893, repr. p. 262; José Gudiol, *Goya*, New York, 1971, vol. 1, pp. 147, 317, no. 561, vol. 4, fig. 906.

Goya loved the theater and the people who acted in it. A charming woman on the stage could captivate his eye and arouse an irresistible desire to perpetuate her beauty. Doña Antonia Zárate, an actress famous throughout Spain, must have done this, for he painted her twice: once in black, seated on a yellow sofa (a portrait now in the Beit Collection in Ireland), and once in gray, wearing a red, fur-lined coat and with her head wrapped in a bluish-gray turban. The two pictures are not far apart in date, though which comes first is disputed; nor is it agreed when either was painted, although critics unanimously place them between 1805 and 1811.

For the Hammer Collection picture, I incline to a date close to 1811, based on the sitter's appearance. Her abnormally large eyes, her pallor, her slightly flushed cheeks seem symptomatic of consumption. We know she died of

this disease in 1811, at the age of thirty-six. If Goya painted her portrait shortly before her death, her wan yet feverish looks are explained. There is in her expression an ineffable sadness, as though she were aware of her fatal illness. Often a bitter satirist, Goya was also a compassionate human being. He understood the pangs of mortality. Those large, questioning eyes of Doña Antonia — were they staring at death approaching so rapidly? A fanciful concept, perhaps, but one in keeping with Goya's well-known morbidity.

The wanderings of Doña Antonia's portrait since its acquisition in Germany by Mr. and Mrs. H. O. Havemeyer, the greatest collectors of Goya in recent times, have been until now incessant. From the Havemeyer Collection in New York, it went to London and was sold at Sotheby's in 1939 as part of the collection of Mrs. Howard B. St. George. Then it traveled back to America when purchased by Marshall Field, only to return to Europe with his daughter, the Comtesse de Flers. Shipped once more to the United States, it was shown at the Metropolitan Museum in 1955. Dr. Hammer bought the painting in 1972.

One last journey remained, to Russia. Dr. Hammer, who spent nine years in the Soviet Union just after the Revolution and who has returned frequently on business trips, came to know the Hermitage Museum in Leningrad as few other visitors. He was always amazed that among its breathtaking treasures there was no example of Goya's work. This startling lacuna he felt must be filled, and on one of his trips to Russia he brought with him the beautiful Goya portrait he had just acquired. His own collection was on loan to the Hermitage and would travel to other Russian museums, and it seemed appropriate that one of its masterpieces should remain behind. He therefore presented the portrait of Doña Antonia Zárate to the Soviet Union, and it now hangs in the Hermitage, the only work by Goya in all Russia, except for the *Portrait of a Woman in a Black Mantilla,* surprisingly enough to be found in a provincial gallery, the Museum of Western and Eastern Art in Kiev!

J. W.

11. THÉODORE GÉRICAULT (1791–1824)
PORTRAIT OF A GENTLEMAN

Oil on canvas: 25⅝ x 21¼″ (65.1 x 54 cm.)
Signed lower left: T.G.

Collections: Mr. Christi, Paris; Le Bohélec, Paris (sold Galerie Charpentier, Paris, June 16, 1955); Drs. Fritz and Peter Nathan, Zurich.

Exhibited: Winterthur, Switz., Kunstmuseum, *Théodore Géricault,* 1953 (no. 92); Los Angeles County Museum of Art, Oct. 12 – Dec. 12, 1971, Detroit Institute of Arts, Jan. 23 – Mar. 7, 1972, and Philadelphia Museum of Art, Mar. 30 – May 14, 1972, *Géricault* (no. 3), repr. in cat.

Hammer Collection exhibitions: see catalogue reference page. First exhibited: XI; not exhibited: XX.

Literature: C. Clement, *Géricault, étude biographique et critique,* Paris, 1868 (3rd ed., enlarged, 1879), p. 307, no. 121; F. H. Lem, "Géricault portraitiste," *L'Arte,* Jan. – June, 1963, p. 68; Mahonri Sharp Young, "The Hammer Collection: Paintings," *Apollo,* vol. 95 (June, 1972), p. 451, repr. plate III in color p. 442.

Signed *T. G.* at the lower left, the picture was traditionally supposed to be a portrait of the composer F. A. Boïeldieu (1775 – 1834), although it does not bear any very pronounced resemblance to his known portraits. Because of its unusually tight and careful finish, the painting has, in Professor Lorenz Eitner's opinion, "no very evident connection with Géricault's characteristic personal manner." He has therefore put forward the ingenious hypothesis that it was "painted probably fairly early in Géricault's career, after the work of an artist of the previous generation." Eitner mentions other equally deceptive copies by Géricault, e.g., the copy after Hyacinthe Rigaud's *Portrait of the Mother of the Artist* (prov. coll., Paris). René Huyghe and Germain Bazin believe, on the other hand, that the unusual execution does not point to a copy but rather to the influence on Géricault of Antoine Jean Gros, whom he admired in his youth.

J. W.

12. JEAN BAPTISTE CAMILLE COROT (1796–1875)
MEDIEVAL RUINS, c. 1828–30

Oil on canvas, mounted on board: 9 x 12″ (23 x 30.5 cm.)
Stamped lower right: Vente Corot
Verso: red wax seal of the Vente Corot

Collections: Vente Corot (Corot sale), Paris, 1875 (no. 329); Comte Armand Doria (sold Paris, May 5, 1899 [no. 108]); Mme. Lazard, Paris; Mr. and Mrs. Eliot Hodgkin, London (sold Sotheby & Co., London, Apr. 29, 1964); Norton Simon, Los Angeles (sold Parke-Bernet Galleries, Inc., New York, May 5, 1971).

Exhibited: Paris, Musée Jacquemart-André, *Le Second Empire,* 1957 (no. 62); Art Institute of Chicago, *Corot,* 1960 (no. 23); London, Marlborough Fine Art, Ltd., *Corot,* 1963 (no. 10).

Hammer Collection exhibitions: see catalogue reference page. First exhibited: IX; not exhibited: XXIII.

Literature: Alfred Robaut, *L'Oeuvre de Corot,* Paris, 1905, vol. 2, p. 75, no. 212, repr.; *Impressionist and Modern Paintings, Drawings and Sculpture,* sale catalogue, Sotheby & Co., London, Apr. 29, 1964, no. 35A, repr.; *Highly Important 19th and 20th Century Paintings, Drawings & Sculpture from the Private Collection of Norton Simon,* sale catalogue, Parke-Bernet Galleries, Inc., New York, 1971, no. 2, repr.; Mahonri Sharp Young, "The Hammer Collection: Paintings," *Apollo,* vol. 95 (June, 1972), p. 451.

Catalogued in the Vente Corot as "Pierrefonds, au pied du Château," this picture has been said by Alfred Robaut to be a view of Arques-la-Bataille. The latter site, near Dieppe, contains the ruins of an eleventh-century fortress built by an uncle of William the Conqueror. The former, near Compiègne, was the site of a fourteenth-century chateau, the remains of which were completely rebuilt by Viollet-le-Duc in the mid-nineteenth century at the order of Napoleon III. Robaut lists two views of Arques painted by Corot about the time of this sketch, three drawings and two paintings of Pierrefonds. Of the latter, three were executed in the 1840s and two in the 1860s. The present picture was probably painted between Corot's first two trips to Italy, that is, about 1828 – 30. It combines his interest in subjects observed on the spot with the luminism he had developed in the south. In this case, the evenness of the northern French light produces two large tonal areas, a light sky and a darker foreground, forecasting the softness of Corot's late work and contrasting with the sharper illumination of his Italian pictures.

C. M.

13. JEAN BAPTISTE CAMILLE COROT (1796–1875)
HARVESTER UNDER TREES, c. 1829

Oil on canvas: 15¹³/₁₆ x 12″ (40.1 x 30.5 cm.)
Stamped lower left: Vente Corot

Collections: Vente Corot (Corot sale), Paris, 1875; M. Mauritz, Paris; Adrien Meunier, Paris; Galerie Daber, Paris.

Hammer Collection exhibitions: see catalogue reference page. First exhibited: I; not exhibited: X, XXIII.

Literature: Alfred Robaut, *L'Oeuvre de Corot,* Paris, 1905, vol. 2, p. 74, no. 219 bis, vol. 4, p. 230, no. 323 bis (sketch by Robaut from posthumous sale catalogue, Paris, 1875); François Daulte, "Hammer en dix chefs-d'oeuvre," *Connaissance des arts,* Sept., 1970, pp. 82 – 83, repr. in color.

Executed at about the same time as the Hammer *Medieval Ruins* (Plate 12) and in a similar, rapid style, this picture is considerably darker in tonality and for that reason more suggestive of the work of the Barbizon School. Only the harvester's white shirt and the light patch of sky relieve the rich greens and browns of the shadows. The serpentine wall connecting foreground and middleground and the diagonally recessive row of trees are unusual devices for Corot. They provide a somewhat more obvious pictorial scaffolding than one finds in the painter's later work. The subject is a scene of unposed action, also unusual for Corot.

C. M.

14. JEAN BAPTISTE CAMILLE COROT (1796–1875)
DISTANT VIEW OF MANTES CATHEDRAL, c. 1855–60

Oil on canvas: 22 1/16 x 18 1/16″ (56 x 45.9 cm.)
Signed lower left: Corot

Collections: M. Knoedler & Co., Paris (sold 1899); Galerie Georges Petit, Paris (sold Paris, Hôtel Drouot, Apr. 27, 1933 [no. 49]); M. Damidot; Ferdinand Blumenthal, Paris; Léfèvre Gallery, London; Count Pecci-Blunt, Rome; C. W. Boise, London.

Exhibited: Paris, Galerie Georges Petit, *Exposition de Chefs-d'oeuvre de l'Ecole Française; vingt peintres du XIXe siècle,* 1910 (no. 7); New York, M. Knoedler & Co., *The Landscape in French Painting, XIXth – XXth Centuries,* 1910; Amsterdam, *Les Peintures Françaises aux XIXe et XXe Siècles,* Apr. – May, 1931.

Hammer Collection exhibitions: see catalogue reference page. First exhibited: I; not exhibited: XXIII.

Literature: Alfred Robaut, *L'Oeuvre de Corot,* Paris, 1905, vol. 2, p. 264, no. 818, repr. p. 265; *Exposition de Chefs-d'oeuvre de l'Ecole Française; vingt peintres du XIXe siècle,* catalogue, Galerie Georges Petit, Paris, 1910, no. 7, repr. p. 103; Horace Shipp, *The French Masters,* London, 1931, repr. p. 112; *Art News,* Apr. 8, 1933, repr. p. 8; *Gazette des beaux-arts,* Apr. 21, 1933, repr. p. 3; *Gazette des beaux-arts,* May 5, 1933, p. 6; Germain Bazin, *Corot,* Paris, 1950, plate 92; Radolphe Walter, "Jean Baptiste Corot et la cathédrale restaurée," *Gazette des beaux-arts,* Apr., 1966, pp. 217 – 28, repr.; *Burlington Magazine,* Apr., 1968, repr. p. VII; *Impressionist and Modern Paintings, Drawings and Sculpture — Various Owners,* sale catalogue, Sotheby & Co., London, Apr. 24, 1968, no. 61, repr.; *Connoisseur,* Aug., 1968, repr. p. XIV; Mahonri Sharp Young, "The Hammer Collection: Paintings," *Apollo,* vol. 95 (June, 1972), p. 452, repr. plate IV in color p. 445.

Mantes (Mantes-la-jolie), a small town east of Paris notable for its magnificent church designed by Pierre de Montreuil, architect of Nôtre Dame at Paris, was painted many times by Corot between the early 1840s and the 1860s. He particularly favored its church and the bridge across the Seine as motifs. The present picture is not dissimilar to one in Reims taken from a slightly different viewpoint (Robaut, no. 1522), although the composition is stronger by virtue of the placement of the trees and the log lying in the foreground. Two drawings in horizontal format (Robaut, nos. 817, 1519) were apparently made at the same spot. The disproportion in the towers of the church has led Radolphe Walter to point out that the painting must have been executed during the rebuilding of the south tower, from 1859 to 1860. He convincingly suggests that it dates to May, 1859, when Corot was at nearby Rosny. The tonality of the picture is somewhat lighter and more even than one is used to from Corot, although he has been careful to add his usual small touch of red to spark the blue-green of the overall composition.

C. M.

15. JEAN BAPTISTE CAMILLE COROT (1796–1875)
PORTRAIT OF A GIRL, c. 1860

Oil on canvas: 12¼ x 9³/₁₆″ (31.1 x 23.3 cm.)
Signed upper right: Corot
    Collections: Emile Bernheim, Paris; André Pacitti, Paris.
    Hammer Collection exhibitions: see catalogue reference page. First exhibited: IV; not exhibited: XXIII.
    Literature: André Schoeller and Jean Dieterle, *Corot, deuxième supplément à "L'Oeuvre de Corot" par Alfred Robaut et Moreau-Nélaton,* Paris, 1956, no. 28; Mahonri Sharp Young, "The Hammer Collection: Paintings," *Apollo,* vol. 95 (June, 1972), p. 451, fig. 2 p. 443.

Degas was among the first to appreciate Corot's abilities as a figure painter, abilities that have generally gone unrecognized because of the popularity of the artist's landscapes. Toward the end of his life, Corot's figures became generalized into national or allegorical types, and individualized portraits such as this became increasingly rare. During the same period, the artist showed a marked predilection for a Leonardesque type, its softly modeled face gazing abstractedly outward, its arms folded across each other. The Louvre's *Woman with the Pearl* is the best example of this type, and the *Figures de Corot* catalogue (Louvre, 1962) suggests a relationship between this painting and both the *Mona Lisa* and the *Belle Ferronnière.* A portrait of a young woman in the Hirschland Collection represents an intermediate compositional step between the *Woman with the Pearl* and this picture.

C. M.

16. JEAN BAPTISTE CAMILLE COROT (1796–1875)
MORNING, 1865

Oil on canvas: 69 $^{11}/_{16}$ x 52⅜″ (177 x 133 cm.)
Signed and dated lower left: Corot 1865
  Collections: M. Larrieu, Bordeaux; E. Secrétan, Paris (sold July 1, 1889 [no. 2]).
  Exhibited: Paris, *Salon de 1865* (no. 506), under the title *Le Matin;* Paris, Ecole Nationale des Beaux-Arts, 1875 (no. 148), lent by M. Larrieu; Paris, Arnold & Tripp, Feb., 1883.
  Hammer Collection exhibitions: see catalogue reference page. First exhibited: II; not exhibited: X, XX, XXIII.
  Literature: Alfred Robaut, "La 'Bacchante' de Corot," *L'Art,* Feb. 18, 1883; Alfred Robaut, *L'Oeuvre de Corot,* Paris, 1905, vol. 3, no. 1635, repr. p. 145; Etienne Moreau-Nélaton, *Corot, raconté par lui-même,* Paris, 1924, vol. 2, fig. 191; Mahonri Sharp Young, "The Hammer Collection: Paintings," *Apollo,* vol. 95 (June, 1972), p. 451.

Seeing this picture in the Salon of 1865, Paul Mantz wrote,

"No landscape is as fresh, as tender, as bathed in the dawn as *Morning*," and in 1883, Alfred Robaut, decrying the small number of Corot paintings in French public collections, unsuccessfully demanded that the state allot one hundred thousand francs for its purchase. Robaut maintained that the composition had resulted from Corot's experience of an early morning in the country at Isigny and that a sketch made on the spot (Robaut, no. 846) was preparatory to it. The sketch, however, bears only slight resemblance to the final composition. Of unusual importance because of its size, *Morning* combines Corot's favorite motifs of classical figures and a dark but luminous setting seen against the light. The touch of red in the hair ribbon of the bacchante is typical of him. The darkening of the picture in the century since it was painted somewhat obscures the original transparency of the coloring. The work has been known variously as *Morning, Bacchante,* and *Bacchante Detaining an Amoretto.*

C. M.

17. JEAN BAPTISTE CAMILLE COROT (1796–1875)
PLEASURES OF EVENING, 1875

Oil on canvas: 44½ x 65³/₁₆" (113 x 165 cm.)
Signed and dated lower left: Corot 1875

Collections: Jay Gould, New York; Edwin J. Gould, New York.

Exhibited: Paris, *Salon de 1875* (no. 520); Paris, *Exposition Universelle Internationale de 1878* (no. 201); New York, American Art Galleries, *Exhibition of the Works of Antoine Barye and also Paintings by his Contemporaries and Friends, for the Benefit of the Barye Monument Fund,* Nov. 15, 1889 – Jan. 15, 1890 (no. 169), lent by Jay Gould.

Hammer Collection exhibitions: see catalogue reference page. First exhibited: I; not exhibited: X, XX, XXIII.

Literature: Ministère de l'Instruction Publique et des Beaux-Arts, *Salon de 1875, 92e exposition officielle,* Paris, 1875, p. 77, no. 520; A. de la Fizelière, *Memento du salon de peinture, de gravure, et des sculptures en 1875,* Paris, 1875, pp. 32, 65, no. 520; Paul Leroi, "Salon de 1875, XV: Corot," *L'Art,* vol. 2 (1875), p. 269, repr. in lithograph; *L'Exposition de l'oeuvre de Corot* (biographical note by P. Burty), Paris, 1875, p. 31; Anatole de Montaiglon, "Salon de 1875," *Gazette des beaux-arts,* ser. 2, vol. 12 (1875), p. 23; Henri Dumesnil, *Corot, souvenirs intimes,* Paris, 1875, pp. 102, 130, no. 120; *L'Alliance des lettres et des arts,* Apr. 1, 1875, repr. in pen drawing; *L'Univers illustré,* May 1, 1875, repr. in woodcut; Jules Claretie, *L'Art et les artistes français contemporains, Salon de 1875,* Paris, 1876, p. 356; *Catalogue officiel de l'Exposition Universelle Internationale de 1878 à Paris,* Paris, 1878, vol. 1, section 1 (Oeuvres d'Art), p. 20, no. 201; *Exposition Universelle Internationale de Paris, 1878, le livre d'or des exposants,* Paris, 1878, p. 8; Jules Claretie, "C. Corot," *Peintres et sculpteurs contemporains,* ser. 1, Paris, 1882, pp. 97 – 120; Jules-Antoine Castagnary, *Salons, 1857 – 1879,* Paris, 1892, vol. 2, p. 41; *Corot and Millet, with critical essays by Gustave Geffroy and Arsène Alexandre,* London and New York, 1902, p. CXXVIII; Etienne Moreau-Nélaton, *Histoire de Corot et de ses oeuvres,* Paris, 1905, pp. 342, 359, fig. 260; Alfred Robaut, *L'Oeuvre de Corot,* Paris, 1905, vol. 1, p. 333, vol. 3, pp. 322 – 23, no. 2195, repr., vol. 4, pp. 170, 278, 378, table p. 34; Etienne Moreau-Nélaton, *Corot, raconté par lui-même,* Paris, 1924, pp. 89, 105, fig. 258, repr. p. 175; Germain Bazin, *Corot,* Paris, 1951 (2d ed.), p. 115; Daniel Band-Bovy, *Corot,* Geneva, 1957, p. 251; *Apollo,* May, 1967, p. LXXXIV, repr.

Jules-Antoine Castagnary wrote of this picture and the *Woodcutters,* both exhibited posthumously in the Salon of 1875, that they were "worthy of the most beautiful among their predecessors." Among the last of Corot's paintings, *Pleasures of Evening* repeats the theme of an antique dance in the forest that he had treated more than once before. Begun at Courbron, a small town just east of Paris where, toward the end of his life, Corot was in the habit of visiting friends and working, the picture was finished in Paris. Between its inception and its completion it was sketched by Alfred Robaut (2195 [A]). It is clear from the sketch that Corot made several changes after his return to Paris, apparently reworking the figures in the group at right center and adding the two figures at the left.

C. M.

18. HONORÉ DAUMIER (1808–1879)
THE LAWYERS (THE BAR)

Oil on canvas: 12⁹/₁₆ x 19¾″ (32.5 x 50.2 cm.)
Signed lower right: h. Daumier

Collections: Camille Corot; Vente Corot (Corot sale), Paris, 1875 (no. 664), purchased by M. Geoffroy-Dechaume, Paris, for 1,160 francs; Vente Geoffroy-Dechaume (Geoffroy-Dechaume sale), 1893 (no. 23), purchased by Mme. Bureau, Paris, for 3,250 francs; Paul Bureau, Paris; Vente Bureau (Bureau sale), 1927 (no. 98), purchased by M. Baudouin, Paris; sale, Drouot Rive Gauche, Paris, May 26, 1977 (no. 23).

Exhibited: Paris, Galerie Durand-Ruel, 1878 (no. 39); Paris, Ecole Nationale des Beaux-Arts, *La Caricature,* 1888 (no. 374); Paris, *Exposition Internationale Universelle,* 1900 (no. 186); Paris, Ecole Nationale des Beaux-Arts, 1901 (no. 17).

Hammer Collection exhibitions: see catalogue reference page. First exhibited: XXXIV.

Literature: *Catalogue de la Vente Corot,* sale catalogue, Paris, 1875, no. 664; Arsène Alexandre, *Honoré Daumier —l'homme et l'oeuvre,* Paris, 1888, pp. 355 – 56, 375; *Catalogue de la Vente Geoffroy-Dechaume,* sale catalogue, Paris, 1893, no. 23; Erich Klossowski, *Honoré Daumier,* Munich, 1923 (2d ed.), no. 110; *Catalogue de la Vente P. Bureau,* sale catalogue, Paris, 1927, no. 98; *L'Amour de l'art,* vol. 8 (1927), p. 155; Eduard Fuchs, *Der Maler Daumier,* Munich, 1927 (2d ed., 1930, with supplement), p. 46, no. 20b; Raymond Echolier, *Daumier,* Paris, 1930, plate 19; Giovanni Scheiwiller, *Honoré Daumier* (Arte Moderna Staniera series), Milan, 1936, plate XX; Benno Fleischmann, *Honoré Daumier: Gemälde und Graphik,* Vienna, 1937, plate 21 (French ed., trans. Maurice Sachs, *Honoré Daumier,* Paris, 1939); Claude Roger-Marx, *Daumier,* Paris, 1938, p. 30; Jean Adhémar, *Honoré Daumier,* Paris, 1954, pp. 68, 110, no. 39, plate 27, as between 1860 and 1863; K. E. Maison, *Honoré Daumier, Catalogue Raisonné of the Paintings, Watercolours and Drawings,* London, 1968, vol. 1, p. 125, no. 139, plate 114, as about 1860.

This painting, which once belonged to Corot, is a souvenir of a remarkable friendship between two artists. Daumier longed to escape the drudgery of supplying lithographs to the satiric journal *Charivari.* His first love was painting, and Corot helped him to achieve it. He gave Daumier a small house and wrote his friend a letter that remains a masterpiece of tact.

My old comrade – I had a little house for which I had no use at Valmodois near the Isle-Adam. The idea came into my head of offering it to you, and, as I think it is a good idea, I have placed it in your name at the notary's. It is not for you that I do this, it is merely to annoy your landlord.

In return for this gift, the destitute Daumier had nothing to offer except his own paintings.

Much of Daumier's best lithographic work was devoted to the subject of the legal profession. The series that he began in 1845, *Les Gens de Justice,* remains his most popular cartoon sequence. He also used the subject in his paintings. The Hammer collection picture of a group of attorneys waiting to enter the courtroom was shown at every important Daumier exhibition from 1878 to 1901. In 1878 Geoffroy-Dechaume, who had bought the picture three years earlier at the Corot sale, accompanied his friend the great politician and lawyer Léon Gambetta to the first retrospective exhibition of Daumier's work. As Gambetta gazed at *The Lawyers,* which was prominently shown, he began to identify his colleagues. Geoffroy-Dechaume stopped him and pointed out that Daumier had not been in the Palais de Justice for ten years. What Gambetta was looking at were archetypal legal faces, in which he could see resemblances to the lawyers he knew. Daumier, having endlessly scrutinized these denizens of the courts, was able to find the universal in the individual and to achieve the ultimate aim of portraiture.

M. E.

Oil on canvas: 17¾ x 25⁵/₁₆″ (45.1 x 64.3 cm.)
Signed and dated lower left: E. Boudin 1869

Collection: Allard et Noël, Paris (sold Palais Galliéra, Paris, May 30, 1967).

Hammer Collection exhibitions: see catalogue reference page. First exhibited: I; not exhibited: XX, XXIII.

Literature: *Deux importants tableaux par Eugène Boudin,* sale catalogue, Palais Galliéra, Paris, 1967, letter A, repr.; Mahonri Sharp Young, "The Hammer Collection: Paintings," *Apollo,* vol. 95 (June, 1972), p. 452; Robert Schmit, *Eugène Boudin, 1824 – 1898,* Paris, 1973, vol. 1, p. 132, no. 467, repr.

Descended from seventeenth-century Holland by way of eighteenth-century Venetian *vedute,* Boudin's paintings contrast towering, broadly brushed skies with more precisely rendered, flickering groups of figures, ships, and buildings stretched out along the horizon. The precision of their naturalistic observation and their narrow tonal range of grayed blue, green, and ocher, sparked with occasional accents of red, attracted the attention of the young Impressionists, most notably Monet. In 1869, the year of this picture, Boudin mentioned "the sun-drenched beaches and the stormy skies, and of the joy of painting them in the sea breezes."

C. M.

20. EUGÈNE BOUDIN (1824–1898)
QUAY AT CAMARET, 1873

Oil on canvas: 14½ x 23″ (36.8 x 58.4 cm.)
Signed and dated lower left: Boudin '73
Inscribed lower right: Camaret

    Collections: Galerie Bernheim-Jeune, Paris; L. Bernard, Paris (sold Hôtel Drouot, Paris, May 11, 1901 [no. 7]); Théodore Révillon, Paris (sold Hôtel Drouot, Paris, May 8, 1924 [no. 11], repr. in cat.); Galerie Georges Petit, Paris; Galerie Schmit, Paris.

    Hammer Collection exhibitions: see catalogue reference page. First exhibited: I; not exhibited: XX, XXIII.

    Literature: Robert Schmit, *Eugène Boudin, 1824 – 1898,* Paris, 1973, vol. 1, p. 316, no. 893, repr.

In 1872 and 1873 Boudin worked at Camaret, at the extreme western tip of Brittany. This picture, somewhat stronger in its tonal contrasts than is common for him, seems almost an illustration of Gustave Geffroy's statement that "Eugène Boudin is one of the immediate precursors of Impressionism. . . . He has perceived that opaque black does not exist, and that air is transparent. He observes the value that objects acquire when exposed to light, and how planes fall into place and lead to the horizon." Boudin himself, constantly conscious of the gap between his perceptions and his expressive powers, wrote, "Sometimes, as I walk sunken in melancholy, I look at the light inundating the earth, trembling on the water, playing on clothing, and I become faint when I realize how much genius is needed to grasp so many difficulties."

C. M.

21. EUGÈNE BOUDIN (1824–1898)
BEACH AT TROUVILLE, c. 1888–95

Oil on canvas: 7⅝ x 12⅞″ (18.6 x 32.7 cm.)
Signed lower right: a Mns Sonnerville [*sic*] Souvenir de E. Boudin
Inscribed lower left: Trouville

Collections: de Sonneville, Bordeaux; William Hallsborough, Ltd., London; Lock Galleries, New York.

Hammer Collection exhibitions: see catalogue reference page. First exhibited: I; not exhibited: XX, XXIII.

Literature: *Art News,* Feb., 1967, repr. p. 53; Mahonri Sharp Young, "The Hammer Collection: Paintings," *Apollo,* vol. 95 (June, 1972), p. 452, fig. 3, p. 444; Robert Schmit, *Eugène Boudin, 1824 – 1898,* Paris, 1973, vol. 3, p. 392, no. 2346, repr.

The horizontal format of this sketch and the friezelike arrangement of people midway in the composition are characteristic of Boudin's beach scenes. This one was made at Trouville, one of his favorite haunts and among the most fashionable of the Second Empire resorts.

C. M.

22. GUSTAVE CAILLEBOTTE (1848–1894)
SQUARE IN ARGENTEUIL

Oil on canvas: 23¹³/₁₆ x 27¾" (60.5 x 70.5 cm.)
Signed lower left: G. Caillebotte

Exhibited: Manila, National Museum of Manila, Oct., 1976.

Hammer Collection exhibitions: see catalogue reference page. First exhibited: V; not exhibited: XX, XXIII.

Literature: *Importants tableaux modernes,* sale catalogue, Palais Galliéra, Paris, June 17, 1970, no. 9; Mahonri Sharp Young, "The Hammer Collection: Paintings," *Apollo,* vol. 95 (June, 1972), p. 452.

Known principally as the collector who bequeathed the first great group of Impressionist pictures to the French state, Caillebotte was among the organizers of, and participants in, many of the original Impressionist exhibitions. As a painter, his vision was almost always advanced, and he favored subjects from daily life in natural poses, although his execution was often tight and linear to the point of academicism. Caillebotte was at his best in his broadly conceived and freely brushed canvases, many of which, like this one, were executed at Argenteuil. This fresh and unexpected work probably dates from the early 1880s.

C. M.

23. ALFRED SISLEY (1839–1899)
TIMBER YARD AT ST.-MAMMÈS, 1880

Oil on canvas: 21½ x 28¾″ (55.6 x 72.9 cm.)
Signed lower right: Sisley

Collections: M. Feder, Paris; Galerie Durand-Ruel, Paris, purchased June 25, 1892; Paul Cassirer, Berlin; Galerie Europe, Brussels; sold Sotheby & Co., London, Nov. 29, 1967 (no. 28).

Exhibited: Paris, Galerie Durand-Ruel, *Monet, Pissarro, Renoir et Sisley,* Apr., 1899 (no. 136); London, Grafton Gallery, *Paintings by Boudin, Sisley,* Jan. – Feb., 1905 (no. 303); Paris, Galerie Durand-Ruel, *Sisley,* June, 1910 (no. 71).

Hammer Collection exhibitions: see catalogue reference page. First exhibited: I; not exhibited: XX, XXIII.

Literature: Gustave Geffroy, *Sisley, Cahiers d'Aujour-d'hui,* no. 16, 1927, pp. 7 – 33, plate 28; Gotthard Jedlicka, *Sisley,* Bern, 1949, plate 37; François Daulte, *Alfred Sisley, catalogue raisonné de l'oeuvre peint,* Lausanne, 1959, no. 368, repr. p. 372; *Impressionist and Modern Paintings, Drawings and Sculpture,* sale catalogue, Sotheby & Co., London, 1967, no. 28, p. 47, repr. in color p. 46; *Burlington Magazine,* Nov., 1967, p. 1, repr.; *Apollo,* Nov., 1967, p. CXVIII, repr.; *Art News,* Nov., 1967, p. 17, repr.; *Apollo,* June, 1968, p. CII, repr.; *Connoisseur,* June, 1968, p. XIV, repr.

Sisley was at his best in broad, close-valued, tonal painting. The typical comma-like Impressionist facture tended to be disruptive of such painting, and Sisley used it most effectively when his strokes were of fairly uniform size and shape, and his colors within one or two narrow ranges of tone, as in this picture. St.-Mammès, to which Sisley eventually retired, was a small town on the banks of the Loing in the area southeast of Fontainebleau. Francois Daulte lists at least three other compositions directly related to this (nos. 369, 370, 372) and one of the same scene from the opposite direction (no. 371).

C. M.

24. CLAUDE MONET (1840–1926)
VIEW OF BORDIGHERA, 1884

Oil on canvas: 26 x 32¼" (66 x 81.9 cm.)
Signed and dated lower left: Claude Monet '84

Collections: Galerie Durand-Ruel, Paris; M. Montaignac, Paris; James F. Sutton, New York (sold American Art Association at the Plaza Hotel, New York, Jan. 16 – 17, 1917 [no. 143]); James B. Hastings, New York; Nils B. Hersloff, Baltimore; Estate of Sigmund N. Hersloff, Baltimore (sold Parke-Bernet Galleries, Inc., New York, Oct. 28, 1970 [no. 5], p. 8 in cat., repr. in color).

Exhibited: Paris, Galerie Georges Petit, *Claude Monet et A. Rodin,* 1889, lent by M. Montaignac; New York, Acquavella Galleries, Inc., *Claude Monet Exhibition,* Oct. 26 – Nov. 28, 1976.

Hammer Collection exhibitions: see catalogue reference page. First exhibited: VII; not exhibited: XXIII.

Literature: Theodore Robinson, "Monet," in *Modern French Masters, a series of biographical and critical reviews by American artists with 37 wood engravings and 28 half-tone illustrations,* edited by John Charles Van Dyke, wood engraving by Michael Haider, New York, 1896, p. 170; *Apollo,* Oct., 1970, p. 141, repr.; *Burlington Magazine,* vol. 112 (Oct., 1970), p. lxxiv, repr.; *Art News,* Oct., 1970, repr.; L. Rossi Bortolatto, *Claude Monet,* Milan, 1972, pp. 105–6, no. 269, repr.; Mahonri Sharp Young, "The Hammer Collection: Paintings," *Apollo,* vol. 95 (June, 1972), p. 452, repr. plate V in color p. 446.

During the 1880s, Monet's palette darkened, a fact that, combined with the discreteness and small size of his brushstrokes and the intensity and value contrasts of his color, tended to give his pictures a woolly texture that is especially noticeable in the Creuse and Belle-Ile paintings. This picture contrasts that roughness with an atmospheric distance and is therefore somewhat less surface-oriented than the similar painting in Chicago. Monet had been attracted to the south on a visit there with Renoir in 1883, and in January of 1884 he returned to paint first at Bordighera, on the Italian Riviera, and then at Menton.

C. M.

25. CAMILLE PISSARRO (1830–1903)
BOULEVARD MONTMARTRE, MARDI GRAS, 1897

Oil on canvas: 25 x 31½″ (63.5 x 80 cm.)
Signed and dated lower left: C. Pissarro '97

Collections: Maurice Barret-Décap, Paris; Mr. and Mrs. Henry R. Luce, New York; Marlborough Alte und Moderne Kunst, Zurich; Norton Simon, Los Angeles (sold Parke-Bernet Galleries, Inc., New York, May 5, 1971 [no. 24]).

Exhibited: Paris, Galerie Durand-Ruel, *C. Pissarro*, 1898 (no. 20); Paris, Galerie Durand-Ruel, *Tableaux, Pastels et Gouaches de C. Pissarro*, 1921 (no. 9); Paris, Galerie Durand-Ruel, *C. Pissarro*, 1928 (no. 78); New Haven, Yale University Art Gallery, *Paintings, Drawings, and Sculpture Collected by Yale Alumni*, May 19 – June 26, 1960 (no. 58), repr. in cat.; New York, Wildenstein & Co., Inc., *C. Pissarro*, Mar. 25 – May 1, 1965 (no. 65), repr. in cat.; Pittsburgh, Carnegie Institute, The Sarah Scaife Gallery of the Museum of Art, *Inaugural Celebration Exhibition*, Oct. 26 – Dec. 9, 1974.

Hammer Collection exhibitions: see catalogue reference page. First exhibited: IX; not exhibited: XXIII.

Literature: Ludovic-Rodo Pissarro and Lionello Venturi, *Camille Pissarro, son art – son oeuvre*, Paris, 1939, no. 995, vol. 2, plate 200; *Highly Important 19th and 20th Century Paintings, Drawings & Sculpture from the Private Collection of Norton Simon*, sale catalogue, Parke-Bernet Galleries, Inc., New York, 1971, p. 40, no. 24, repr. in color.

Pissarro produced several paintings of the Boulevard Montmartre in 1897 (Pissarro and Venturi, nos. 986 – 998), three of which (Pissarro and Venturi, nos. 995 – 997) seem to represent successive stages of a Lenten parade. Although the three are surely related, two, including this one, are catalogued by Pissarro and Venturi as Mardi Gras scenes and the third as a Mi-Carême. This picture is characteristic of Pissarro's late city scenes, particularly views of Paris, seen at sharp downward angles. Characteristic, too, are the blond tonality and obvious feathery or calligraphic brushwork he used toward the end of his life. Partly because of the nature of the subject, this picture has somewhat more color than some other Paris views by the artist.

C. M.

26. PIERRE-AUGUSTE RENOIR (1841–1919)
GRAPE PICKERS AT LUNCH

Oil on canvas: 21⅞ x 18¼″ (55.5 x 46.4 cm.)
Signed lower left: Renoir

Collections: Arsène Alexandre, Paris; Rosenberg & Stiebel, New York.

Hammer Collection exhibitions: see catalogue reference page. First exhibited: II; not exhibited: X, XX, XXIII, XXVIII, XXIX.

Literature: sale catalogue, Galerie Georges Petit, Paris, May, 1903, no. 54; François Daulte, *Auguste Renoir: catalogue raisonné de l'oeuvre peint,* Lausanne, 1971, vol. 1, no. 467, repr., as Renoir, 1884.

This picture, with its sharp contrasts of hue and its carefully drawn forms, is a product of the mid-1880s — a period of experimentation and reevaluation for Renoir. He had earlier questioned the validity of recording purely visual impressions, and, after studying the Raphael paintings in Rome and the ancient frescoes from Pompeii in the Naples Museum during an Italian trip in 1881 – 82, Renoir sought to reassess the importance of drawing, line, modeled form, and compositional reorganization of nature. He even questioned the soundness of painting in the open air directly from nature as opposed to composing in the studio. Like Cézanne, but in his own way, he devoted himself at this time to establishing harmony between Impressionism and the "art of the museums."

The *Grape Pickers at Lunch* is a product of Renoir's exploration of some of these concepts. Instead of his usual soft brushwork, he uses smaller, sharper, more graphic strokes, which define and model the figures. Instead of merging his figures with the landscape, as in the Impressionist works of the 1870s, he arranges his figures to form a closed concentric group, which establishes a real, but limited foreground space, reminiscent of Renaissance "stagelike" space, to which the landscape forms a backdrop.

The probability that the painting is a studio composition is reinforced by the reappearance of the girl with the basket on her back, who had been used by Renoir in the *Mussel Gatherers at Berneval,* painted in 1879 and shown in the Salon of 1880. The three girls in the foreground are said to be the daughters of Paul Alexis.

C. M.

27. PIERRE-AUGUSTE RENOIR (1841–1919)
ANTIBES, 1888

Oil on canvas: 25½ x 32″ (64.8 x 81.3 cm.)
Signed and dated lower right: Renoir '88

Collections: Galerie Durand-Ruel, Paris, 1910; Baroness von Brenin, Berlin, 1931; Parke-Bernet Galleries, Inc., New York (sold Feb. 25, 1970 [no. 21]).

Exhibited: Paris, Galerie Durand-Ruel, *Exposition de Tableaux par Renoir,* Apr. 27 – May 15, 1912 (no. 5); Akron Art Institute, 1947; Milwaukee Art Institute, *Masters of Impressionism,* 1948 (no. 38); Art Institute of Chicago, *Renoir Exhibition,* Jan. 30 – Apr. 1, 1973.

Hammer Collection exhibitions: see catalogue reference page. First exhibited: IV; not exhibited: XVI – XIX, XX, XXIII, XXVIII, XXIX.

Literature: *Highly Important Impressionist, Post-Impressionist & Modern Paintings and Drawings,* sale catalogue, Parke-Bernet Galleries, Inc., New York, 1970, no. 21, repr. in color; Mahonri Sharp Young, "The Hammer Collection: Paintings," *Apollo,* vol. 95 (June, 1972), p. 452.

During the 1880s, Renoir's efforts to restudy his draftsmanship resulted in a hard and carefully outlined figure style usually at variance with the continued softness of his backgrounds. Only in the nonfigural subjects, such as this view of Antibes, did he maintain and develop his feathery brush style, suppressing contour to an extent that makes the subjects of these pictures seem almost to evaporate. A similar composition is recorded in the collection of Sir Simon and Lady Marks.

C. M.

28. PIERRE-AUGUSTE RENOIR (1841–1919)
TWO GIRLS READING, 1890–91

Oil on canvas: 22 x 18⅝" (55.9 x 47.2 cm.)
Signed lower right: Renoir

Collections: Galerie Durand-Ruel, Paris, purchased 1895 from Renoir; H. O. Niethke Gallery, Vienna, purchased 1912; Dr. Herman Eissler, Vienna; Hugo Moser, Heemstede; Mrs. Maria Moser, New York; Dr. and Mrs. Armand Hammer, Los Angeles; Los Angeles County Museum of Art, gift of Dr. and Mrs. Armand Hammer, 1968.

Exhibited: Zurich, Kunsthaus, 1933; Haarlem, Frans Hals Museum, 1936; Baltimore Museum of Art, Summer, 1939; New York, Wildenstein & Co., Inc., *Renoir,* Apr. 8 – May 10, 1958 (no. 53), p. 67 in cat., repr.; New York, Metropolitan Museum of Art, 1959 – 67; New York, Wildenstein & Co., Inc., *Renoir,* Mar. 27 – May 3, 1969 (no. 77); Manila, National Museum of Manila, Oct., 1976.

Hammer Collection exhibitions: see catalogue reference page. First exhibited: I; not exhibited: IV, VI, VII, IX, XXIII.

Literature: *Quarterly,* Baltimore Museum of Art, July 1, 1939, p. 8, repr.; Los Angeles County Museum of Art, *Annual Report,* 1968 – 69, pp. 18 – 19, repr.; Alfred Werner, "Renoir's Daimon," *Arts Magazine,* Apr. 1969, p. 40, repr.; *Gazette des beaux-arts,* Feb., 1970, supplement, p. 87, repr.; Mahonri Sharp Young, "The Hammer Collection: Paintings," *Apollo,* vol. 95 (June, 1972), p. 452, fig. 4 p. 447.

This gentle and slightly nostalgic subject is of the kind that most appealed to Renoir and that he was best able to execute successfully. The consistency of the brushwork and the warmth of color help unify the composition, and the painting shows the renewed softness of Renoir's work toward the end of the century. The girl at the left is said to be Julie Manet, daughter of Berthe Morisot and Eugène Manet, while the one at the right is possibly her cousin Paule Gobillard. A less satisfying variation of this composition is recorded in a Scottish private collection (repr. *Scottish Art Review,* vol. 4, no. 4 [1953], p. 19), and there is also a three-quarter-length variation of a similar subject (repr. *Beaux-Arts,* Feb. 22, 1935, p. 4).

C. M.

29. BERTHE MORISOT (1841–1895)
PAULE GOBILLARD—NIECE OF BERTHE MORISOT, c. 1887

Oil on canvas: 28¾ x 23¾″ (72.8 x 60.1 cm.)

Collections: Paule Gobillard, Quimperlé; Morisot Family, Paris.

Exhibited: Paris, Galerie Durand-Ruel, *Berthe Morisot,* March, 1896 (no. 29); Paris, Galerie Marcel Bernheim, *Berthe Morisot,* June – July, 1922 (no. 27); Copenhagen, Ny Carlsberg Glyptotek, *Berthe Morisot,* Aug. – Sept., 1949 (no. 37); Musée de Dieppe, *Exposition Berthe Morisot,* July – Sept., 1957 (no. 38); New York, Wildenstein & Co., Inc., *Berthe Morisot,* Nov., 1960 (no. 45).

Hammer Collection exhibitions: see catalogue reference page. First exhibited: XXXV.

Literature: M. L. Bataille and G. Wildenstein, *Berthe Morisot,* Paris, 1961, p. 36, no. 209, plate 63, as painted in 1887.

Paule Gobillard and her younger sister were daughters of Berthe Morisot's sister and, like her own daughter, Julie, were among her favorite models. Berthe Morisot had a warm, maternal feeling for children and young people. This, coupled with her keen intelligence, produced some of the most sympathetic portraits of the Impressionist School. Hers was an essentially feminine vision and, indeed, most of her subjects were women. Denis Rouart, her grandson, described the sitters who most appealed to her: beloved friends and family, frequent guests, and favorite children.

The Hammer portrait, of about 1887, is one of the last pictures she painted in the style of her highly successful first period (1878 – 88). In this decade, more assured of herself as a painter than at any other time, Berthe Morisot brought together the two main influences of her life. On the one hand, she explored the lessons of the 1860s learned from her friend Corot. At the age of sixty-four, he had inspired her to see the effects of natural light and atmosphere. On the other hand, since meeting in 1868 her future brother-in-law, Edouard Manet, she had been increasingly liberated by his unconventional approach to painting. It was his freedom of brushwork and his volatile spirit that attracted her to his style and to him. In this period, there are no preliminary sketches or even superficial outlines on the canvas; there are only bold, irregular, and rapid strokes of paint. Like most Impressionists, Berthe Morisot worked with speed and spontaneity directly on the canvas. Rouart described her particular technique as "brushwork like fireworks." His phrase is brilliantly exemplified by the Hammer picture. Within a year of this picture, Berthe Morisot's style was to change radically. She became interested in mass and form. The explosive slashes of color typical of her work until 1888 gave way to long, continuous lines enclosing smooth, serene shapes.

M. E.

30. PAUL CÉZANNE (1839–1906)
BOY RESTING, c. 1885

Oil on canvas: 21⁷/₁₆ x 25¹³/₁₆″ (54.5 x 65.5 cm.)

Collections: Ambroise Vollard, Paris; Galerie Bernheim-Jeune, Paris; Galerie Thannhauser, Lucerne; Josef Stransky, New York; Estate of Josef Stransky (on loan to the Worcester Art Museum, Worcester, Mass., June 1, 1932 – Mar. 9, 1936); Wildenstein & Co., Inc., New York; Arnold Kirkeby, New York (sold Parke-Bernet Galleries, Inc., New York, Nov. 19, 1958 [no. 16]); Mrs. Arnold Kirkeby, Los Angeles.

Exhibited: Paris, Galerie Bernheim-Jeune, *Retrospective Paul Cézanne,* June 1 – 30, 1926 (no. 5); New York, Museum of Modern Art, *1st Loan Exhibition,* Nov., 1929 (no. 13); Art Institute of Chicago, *A Century of Progress,* June 1 – Nov. 1, 1933 (no. 318A); Worcester, Mass., Worcester Art Museum, *The Loan Exhibition of the New Museum Building,* 1933 – 1934; San Francisco, California Palace of the Legion of Honor, *French Painting from the 15th Century to the Present Day,* June 8 – July 8, 1934 (no. 65); Kansas City, William Rockhill Nelson Gallery of Art, *Nineteenth Century French Painting,* Mar. 15 – Apr. 12, 1936; London, Wildenstein & Co., Ltd., *Collection of a Collector, Modern Painting from Ingres to Matisse, The Private Collection of the Late Josef Stransky,* July, 1936 (no. 18); Toledo, Ohio, Toledo Museum of Art, *Cézanne, Gauguin,* Nov. 1 – Dec. 13, 1936 (no. 29); San Francisco Museum of Art, *Paul Cézanne,* Sept. 1 – Oct. 4, 1937 (no. 16), repr. in cat.; London, Wildenstein & Co., Ltd., *Homage to Paul Cézanne,* July, 1939 (no. 30); New Haven, Yale University Art Gallery, *Cézanne and the French Tradition,* Jan. 29 – Feb. 18, 1945; Cincinnati Art Museum, *Paintings by Paul Cézanne,* Feb. 5 – Mar. 9, 1947 (no. 4); New York, Wildenstein & Co., Inc., *A Loan Exhibition of Paul Cézanne for the Benefit of the New York Infirmary,* Mar. 27 – Apr. 26, 1947 (no. 19); Los Angeles, Art Galleries, University of California, *California Collects: North and South,* Jan. 20 – Feb. 23, 1958 (no. 29), repr. in cat.; Tokyo, National Museum of Western Art, Mar. 20 – Apr. 19, 1974, Kyoto, Municipal Museum, June 1 – July 17, 1974, Fukuoka, Prefectural Cultural Center Museum, July 24 – Aug. 18, 1974, *Cézanne Exhibition.*

Hammer Collection exhibitions: see catalogue reference page. First exhibited: IX; not exhibited: XX, XXIII.

Literature: *Kunst und Kunstler,* vol. 24 (1926), pp. 448 – 49; *International Studio,* Nov., 1929, p. 66, repr.; Eugenio d'Ors, *Paul Cézanne,* Paris, 1930, p. 25, repr., table VI; Ralph Flint, "The Private Collection of Josef Stransky," *Art News,* May 16, 1931, p. 8, repr.; Perry B. Cott, "The Stransky Collection of Modern Art," *Bulletin of the Worcester Art Museum,* Winter, 1933, p. 157; Nina Iavorskaïa, *Paul Cézanne,* Milan, 1935, plate VI; *Art Digest,* Apr. 1, 1936, p. 5, repr.; *Parnassus,* Dec., 1936, p. 26, repr.; Maurice Raynal, *Cézanne,* New York, 1936, plate 51; Lionello Venturi, *Cézanne, son art — son oeuvre,* Paris, 1936, vol. 1, p. 150, no. 391, vol. 2, no. 391, plate 107; Ambroise Vollard, *Paul Cézanne, His Life and Art* (trans. Harold L. Van Doren), New York, 1937, plate 9; *Art News,* Oct., 1958, p. 41, repr.; "Kirkeby Collection at Auction," *Arts,* Nov., 1958, p. 27, repr.; *Connoisseur,* Nov., 1958, p. 124, repr.; *Connoisseur,* Jan., 1959, p. 254, repr.; *Apollo,* June, 1959, p. 215, repr.; Robert Melville, "Exhibitions," *Architectural Review,* Aug., 1959, pp. 131 – 33, repr.; Mark Roskill, *Van Gogh, Gauguin, and the Impressionist Circle,* London, 1970, p. 231, plate 179; M. Brion, *Paul Cézanne,* Milan, 1971, p. 77, repr.; Elie Faure, *Cézanne,* Paris, n.d., plate 7.

The subject of this picture of a reclining clothed figure, unique in Cézanne's oeuvre, was considered by Ambroise Vollard to be the artist's son, Paul. The composition exemplifies the artist's struggle to reconcile pictorial and naturalistic scale and effect. The broad rectilinear paint areas at the top of the canvas were clearly conceived as flat elements directly related to the size and shape of that canvas. Their two-dimensional strength creates a pictorial pressure that jeopardizes the human identity of the figure, makes its location in depth ambiguous, and mitigates its three-dimensionality. That Cézanne could explore such complex problems without sacrificing the quality of his art is an index of his genius.

C. M.

32. HENRI FANTIN-LATOUR (1836–1904)
PORTRAIT OF MISS EDITH CROWE, 1874

Oil on canvas: 28¾ x 23⁵⁄₁₆″ (73 x 59.2 cm.)
Signed and dated upper left: Fantin '74

Collections: Mme. Paul Paix; Mrs. D. Bergen-Hayn; Galerie l'Oeil, Paris.

Exhibited: Paris, *Salon de 1875* (no. 783); Paris, Ecole National des Beaux-Arts, *Exposition de l'Oeuvre de Fantin-Latour,* May – June, 1906 (no. 41); Amsterdam, Stedelijk Museum.

Hammer Collection exhibitions: see catalogue reference page. First exhibited: II; not exhibited: X, XX, XXIII.

Literature: Ministère de l'Instruction Publique et des Beaux-Arts, *Salon de 1875, 92e exposition officielle,* Paris, 1875, p. 115, no. 783; Paul Leroi, *L'Art, Salon de 1875,* Paris, 1875, vol. 1, p. 137, no. 783; Adolphe Jullien, *Fantin-Latour, sa vie et ses amitiés,* Paris, 1909, p. 199; Mme. Fantin-Latour, *Catalogue de l'oeuvre complète de Fantin-Latour,* Paris, 1911, p. 81, no. 739; *Connoisseur,* Nov., 1970, p. 210, repr.; Mahonri Sharp Young, "The Hammer Collection: Paintings," *Apollo,* vol. 95 (June, 1972), p. 452.

This picture was exhibited as "Portrait of Mlle. E. C—" in the Salon of 1875 along with Fantin's superb double portrait of his English friends and patrons, Mr. and Mrs. Edwin Edwards, to whom he had been introduced by Whistler. Miss Crowe was presumably a friend of the Edwardses, or of someone whom they had introduced to Fantin. It has been reported that she was the youngest of a large family that lived in Paris. Apparently, her house was like a salon for many of the artists of that time. Broader in technique than Fantin's flower pieces, this picture is not yet as free as the allegories and Wagnerian paintings. The placement of the figure against an unmodulated dark ground suggests what Fantin may owe to Manet, although the head is developed in a more traditional chiaroscuro. Speaking of another of Fantin's portraits, Zola noted that "Each of his canvases is an act of conscience. He excels at painting figures in the atmosphere in which they live, in giving them a warmth and supple life; it is that which means that, despite the restraining frame in which it is enclosed, this hardly seems to be a portrait, it is nothing less than a thing apart, very elevated."

C. M.

33. HENRI FANTIN-LATOUR (1836–1904)
ROSES, 1884

Oil on canvas: 26¹/₁₆ x 22¹¹/₁₆″ (66.2 x 57.7 cm.)
Signed and dated upper left: Fantin '84

Collections: Mrs. Edwards, London; Miss R. Bryant, London; Arthur Tooth & Sons, Ltd., London; Mrs. Hazel C. Boise, London (sold Sotheby & Co., London, Apr. 26, 1967 [no. 7]).

Exhibited: Musée de Grenoble, *Exposition du Centenaire de la Naissance de Fantin-Latour,* Aug. – Oct., 1936 (no. 145); London, Arthur Tooth & Sons, Ltd., *French Pictures from Private Collections,* June, 1949 (no. 19).

Hammer Collection exhibitions: see catalogue reference page. First exhibited: I; not exhibited: XX, XXIII.

Literature: Mme. Fantin-Latour, *Catalogue de l'oeuvre complète de Fantin-Latour,* Paris, 1911, no. 1167; *Burlington Magazine,* Apr., 1967, p. XVI, repr.; *Connoisseur,* Apr., 1967, p. XCIII, repr.; *Impressionist and Modern Paintings and Sculpture,* sale catalogue, Sotheby & Co., London, 1967, p. 15, no. 7, repr. p. 14; Mahonri Sharp Young, "The Hammer Collection: Paintings," *Apollo,* vol. 95 (June, 1972), p. 452.

The Mrs. Edwards who originally owned this picture is presumably Mrs. Edwin Edwards, wife of Fantin's English friend and patron. Although Fantin's portraits and genre subjects were favored in France, his flower pictures were particularly popular in England, and his submissions to the Royal Academy between 1862 and 1900 consisted almost entirely of such subjects. Many of these had poetic titles such as *Here Without a Thorn, the Rose.* Although this picture seems originally to have been called simply *Roses,* it has been known as *All the Roses of the Garden,* probably because of Mme. Fantin-Latour's description of it in her catalogue. *Roses* is a "poetic," close-valued painting, somewhat more broadly brushed than the Hammer *Peonies* (Plate 31), the pastel pinks and yellows mediating between the white highlights and the deep red and dark greens to soften the picture's general appearance. This atmospheric facture is particularly appropriate in view of the literary associations roses seem regularly to have evoked in Fantin.

C. M.

34. EDGAR DEGAS (1834–1917)
THREE DANCERS IN YELLOW SKIRTS, c. 1891

Oil on canvas: 32 x 25⅝″ (81.3 x 65.1 cm.)
Signed lower right: Degas

Collections: Atelier Degas (sold Galerie Georges Petit, Paris, first sale, May 6 – 8, 1918 [no. 92], repr. in cat.); MM. Nunès and Fiquet, Paris; F. R. (sold Paris, Mar. 8, 1930 [no. 74]); sold Galerie René Drouet, Paris; Erwin Swann, Pennsylvania (sold Sotheby & Co., London, Dec. 10, 1969 [no. 20]).

Exhibited: New York, Gallery of Modern Art, *The Pleasure of the Eye — The Collection of Caroline and Erwin Swann,* 1964 – 65 (no. 9).

Hammer Collection exhibitions: see catalogue reference page. First exhibited: III; not exhibited: XX, XXIII.

Literature: *Catalogue des tableaux, pastels et dessins par Edgar Degas,* catalogue of first sale, Galerie Georges Petit, Paris, 1918, p. 51, no. 92, repr.; *Catalogue de la Vente F. R.,* sale catalogue, Hôtel Drouot, Paris, 1930, 2d part, no. 74, p. 20, repr.; P. A. Lemoisne, *Degas et son oeuvre,* Paris, 1947, vol. 3, p. 636, no. 1100, repr.; *Impressionist and Modern Paintings,* sale catalogue, Sotheby & Co., London, 1969, no. 20, repr. in color; Mahonri Sharp Young, "The Hammer Collection: Paintings," *Apollo,* vol. 95 (June, 1972), p. 452, repr. plate VII in color p. 449.

This picture is similar in size and conception to the Louvre *Dancers in Blue,* which is, in turn, closely related to the Metropolitan Museum *Dancers in Red and Green.* The Louvre picture and this one seem, in fact, to be coloristic variations on the same theme, the Louvre painting developed in blue-green-purple, this one in red-yellow-orange. The broadly stippled background was explored by Degas in other pictures at this time, both of dancers (Lemoisne, no. 975) and of bathers (Lemoisne, no. 1104). The placement of the figures suggests the same or similar poses seen from different angles of vision, a device increasingly exploited by Degas. Along with his interest in different poses arranged sequentially, the resulting protocinematic effect almost certainly reflects his knowledge of early experiments in motion photography. This effect is enhanced by the suggestion of unstable equilibrium resulting from the eccentric arrangement of the figures. The entire composition is stabilized by Degas's manipulation of his hues and their values.

C. M.

35. HENRI MARIE RAYMOND DE TOULOUSE-LAUTREC (1864–1901) IN THE SALON, 1894

Oil on cardboard: 23⅞ x 15¾″ (60.6 x 40 cm.)
Signed lower left: H.-T. Lautrec

Collections: Octave Maus, Brussels; Tetze-Lund, Copenhagen; J. K. Thannhauser, New York; Paul Rosenberg, New York (sold Sotheby & Co., London, Nov. 7, 1962 [no. 85]); Galerie Beyeler, Basel.

Exhibited: Paris, Galerie Manzi et Joyant, *Toulouse-Lautrec,* 1896; Brussels, *Exposition Toulouse-Lautrec,* organized by La Libre Esthétique, Mar., 1902; Paris, Galerie Manzi et Joyant, *Exposition Retrospective de L'Oeuvre de H. Toulouse-Lautrec,* June 15 – July 11, 1914 (no. 39).

Hammer Collection exhibitions: see catalogue reference page. First exhibited: I; not exhibited: XX, XXIII, XXXI, XXXII.

Literature: Maurice Joyant, *Henri de Toulouse-Lautrec,* Paris, 1926, p. 286; Gotthard Jedlicka, *Henri de Toulouse-Lautrec,* Erlenbach-Zurich, 1943, p. 321, repr. opp. p. 218; Francis Jourdin and Jean Adhémar, *Toulouse-Lautrec,* Paris, 1952, plate 84; *Impressionist and Modern Paintings, Drawings and Sculpture,* sale catalogue, Sotheby & Co., London, 1962, no. 85, repr. in color; P. Huisman and M. G. Dortu, *Lautrec by Lautrec,* New York, 1964, pp. 130 – 131, repr. in color; *Apollo,* Sept. 1966, p. LXXV, repr.; "On the Market," *Apollo,* Nov., 1968, p. 395, repr.; François Daulte, "Hammer en dix chefs-d'oeuvre," *Connaissance des arts,* Sept., 1970, p. 79, repr.; *Connoisseur,* Nov., 1970, p. 210, repr.

From 1892 until 1895, Toulouse-Lautrec produced a series of pictures of prostitutes and bordello scenes. The summation of this work was the large canvas *In the Salon,* painted in 1894 and now in the museum at Albi. There is a pastel version of the complete composition in the same museum and a large group of related studies, of which this picture is one. Presumably also executed in 1894, it represents the same two women who are seated at the left rear center of the Albi painting. According to Maurice Joyant, the woman seen in profile is the Rolande of several of the other studies. In transferring the figures to the larger work, Lautrec has altered only the position of the arms. The technique of this study is much broader than that of the finished picture, and its color is worked out in terms of close-valued, close-hued, and astringent contrasts in Lautrec's most expressive manner. Octave Maus is said to have acquired this picture in 1896, perhaps directly from the Manzi-Joyant exhibition, at which the bordello scenes were shown by Lautrec in two small locked rooms.

C. M.

36. GUSTAVE MOREAU (1826–1898)
SALOME, 1876

Oil on canvas: 56⅝ x 41¹/₁₆″ (143.8 x 104.2 cm.)

Collections: Louis Mante, Marseilles (sold Galerie Charpentier, Paris, Nov. 28, 1956 [no. 10]); Robert Lebel, Paris; Julius Weitzner, London; Huntington Hartford, New York.

Exhibited: Paris, *Salon de 1876* (no. 1506); Paris, *Exposition Universelle Internationale de 1878* (no. 657); Paris, Galerie Georges Petit, *Gustave Moreau Exposition au profit des oeuvres du travail et des pauvres honteux,* 1906 (no. 76), lent by Louis Mante; Paris, Louvre, *Gustave Moreau,* June, 1961 (no. 22), lent by Huntington Hartford; New York, Museum of Modern Art, Dec. 4, 1961 – Feb. 4, 1962, and Art Institute of Chicago, Mar. 2 – Apr. 15, 1962, *Odilon Redon — Gustave Moreau — Rudolphe Bresdin* (no. 177), lent by Huntington Hartford; Los Angeles County Museum of Art, July 23 – Sept. 1, 1974, and San Francisco, California Palace of the Legion of Honor, Sept. 14 – Nov. 3, 1974, *Gustave Moreau.*

Hammer Collection exhibitions: see catalogue reference page. First exhibited: IX; not exhibited: XX, XXIX.

Literature: *Salon de 1876, Palais de Champs Elysées, explication des ouvrages,* Paris, May 1, 1876, p. 187, no. 1506; P. de Saint Victor, *La Liberté,* May 19, 1876; *Zigzags, Salon de 1876, Gustave Moreau,* June 25, 1876, p. 2, no. 9; Charles Yriarte, "Le Salon de 1876," in *Gazette des beaux-arts,* vol. 13, Paris, 1876, pp. 705 – 8, repr. p. 698 (sketch for *Salome*); Pierre de Savarus, *Le Salon de 1876, à vol d'oiseau,* Paris, 1876, pp. 43 – 44; George Dufour, "Salon de 1876; le grand art et le petit art," *L'Artiste,* July, 1876, pp. 43 – 44; Victor de Swarte, *Lettres sur le Salon de 1876,* St.-Omer, 1876, p. 79; *Catalogue officiel de l'Exposition Universelle Internationale de 1878 à Paris,* 1878, vol. 1, section 1 (Oeuvres d'Art), p. 51, no. 657; Paul Mantz, "Paris Exposition Universelle, la peinture française," *Gazette des beaux-arts,* vol. 1 (Dec. 1, 1878), p. 47; Charles L. Duval, *Les Beaux-Arts à l'Exposition de 1878, impression et notes d'artistes,* Meaux, 1878, p. 127 (from *Le Publicateur,* Arrondissement de Meaux); *Exposition Universelle de Paris, 1878, le livre d'or des exposants,* section 1 (Beaux-Arts), Paris, 1878, p. 10; Hippolyte Gautier and Adrien Desprez, *Les Curiosités de l'Exposition de 1878,* Paris, 1878, p. 87; M. E. Bergerat, *Les Chefs-d'oeuvre d'art à l'Exposition Universelle, 1878,* Paris, 1878, p. 156, plate 20 (photogravure Goupil et Cie); Pierre de Savarus, *Dix Années d'art (souvenir des expositions),* Paris, 1879, pp. 89 – 91;

J. C. L. Dubosc de Pesquidoux, *L'Art au XIXe siècle. L'Art dans les deux mondes — peinture et sculpture,* Paris, 1881, vol. 1, p. 82, no. IV; J. K. Huysmans, *A Rebours,* Paris, 1884, pp. 71 – 76 (Engl. ed., trans. Robert Baldick, *Against Nature,* Baltimore, 1959, pp. 63 – 67); Paul Leprieur, "Gustave Moreau," *L'Artiste,* Mar., 1889, pp. 175, 177, 180, May, 1889, pp. 339, 350, 351, June, 1889, pp. 444, 449, 450, 452; Jules-Antoine Castagnary, *Salons, 1857 – 1879,* Paris, 1892, vol. 2, pp. 227 – 28; Gustave Larroumet, *Etudes de littérature et d'art,* Paris, 1896, pp. 227 – 78; Léon Thévenin, *L'Esthétique de Gustave Moreau,* Paris, 1897, pp. 9, 12 – 13; Gleeson White, "The Pictures of Gustave Moreau," *The Pageant,* 1897, p. 11; Léonce Bénédite, "Deux idéalistes, Gustave Moreau et E. Burne-Jones," *La Revue de l'art ancien et moderne,* Apr., 1899, pp. 265 – 90, repr.; Ary Renan, "Gustave Moreau," *Gazette des beaux-arts,* July, 1899, pp. 62 – 63, repr. (heliogravure by J. Chauvet); Gustave Geffroy, *La Vie artistique,* ser. 6, chap. XVI, Paris, 1900, pp. 143 – 47; Henri Frantz, "The New Gustave Moreau Gallery," *Magazine of Art,* vol. 24 (1900), pp. 99 – 104; Gustave Larroumet, Institut de France, Académie des Beaux-Arts, *Notice historique sur la vie et les oeuvres de M. Gustave Moreau,* Paris, 1901, pp. 21 – 22, 29 – 30, repr. p. 36; *Principales Oeuvres de maître dans les musées et collections particulières* (intro. Georges Desvallières), Musée National Gustave Moreau, Paris, 1906, no. 9 (heliogravure by J. Chauvet; Mante Coll.); Gustave Geffroy, *L'Oeuvre d'art, l'oeuvre de Gustave Moreau,* Paris, 1906, pp. 5, 9, 26 – 27; *Gustave Moreau Exposition au profit des oeuvres du travail et des pauvres honteux* (preface Robert de Montesquiou), catalogue, Galerie Georges Petit, Paris, 1906, no. 76, p. 38 (Mante Coll.); Arthur Symons, *Studies in Seven Arts,* London, 1910, pp. 73 – 77; Jean Laran and León Deshairs, *L'Art de nôtre temps, Gustave Moreau,* Paris, 1912, pp. 71 – 72, plate 28; *L'Oeuvre de Gustave Moreau* (intro. Georges Desvallières), Musée National Gustave Moreau, Paris, 1913, no. 9, repr.; Anon., *Gustave Moreau (Les Peintres illustrés,* no. 55), Paris, 1914, pp. 69 – 70; "Lettres de Georges Rouault à André Suarès," in *L'art et les artistes,* vol. 13, no. 66, Paris, 1926, p. 223, repr.; *Catalogue de la Vente Collection Louis Mante,* sale catalogue, Galerie Charpentier, Paris, 1956, no. 10, plate 111; Ragnar von Holten, *L'Art fantastique de Gustave Moreau,* Paris, 1960, pp. 19 – 20, repr. plate III in color; *Catalogue de l'Exposition Gustave Moreau,* Musée de Louvre, Paris,

1961, p. 22, no. 22, plate 11 (Huntington Hartford Coll.); Ragnar von Holten, "Le développement du personnage de Salomé à travers les dessins de Gustave Moreau," *L'Oeil,* Aug., 1961, pp. 44 – 51, 72; John Rewald, Dore Ashton, and Harold Joachim, *Odilon Redon — Gustave Moreau — Rudolphe Bresdin* (Museum of Modern Art, New York, in collaboration with the Art Institute of Chicago), New York, 1962, p. 116, no. 177; John Simon, "The Torments of Imagination," *Arts,* Feb., 1962, pp. 20 – 27, repr.; Daniel Grojnowski, "Les Mystères Gustave Moreau," *Revue générale des publications françaises et étrangères* (Editions de Minuit), vol. 19 (Mar., 1963), no. 190, pp. 225 – 38, sketch p. 237; *Catalogue of Paintings from the Huntington Hartford Collection in the Gallery of Modern Art,* New York, 1964, no. 14, repr. in color; Ragnar von Holten, *Gustave Moreau, Symbolist,* Stockholm, 1965, pp. 48 – 65, repr. p. 49; Max Gérard, *Dali,* New York, 1968, no. 169, detail repr. in color; *Important Impressionist and Modern Paintings and Drawings,* sale catalogue, Parke-Bernet Galleries, Inc., New York, Mar. 10, 1971, p. 52, no. 29, repr. in color; Mahonri Sharp Young, "The Hammer Collection: Paintings," *Apollo,* vol. 95 (June, 1972), p. 452, repr. in color on cover; P.-L. Mathieu, *Gustave Moreau: sa vie, son oeuvre; catalogue raisonné de l'oeuvre achevé,* Fribourg, 1976, pp. 121 – 24, repr. pp. 126, 127 (detail), 315 (cat. no. 157).

Salome represents the full flower of the tendency toward accumulation in Moreau's art as well as the apotheosis of one of the most notable and hermetic tendencies in late nineteenth-century French art and literature. This tendency, which involved a slightly overripe enumerative presentation in both visual and verbal media, culminated in and was transformed by the work of Marcel Proust. More than one hundred related drawings are known for Moreau's *Salome* and its variant, *The Apparition,* of which the finished watercolor, now in the Louvre, was also exhibited in the Salon of 1876. The figure of Salome herself was studied in a wooden figure covered with wax and dressed, one of the dozen or so surviving pieces of sculpture by Moreau. Ragnar von Holten believes the subject to have been inspired by Flaubert's *Salammbô,* while Georges Duthuit traces it to Mallarmé's *Hérodiade,* but perhaps no specific source is needed for this theme of the *belle dame sans merci* (see Mario Praz, *The Romantic Agony)* so common to the *fin de siècle.* The scene takes place under the surveillance of the Ephesian Artemis in a fantastic architecture of Moorish inspiration. J. K. Huysmans, who placed the painting in the possession of Des Esseintes, hero of *A Rebours,* described Salome as follows: "Her face composed, solemn, almost august, she begins the lascivious dance which must awaken the deadened senses of the aged Herod. . . . Concentrating, her eyes fixed like those of a sleepwalker, she sees neither the trembling Tetrarch nor her mother, the fierce Herodiade, who watches her, nor the hermaphrodite, or eunuch, who stands, sword in hand, at the foot of the throne." Moreau himself described Salome as "that woman nonchalantly strolling . . . in the gardens recently stained by that horrible murder which terrified the executioner himself." Kaplan has called this picture, which has been known variously as *Salome,* the *Dance of Salome,* and *Salome Dancing Before Herod,* Moreau's "most successful synthesis of precise delineation and free handling of oil pigment."

C. M.

37. GUSTAVE MOREAU (1826–1898)
KING DAVID

Oil on canvas: 90^9/₁₆ x 54^5/₁₆″ (230 x 137.6 cm.)

Collections: Comtesse Roederer, Paris; Hector Brame, Paris; Walter P. Chrysler, Jr., New York.

Exhibited: Paris, *Exposition Universelle Internationale de 1878* (no. 659); Toronto, The Art Gallery of Ontario, *The Sacred and Profane in Symbolist Art,* Nov., 1969 (no. 64); New York, Spencer A. Samuels & Co., Ltd., *Symbolists,* Nov., 1970 (no. 116); Los Angeles County Museum of Art, July 23 – Sept. 1, 1974, and San Francisco, California Palace of the Legion of Honor, Sept. 14 – Nov. 3, 1974, *Gustave Moreau.*

Hammer Collection exhibitions: see catalogue reference page. First exhibited: VIII; not exhibited: X, XX, XXIII, XXVIII, XXIX.

Literature: *Catalogue Officiel de l'Exposition Universelle Internationale de 1878 à Paris,* Paris, 1878, vol. 1, section 1 (Oeuvres d'Art), p. 51, no. 659; Pierre de Savarus, *Dix années d'art (souvenir des expositions),* Paris, 1879, pp. 94 – 95; J. C. L. Dubosc de Pesquidoux, *L'Art au XIXe siècle. L'Art dans les deux mondes — peinture et sculpture,* Paris, 1881, vol. 1, p. 84, no. VI; Claude Phillips, "Gustave Moreau," *Magazine of Art,* vol. 8, 1885, pp. 228 – 33, repr.; Paul Leprieur, "Gustave Moreau," *L'Artiste,* Mar., 1889, p. 175, May, 1889, p. 357, June, 1889, pp. 450 – 51; Jean Lorrain, *Sensations et Souvenirs,* Paris, 1895, p. 67; Ary Renan, "Gustave Moreau," *Gazette des beaux-arts,* Mar., 1899, pp. 192, 194, repr. (etching by M. Bracquemond); Henri Frantz, "The New Gustave Moreau Gallery," *Magazine of Art,* vol. 24 (1900), pp. 97 – 104, repr. p. 98 (engraving by Jonnard reprinted from Claude Phillips, "Gustave Moreau," *Magazine of Art,* 1885, pp. 228 – 33); Gustave Larroumet, Institut de France, Académie des Beaux-Arts, *Notice historique sur la vie et les oeuvres de M. Gustave Moreau,* Paris, 1901, p. 36; *Catalogue sommaire des peintures, dessins, cartons et aquarelles du Musée Gustave Moreau,* Paris, 1902, pp. 9, 22, 33, 49 – 50, 55, 113; Louis Dimier, "L'Inspiration de Gustave Moreau," *Minerva,* Nov. 15, 1902, pp. 275 – 76; Camille Mauclair, "The Gustave Moreau Museum in Paris," *Art Journal* (London), 1905, p. 255, repr.; *Principales Oeuvres de maître dans les musées et collections particulières* (intro. Georges Desvallières), Musée National Gustave Moreau, Paris, 1906, no. 22 (heliogravure by J. Chauvet); Jean Laran and Léon Deshairs, *L'Art de Notre Temps, Gustave Moreau,* Paris, 1912, pp. 79 – 80, plate 33; Anon., *Gustave Moreau (Les Peintres illustrés,* no. 55), Paris, 1914, p. 74; Ragnar von Holten, *L'Art fantastique de Gustave Moreau,* Paris, 1960, plate 37; *Symbolists,* catalogue, Spencer A. Samuels & Co., Ltd., New York, 1970, p. 56, no. 116, repr.; J. Paladilhe and J. Pierre, *Gustave Moreau,* London, 1972, pp. 40, 122; P.-L. Mathieu, *Gustave Moreau: sa vie, son oeuvre; catalogue raisonné de l'oeuvre achevé,* Fribourg, 1976, pp. 132L – 132R, repr. p. 135 (detail), 318 (cat. no. 171).

Originally known simply as *David,* this picture has more recently borne the title *King David Meditating.* In it one sees that juxtaposition of disparate architectural and decorative elements so dear to Moreau. The cross-decorated temple lamp and the evangelist symbols on the capitals may refer to David as lineal ancestor of Christ. The painting comes close to being an allegory of the senses, with the aged psalmist surrounded by flowers, incense, and a burning lamp and clothed in jewels and rich materials. The subtle rhythms of the asymmetrical composition and the softening of the delicate and intricate detail in a poetic atmosphere distinguish Moreau's *King David* and other salon paintings from the works of empty formalism and banal sentiment by so many of his academic contemporaries. Of this kind of picture, Ary Renan wrote in the *Gazette des beaux-arts* in 1899, "His [Moreau's] idea was to equal, without deranging the harmony of line, and by the prestige alone of environing decorations, all the suggestions provoked in literature, music, and the theater."

C. M.

38. SIR JOHN EVERETT MILLAIS (1829–1896)
CALLER HERRIN', 1881

Oil on canvas: 43½ x 31" (110.5 x 79 cm.)
Signed with a monogram and dated lower right

Collections: Fine Art Society, London (bought from the artist Feb. 15, 1882); bought by Walter Dunlop, June 21, 1882 (sold Christie's, London, Mar. 12, 1904 [no. 78]); bought by Thomas Agnew & Sons, Ltd., London, and sold to Stephen G. Holland (sold Christie's, London, June 25, 1908 [no. 77]); bought by Thomas Agnew & Sons, Ltd., London, and sold to Sir Thomas Dewar (sold Christie's, London, Nov. 29, 1918 [no. 91]); bought by Gooden & Fox, London, and sold to Viscount Leverhulme (sold Anderson Galleries, New York, Feb. 17, 1926 [no. 179]); Alvan T. Fuller, Boston.

Exhibited: London, Fine Art Society, 1882; Edinburgh, Royal Scottish Academy, 1883 (no. 322); Manchester, Corporation of Manchester Art Galleries, 1885; London, Grosvenor Gallery, 1886 (no. 52); Boston, Boston Art Club, *Fuller Collection,* 1928 (no. 14); Boston, Museum of Fine Arts, *A Memorial Exhibition of the Collection of the Honorable Alvan T. Fuller,* 1959 (no. 34).

Literature: Sir W. Armstrong, "Sir John Millais," *The Art Annual,* 1885, p. 19; John Ruskin, *Notes on the Principal Pictures of Sir John Everett Millais Exhibited at the Grosvenor Gallery, 1886,* London, 1886, pp. 17 – 18; J. G. Millais, *The Life and Letters of Sir John Everett Millais,* London, vol. 2, 1899, pp. 128, 480; M. H. Spielmann, *Millais and His Works,* Edinburgh and London, 1898, pp. 38, 122, 146, 175, 179.

Few of Millais's paintings so brilliantly display his control of the brush, his superb ability as a pure painter. But looking at this ravishingly beautiful girl, chin in hand, gazing into the distance, pensive and melancholy, makes one forget all technical virtuosity, just as one ignores the marvelous execution of the herrings, which so impressed John Ruskin. Beatrice Buckstone, the focus of the picture, was the daughter of a well-known actor and became one of Millais's favorite models. The painter envisages her as having just sung an old Scottish folk song:

> Come buy my bonny caaler herrin'
> Six a penny caaler from the sea.

"Caaler" means fresh, and this gives the painting its title.

Ruskin, who also loved adolescent beauty, was enthralled by the painting. In a lecture he said, "As a piece of art, I should myself put [it] highest of all yet produced by the Pre-Raphaelite school." In a letter of June 2, 1882, to Mrs. Arthur Stevens he went further. "*Caller Herrin'* is a life-size sketch — or little more than a sketch — but with all the power of a finished picture, of a fisher girl about fourteen sitting with loose hair under a bank at the edge of the beach, with one hand on her basket (with two fish in it), her chin resting on the other, — and her dark eyes lifted to the sky — the most pathetic single figure I ever saw in my life — though there is no sign of distress about the girl. She has good strong shoes, and dress — nothing to indicate hard life but a little bloodstain on the hand from the fish — but quite unspeakably tragic — and such painting as there has not been since Tintoret."

One must admire Ruskin. He did not let his personal feelings interfere with his appreciation. Could more sympathetic lines be dashed off about a painter's work, especially when one remembers that the painter in question had run off with the writer's wife?

J. W.

39. PAUL GAUGUIN (1848–1903)
BONJOUR M. GAUGUIN, 1889

Oil on canvas, mounted on panel: 29½ x 21½″ (74.9 x 54.6 cm.)

Inscribed lower left: Bonjour M. Gauguin

Collections: Mme. Marie Henry, Le Pouldu, France; Galerie Barbazanges, Paris; Meyer Goodfriend, New York (sold American Art Galleries, New York, Jan. 4 – 5, 1923 [no. 107]); B. M. Alexander, New York; Howard Young Galleries, New York; Carlton Mitchell, Annapolis; Count Ivan Podgoursky, San Antonio; Mrs. Mary Ermolaev, Princeton, N.J. (sold Christie, Manson & Woods, Geneva, Switz., Nov. 6, 1969 [no. 169], repr. in cat.).

Exhibited: Paris, Galerie Barbazanges, *Exposition d'Oeuvres Inconnues,* Oct. 10 – 30, 1919 (no. 2); New York, Wildenstein & Co., Inc., *A Retrospective Loan Exhibition for the Benefit of Les Amis de Paul Gauguin and the Penn Normal Industrial and Agricultural School,* Mar. 2 – Apr., 18, 1936 (no. 14); Montreal, Museum of Fine Arts, *Manet to Matisse,* May – June, 1949 (no. 14); Paris, Galerie Loize, *Les Amitiés du Peintre Georges-Daniel de Monfried et ses Reliques de Gauguin,* May, 1951 (no. 108); Houston, Museum of Fine Arts, *Paul Gauguin, His Place in the Meeting of East and West,* Mar. 27 – Apr. 25, 1954 (no. 15); Wichita Falls, Tex., The Museum Association of Midwestern Universities, Sept. – Oct., 1955 (no. 16); Tulsa, Philbrook Art Center, *Four Centuries of European Art,* Oct., 1956 (no. 34); Oklahoma City, Oklahoma Art Center, Nov., 1957 (no. 23), and Little Rock, Museum of Fine Arts, Dec., 1958 (no. 30), *Four Centuries of European Art;* Phoenix, Phoenix Art Museum, Feb. 1 – 26, 1961, and Oakland, Calif., Oakland Art Museum, Mar. 5 – 31, 1961, *One Hundred Years of French Painting, 1860 – 1960* (no. 42), lent by Count Ivan Podgoursky; *Van Gogh, Gauguin and Their Circle,* catalogue, Christie, Manson & Woods (U.S.A.), Ltd., New York, Nov. 1968 (no. 9).

Hammer Collection exhibitions: see catalogue reference page. First exhibited: II.

Literature: Charles Chassé, *Gauguin et le groupe de Pont-Aven,* Paris, 1921, pp. 48 – 50; *American Art Journal,* vol. 20 (1923 – 24), p. 275; Jean de Rotonchamp, *Gauguin,* Paris, 1925, p. 70; *Canadian Art,* vol. 6 (Summer, 1949), p. 176, repr.; J. Loize, *Les Amitiés du peintre Georges-Daniel de Monfried et ses reliques de Gauguin,* catalogue, Galerie Loize, Paris, 1951, pp. 86 – 87, no. 108; Charles Chassé, *Gauguin et son temps,* Paris, 1955, pp. 70, 79; M. Malingue, "Du Nouveau sur Gauguin," *L'Oeil,* July – Aug., 1959, p. 38; John Rewald, *Le Post-Impressionisme,* Paris, 1961, p. 176; George Boudaille, *Gauguin,* London, 1964, pp. 89, 130, repr. in color; Georges Wildenstein, *Gauguin,* Paris, 1964, pp. 121 – 22, no. 321; *Art in America,* Sept., 1969, p. 15, repr.; *Art News,* Sept., 1969, p. 26, repr.; *Apollo,* Oct., 1969, p. IX, repr.; *Connaissance des arts,* Oct., 1969, p. 67, repr.; *Apollo,* Feb., 1970, p. 170, repr.; *Connoisseur,* Feb., 1970, p. 116, repr.; Frank Davis, "A Royal Record of Portraiture," *Country Life,* Feb. 5, 1970, pp. 302 – 3, repr.; Mahonri Sharp Young, "The Hammer Collection: Paintings," *Apollo,* vol. 95 (June, 1972), p. 452.

In 1889 Gauguin and the painters working with him transferred their Breton activities from Pont-Aven to Le Pouldu, which they found more primitive. In October of that year, they moved to an inn kept by Marie Henry and soon thereafter began decorating its walls with paintings and sculpture. Gauguin's *Bonjour Monsieur Gauguin* occupied the upper panel of a door in the inn. There are two existing versions of the composition, and both Georges Wildenstein and Denys Sutton are agreed that the Hammer picture is the one originally fastened to the door at Le Pouldu, while the Prague version precedes it or is a later replica. In any case, the two pictures cannot have been created more than a few weeks apart. This picture is distinguished from the Prague version by a somewhat more unified composition and more consistent brushwork. The subject was almost certainly inspired by Courbet's *Bonjour Monsieur Courbet,* which Gauguin and Van Gogh had seen on a visit to Montpellier in December, 1888. A related watercolor on silk (John Rewald, *Gauguin Drawings,* New York, 1958, no. 18) is apparently a study for the righthand figure in the Prague version.

C. M.

40. EMILE BERNARD (1868–1941)
WHEAT HARVEST, 1889

Oil on canvas: 28½ x 35⅞" (72.4 x 91.1 cm.)
Signed and dated lower left: E. Bernard 1889

Collections: Clement Altarriba (son-in-law of the artist), Paris; Wildenstein & Co., Inc., New York; Mr. and Mrs. Richard Sussman, New York; Findlay Galleries, Inc., Chicago.

Hammer Collection exhibitions: see catalogue reference page. First exhibited: II; not exhibited: XX, XXIII.

Literature: John Rewald, *Post Impressionism,* New York, 1956, repr. p. 285; *Connoisseur,* Nov., 1966, repr. p. XCIII; *Art Journal,* Winter, 1966 – 67, repr. p. 195; Mahonri Sharp Young, "The Hammer Collection: Paintings," *Apollo,* vol. 95 (June, 1972), p. 452.

The harvesting of wheat was among the favorite themes of the group gathered around Gauguin in Brittany during the years 1889 – 90. Bernard treated the subject in painting in 1888 and in a print in 1889, the year of this picture, and Gauguin also painted Breton haymakers in 1889 (see his *Breton Landscape* in the de Sylva Collection of the Los Angeles County Museum of Art). Bernard, forbidden by his father to join Gauguin at Pont-Aven, passed the summer of 1889 at St.-Briac, where this picture was probably painted. One sees in the flat color areas reminiscences of the Japanese prints so popular with the Pont-Aven group, and in the outlining of the shapes the "cloisonnism" identified in their work by Edouard Dujardin. At this particular moment, Bernard had carried flatness and clear separation of colors considerably farther than Gauguin, although his facture (and Gauguin's of the period) recalls Cézanne's version of the Impressionist comma-like brushwork with its groups of parallel strokes. In the cross on the distant hill, one can perhaps see a forecast of the mystical Catholicism that was increasingly to occupy Bernard.

C. M.

41. VINCENT VAN GOGH (1853–1890)
GARDEN OF THE RECTORY AT NUENEN, 1885

Oil on canvas, mounted on panel: 20⅞ x 30¾" (53 x 78.2 cm.)

Collections: Oldenzeel Gallery, Rotterdam, 1903; Jan Smit, Alblasserdam (sold Mak van Waiij, Amsterdam, Feb. 10, 1919 [no. 30]), repr. in cat.; L. J. Smit, Kinderdijk; Leo C. Smit, Kinderdijk, 1952 (sold Parke-Bernet Galleries, Inc., New York, Nov. 20, 1968 [no. 37]); Spencer A. Samuels & Co., Ltd., New York; Fletcher Jones, Los Angeles.

Exhibited: Rotterdam, Oldenzeel Gallery, *Van Gogh,* 1904 (no. 31); The Hague, Gemeentemuseum, *Vincent van Gogh,* Mar. 30 – May 17, 1953 (no. 31); Otterloo, Rijksmuseum Kröller-Müller, *Vincent van Gogh,* May 24 – July 19, 1953 (no. 18); Amsterdam, Stedelijk Museum, *Vincent van Gogh,* July 23 – Sept. 20, 1953 (no. 18); Dordrecht Museum, *Boem, Bloem en Plant,* July 16 – Aug. 31, 1955 (no. 52); Paris, Musée Jacquemart-André, *Vincent van Gogh,* Feb. – Mar., 1960 (no. 11).

Hammer Collection exhibitions: see catalogue reference page. First exhibited: III; not exhibited: XX, XXIII.

Literature: *The Letters of Vincent van Gogh to His Brother, 1872 – 1886,* London, Boston, and New York, 1927, vol. 2, Letter 394, pp. 456 – 58; J. B. de la Faille, *L'Oeuvre de Vincent van Gogh, catalogue raisonné,* Paris and Brussels, 1928, vol. 1, no. 67, vol. 2, plate XX (measurements incorrect); Dr. Walter Vanbeselaere, *De Hollandsche Periode (1880 – 1885) in Het Werk van Vincent van Gogh,* Antwerp, 1937, pp. 294, 352, 414; J. B. de la Faille, *Vincent van Gogh* (preface Charles Terrasse), Paris, 1939, p. 79, no. 73 (measurements incorrect); J. B. de la Faille, *The Works of Vincent van Gogh: His Paintings and Drawings,* Amsterdam, London, and New York, 1970, pp. 66, 614, no. F67, repr. p. 67; *Impressionist and Modern Paintings and Sculptures,* sale catalogue, Sotheby & Co., London, Apr. 15, 1970, p. 55, no. 26, repr. in color.

In the late winter of 1885 – 86, Van Gogh wrote to his brother, "When there was snow, I . . . painted a few studies of our garden," and de la Faille dates this picture to January, 1885. The scene is taken from the presbytery at Nuenen, the small town in which Van Gogh's father was vicar and where Vincent lived with his family for two years before going to France. The distant tower occurs in several pictures of the time, and there exist another painting and two drawings directly related to this scene (de la Faille, nos. 185, 1133, 1234). The picture projects the bleakness Vincent felt around him in the winter of 1885, a bleakness that permeates both his landscapes and his figure studies. It is among the last of his "Dutch" pictures, worked out in the dark tonalities of the Hague School, its drawing perhaps indebted to the English illustrations he knew so well. The extreme lightness of the sky forecasts the future lightening of Van Gogh's palette and suggests that interest in color to which he referred constantly in his letters of the period.

C. M.

42. VINCENT VAN GOGH (1853–1890)
LILACS, 1887

Oil on canvas: 10¾ x 13¹⁵/₁₆″ (27.3 x 35.3 cm.)
　　Collection: Drs. Fritz and Peter Nathan, Zurich.
　　Hammer Collection exhibitions: see catalogue reference page. First exhibited: IX; not exhibited: XXIII.
　　Literature: J. B. de la Faille, *The Works of Vincent van Gogh: His Paintings and Drawings,* Amsterdam, London, and New York, 1970, p. 142, no. 286b.

Van Gogh had been preoccupied with bringing more intense color into his pictures since well before his move to Paris in 1886. It was only under the direct impact of the paintings he saw in the French capital, however, that he began to use color freely, applying it with an increasingly divisionist brushstroke. Toward the fall of 1887, Vincent wrote to the English painter Levens, "I have lacked money for paying models else I had entirely given myself to figure painting. But I have made a series of color studies in painting, simply flowers, red poppies, blue cornflowers and myosotis, white and red roses, yellow chrysanthemums— seeking oppositions of blue with orange, red and green, yellow and violet, seeking *les tons rompus et neutres* to harmonize brutal extremes. Trying to render intense color and not a gray harmony." The present picture is, no doubt, one of these studies.

C. M.

43. VINCENT VAN GOGH (1853–1890)
THE SOWER, c. 1888

Oil on canvas: 13¼ x 15¹⁵/₁₆″ (33.6 x 40.4 cm.)

Collections: Mme. J. van Gogh-Bonger, Amsterdam; Montross Gallery, New York, 1921; the Reverend Theodore Pitcairn, Bryn Athyn, Pa.

Exhibited: New York, Montross Gallery, Oct., 1920; Philadelphia Museum of Art, Summer Loan, 1960, lent by the Reverend Theodore Pitcairn.

Hammer Collection exhibitions: see catalogue reference page. First exhibited: II; not exhibited: X, XX, XXIII.

Literature: *Important Impressionist and Modern Drawings, Paintings and Sculpture,* sale catalogue, Christie, Manson & Woods, London, May 2, 1969, p. 46, no. 58, repr. opp. p. 46; J. B. de la Faille, *The Works of Vincent van Gogh: His Paintings and Drawings,* Amsterdam, London, and New York, 1970, pp. 240, 634, no. 575a, repr.; P. Lecaldano, *Van Gogh,* Milan, 1971, vol. 2, p. 212, no. 566, repr.

The Sower was a theme that fascinated Van Gogh throughout his career, partly because of his Millet-inspired identification with the peasant subject and partly for psychologically more deeply seated associations with fertility and generation. This version of the subject is unique in showing the sower's figure placed against a silhouette of Arles, something Van Gogh otherwise reserved for pictures of reapers or plowed fields (de la Faille, nos. 465, 545). The character of the brushwork and the nature and intensity of the color suggest a date in late 1888 or early 1889, conceivably even one as late in 1889 as Van Gogh's stay in the hospital of St.-Rémy. The size and intensity of the blue-purple field, "compulsive in its excess" (Meyer Schapiro), swallow the figure, adding to the picture's disharmonious scale relationships. These do not, however, detract from the power of this small canvas.

C. M.

44. VINCENT VAN GOGH (1853–1890)
HOSPITAL AT ST.-RÉMY, 1889

Oil on canvas: 35½ x 28″ (90.2 x 71.1 cm.)

Collections: A. Schuffenecker, Paris; Galerie E. Druet, Paris, 1907; Dr. J. Keller, Paris, 1908 – 10; Galerie E. Druet, Paris, 1910; Paul von Mendelssohn-Bartholdy, Berlin, 1911; Paul Rosenberg & Co., New York; Norton Simon, Los Angeles, 1964 (sold Parke-Bernet Galleries, Inc., New York, May 5, 1971 [no. 48]).

Exhibited: Paris, Galerie E. Druet, *Vincent van Gogh,* Jan. 6 – 18, 1908 (no. 16); Berlin, Galerie Paul Cassirer, *Vincent van Gogh,* May – June, 1914 (no. 65); Amsterdam, Stedelijk Museum, *Vincent van Gogh en Zijn Tijdgenooten,* Sept. 6 – Nov. 2, 1930 (no. 92); Frankfurt, Städelsches Kunstinstitut, *Ausstellung von Meisterwerken moderner Malerei, vom Abbild zum Sinnbild,* June 3 – July 3, 1931 (no. 69).

Hammer Collection exhibitions: see catalogue reference page. First exhibited: IX.

Literature: *Aesculape,* 13th year, no. 10 (Nov., 1923), p. 250, repr.; Louis Piérard, *La Vie tragique de Vincent van Gogh,* Paris, 1924, p. 184, repr.; Roch Grey, *Vincent van Gogh,* Rome, 1924, repr.; *Aesculape,* 16th year, no. 6 (June, 1926), p. 158; Florent Fels, *Vincent van Gogh,* Paris, 1928, p. 171, repr.; J. B. de la Faille, *L'Oeuvre de Vincent van Gogh, catalogue raisonné,* Paris and Brussels, 1928, vol. 1, no. 643, vol. 2, plate CLXXIX; Victor Doiteau and Edgar Leroy, *La Folie de van Gogh* (preface Paul Gachet), Paris, 1928, p. 64, repr.; *The Further Letters of Vincent van Gogh to His Brother, 1886 – 1889,* London, Boston, and New York, 1929, vol. 3, Letter 610, p. 400; *Vincent van Gogh en Zijn Tijdgenooten,* catalogue, Stedelijk Museum, Amsterdam, 1930, p. 18, no. 92; *Ausstellung von Meisterwerken moderner Malerei, vom Abbild zum Sinnbild,* catalogue, Städelsches Kunstinstitut, Frankfurt, 1931, p. 26, no. 69; John Rewald, "Van Gogh en Provence," *L'Amour de l'art,* vol. 17 (Oct., 1936), p. 297, repr.; W. Scherjon and W. Jos. de Gruyter, *Vincent van Gogh's Great Period,* Amsterdam, 1937, p. 205, repr.; J. B. de la Faille, *Vincent van Gogh* (preface Charles Terrasse), Paris, 1939, p. 446, no. 648, repr.; Dr. François-Joachim Beer, *Du Démon de Van Gogh* (after *Van Gogh à l'asile,* by Dr. Edgar Leroy), Nice, 1945, p. 75; J. B. de la Faille, *The Works of Vincent van Gogh: His Paintings and Drawings,* Amsterdam and New York, 1970, pp. 256, 636, no. F643, repr. p. 257; *Highly Important 19th and 20th Century Paintings, Drawings & Sculpture from the Private Collection of Norton Simon,* sale catalogue, Parke-Bernet Galleries, Inc., New York, 1971, p. 92, no. 48, repr. in color; P. Lecaldano, *Van Gogh,* Milan, 1971, vol. 2, p. 223, no. 720, repr.; Mahonri Sharp Young, "The Hammer Collection: Paintings," *Apollo,* vol. 95 (June, 1972), p. 452, repr. plate VI in color p. 448.

Van Gogh stayed at the hospital at St.-Rémy for almost exactly one year, from May, 1889, until May, 1890, and took its gardens and surroundings as the subject for many of his pictures. In the fall of 1889, he wrote to his brother Theo that he had "two views of the park and the asylum," one of which was undoubtedly this work. Only one other painting (de la Faille, no. 653) shows a substantial portion of the facade of the hospital. One sees in this picture the remnants of an older style in the squared rendering of the building, while the flamelike brushwork of the trees, which Vincent saw as "warped as in old wood," announces the style for which he has become best known. Few of Van Gogh's pictures show as well as this the tendency of his brushstrokes to cling to the surface of the canvas and the increasing density and intensity of his paint application during the last three years of his life.

C. M.

45. PIERRE BONNARD (1867–1947)
STREET SCENE, c. 1902

Oil on canvas: 21 x 27½″ (53.3 x 69.8 cm.)
Signed lower right: Bonnard

Collections: Viscount Jowitt, London; Noel Coward, London; Sotheby & Co., London (sold Apr. 18, 1956 [no. 144]); Schoneman Galleries, New York; Christie, Manson & Woods, London (sold Dec. 1, 1967 [no. 37]).

Exhibited: Scotland, Edinburgh Festival, *Bonnard and Vuillard,* Aug., 1948 (no. 55), repr. p. 7 in cat.; London, Roland, Browse and Delbanco, *Bonnard,* 1950 (no. 16), repr. in cat.; London, Redfern Gallery, *French Paintings,* Oct. 30 – Nov. 22, 1952 (no. 53).

Hammer Collection exhibitions: see catalogue reference page. First exhibited: I; not exhibited: XXIII.

Literature: *Modern and French 19th Century Drawings, Paintings and Sculpture,* sale catalogue, Sotheby & Co., London, 1956, no. 144, repr.; *L'Oeil,* Sept., 1956, p. 44; *Bonnard* (intro. Denys Sutton), catalogue, Farber Gallery, London, 1957, p. 12, repr. plate 5 in color; Jean and Henry Dauberville, *Bonnard, catalogue raisonné de l'oeuvre peint, 1888 – 1905,* Paris, vol. 1, 1965, p. 26, no. 269, repr.; *Important Impressionist and Modern Drawings, Paintings and Sculpture,* sale catalogue, Christie, Manson & Woods, London, 1967, p. 34, no. 37, repr. in color.

Although the relatively muted tones, small-scale paint application, and areas of bare canvas in this picture recall the early style Bonnard shared with Vuillard, one already senses the richness of his later color in the red-blue contrasts. The tree trunks hold the composition firmly in place, making it almost a triptych, a favorite Nabi format.

C. M.

Oil on canvas: 48¾ x 21½″ (123.8 x 54.6 cm.)
Signed lower left: Bonnard

Collections: Galerie Bernheim-Jeune (acquired from Bonnard Jan. 8, 1909); Henri Bernstein, Paris, purchased Jan. 8, 1910; repurchased by Galerie Bernheim-Jeune, Paris, June 9, 1911; Emile Maysisch, Paris; Marianne Feilchenfeldt, Zurich; Ragnar Moltzau, Oslo; Michel P. Couturier, Neuilly-sur-Seine; Adler Collection, London (sold Parke-Bernet Galleries, Inc., New York, Mar. 21, 1962 [no. 80]); Galerie der Spiegel, Cologne; Alex Léfèvre Gallery, London; Norton Simon, Los Angeles (sold Parke-Bernet Galleries, Inc., New York, May 5, 1971 [no. 59]).

Exhibited: Zurich, Kunsthaus, *Bonnard,* 1949; Copenhagen, Ny Carlsberg Glyptotek, *Fra Renoir til Villon, Franske Malerier eg. Udlaant fra Ragnar Moltzau Samling,* June 21 – Aug. 1, 1956 (hors cat.); The Hague, Gemeentemuseum, *Collection Moltzau,* Apr. – June, 1957 (no. 15); Scotland, Edinburgh Festival, and London, Tate Gallery, *Bonnard,* 1958 (no. 13); Copenhagen, Ny Carlsberg Glyptotek, *Documenta III,* 1959; Paris, Galerie Europe, *Itinéraire sur Trois Génerations,* June – July, 1960 (no. 4); London, Alex Léfèvre Gallery, *XIXth and XXth Century French Paintings,* Oct. 14 – Nov. 13, 1965 (no. 1).

Hammer Collection exhibitions: see catalogue reference page. First exhibited: IX; not exhibited: XXIII.

Literature: Gustave Coquiot, *Bonnard,* Paris, 1922, plate 5; *Art and Auctions,* vol. 6, no. 121 (Feb. 28, 1962), pp. 29, 35; *Important Modern Paintings, Drawings, Bronzes,* sale catalogue, Parke-Bernet Galleries, Inc., New York, 1962, no. 80, repr.; *Arts,* Mar., 1962, repr. p. 13; *Apollo,* Oct. 1965, repr. p. 338; Jean and Henry Dauberville, *Bonnard, catalogue raisonné de l'oeuvre peint, 1888 – 1905,* Paris, vol. 2, 1968, no. 528, repr. p. 140; *Highly Important 19th and 20th Century Paintings, Drawings & Sculpture from the Private Collection of Norton Simon,* sale catalogue, Parke-Bernet Galleries, Inc., New York, 1971, no. 59, p. 114, repr. in color.

Strongest as a colorist, weakest as a draftsman, Bonnard was often at his best when a canvas of firmly marked shape helped him structure his composition. In this picture the rectangular shapes at the top and left side assist in giving firmness, as do the value contrasts caused by the backlighting of the figure. For the rest, Bonnard is free to indulge the lavish richness of his purples, golds, and dark greens. Consistently attracted to the timeless theme of the bather, he has here used a languid pose recalling that of the traditional *La Source.* The picture was said by Gustave Coquiot to date from 1908, although the Daubervilles assign it to 1909.

C. M.

47. EDOUARD VUILLARD (1868–1940)
IN THE BUS, c. 1895

Oil on board: 9¹³/₁₆ x 9″ (25 x 22.9 cm.)
Signed lower right: E. Vuillard

Collections: Georges Seligmann, New York; Dalzell Hatfield Galleries, Los Angeles; Stephen Hahn Gallery, New York.

Hammer Collection exhibitions: see catalogue reference page. First exhibited: I; not exhibited: XX, XXIII.

Literature: Mahonri Sharp Young, "The Hammer Collection: Paintings," *Apollo,* vol. 95 (June, 1972), p. 452.

The *tachiste* paint application, which results in an all-over decorative pattern, and the predominance of low-keyed golden browns are characteristic of Vuillard at this date. The subject of the painting is by no means clear.

C. M.

48. EDOUARD VUILLARD (1868–1940)
AT THE SEASHORE, c. 1904

Oil on panel: 8½ x 8½" (21.6 x 21.6 cm.)
Signed lower left: E. Vuillard

Collections: Joseph Hessel, Paris; Alfred Daber, Paris; Sam Salz, New York; Mr. and Mrs. Henry R. Luce, New York.

Exhibited: Paris, Musée du Louvre, Pavillon Marsan, *Vuillard,* 1938; Paris, Galerie Charpentier, *Vuillard,* 1946; New York, Museum of Modern Art, and Cleveland Museum of Art, *Edouard Vuillard,* 1954, p. 103 in cat.; Toronto, Art Gallery of Ontario, Sept. 11 – Oct. 24, 1971, San Francisco, California Palace of the Legion of Honor, Nov. 18, 1971 – Jan. 2, 1972, and Art Institute of Chicago, Jan. 28 – Mar. 12, 1972, *Edouard Vuillard* (no. 59).

Hammer Collection exhibitions: see catalogue reference page. First exhibited: II; not exhibited: XI, XXIII.

Literature: Jacques Salomon, *Vuillard,* Paris, 1968, no. 100, as *Lucie Hessel Devant la Mer,* repr. in color; Francois Daulte, "Hammer en dix chefs-d'oeuvre," *Connaissance des arts,* Sept., 1970, p. 85, repr. in color; John Russell, *Edouard Vuillard, 1868 – 1940,* catalogue, Art Gallery of Ontario, Toronto, 1971, p. 231, plate 59; Mahonri Sharp Young, "The Hammer Collection: Paintings," *Apollo,* vol. 95 (June, 1972), p. 452, repr. plate VIII in color p. 450.

"This little painting," wrote Jacques Salomon, "is like a cry from the heart, the echo of which ravished me when I admired it on Lucie Hessel's mantelpiece; the touch is so alive, so alert, so completely submissive to the rhythm of Vuillard's feeling." Vuillard first met Mme. Hessel in 1900, and it was in her apartment in the Rue de Rivoli that he henceforth found most of his sitters, the most constant of these being Mme. Hessel herself. She was, in Jacques Salomon's words, "beautiful and elegant, without being pretty. Mme. Hessel joined great qualities of judgment and feeling to a real distinction. Vuillard devoted to her a constant friendship, which for forty years was not troubled by the slightest cloud." Lucie Hessel was the wife of Joseph Hessel, first director of the Galerie Bernheim-Jeune and later an important independent dealer in Rue La Boëtie.

C. M.

49. EDOUARD VUILLARD (1868–1940)
RUE LEPIC, PARIS, 1908

Tempera: 65 x 18½" (165.1 x 47 cm.)
Signed lower right: E. Vuillard

Collections: Sam Salz, New York; Mr. and Mrs. Henry R. Luce, New York.

Hammer Collection exhibitions: see catalogue reference page. First exhibited: II; not exhibited: XXI – XXXIII.

Literature: Claude Roger-Marx, *Vuillard et son temps,* Paris, 1945, p. 140 (original project, with additional twelve inches of sky, repr. p. 161); John Russell, *Edouard Vuillard, 1868 – 1940,* catalogue, Art Gallery of Ontario, Toronto, 1971, p. 232, plate 69; Mahonri Sharp Young, "The Hammer Collection: Paintings," *Apollo,* vol. 95 (June, 1972), p. 452.

The tall, narrow format imposed by projects for decorative screens or room panels seems to have been particularly congenial to the Nabis. In this one, the matte paint application, leaving space for the support to show through, may reflect Vuillard's awareness of Toulouse-Lautrec. The composition, cut down by about a foot from its original dimensions, was one of a series of sketches of streets and squares of Paris for a projected room decoration for Henri Bernstein. Claude Roger-Marx reproduces it in its original state next to a similar panel of a park in Paris. The Rue Lepic runs into the Place Blanche in Montmartre, the center of Nabi activity.

C. M.

50. EDOUARD VUILLARD (1868–1940)
INTERIOR, c. 1910

Oil on board: 21⅛ x 15⅞″ (53.3 x 40.3 cm.)
Stamped lower right: E. Vuillard

Collections: The Hanover Gallery, London; Edward Le Bas, Brighton (sold Christie, Manson & Woods, Geneva, Switz., Nov. 6, 1969 [no. 164]).

Exhibited: London, Royal Academy of Arts, *From a Painter's Collection* (Edward Le Bas Coll.), Mar. 19 – Apr. 28, 1963 (no. 120).

Hammer Collection exhibitions: see catalogue reference page. First exhibited: II; not exhibited: XXIII.

Literature: *Impressionist and Modern Drawings, Paintings and Sculpture,* sale catalogue, Christie, Manson & Woods, Geneva, Switz., 1969, no. 164, repr.

Lighter in tone than is common for Vuillard, this airy composition is held together by the rectangular forms of the window, doorway, and chair and by the strong vertical of the open door. Interiors without figures are rare for Vuillard. In this case, the scene may be that of his studio on the Boulevard Malsherbes.

The stamped signature in the lower righthand corner of the picture is identified in Frits Lugt, *Les Marques de collections, de dessins & d'estampes* (Le Haye, 1956, Supplement, pp. 363 – 64, no. 2497a). After Vuillard's death, his sister and brother-in-law, M. and Mme. K.-X. Roussel, put stamps (E Vuillard or E V) on the works that remained in his studio as well as on a few that belonged to the family or to Vuillard's close friends.

J. W.

51. ANDRÉ DERAIN (1880–1954)
STILL LIFE WITH BASKET, JUG, AND FRUIT, 1911

Oil on canvas: 19⅞ x 23¹¹/₁₆″ (50.5 x 60.1 cm.)
Signed lower right: a derain

   Collections: Galerie Simon, Paris; Galerie Matthieson, Berlin; Edward Le Bas, Brighton (sold Christie, Manson & Woods, Geneva, Switz., Nov. 6, 1969 [no. 165]).

   Exhibited: London, Arts Council, *20th Century French Paintings and Drawings,* 1943 (no. 10); London, Royal Academy of Arts, *From a Painter's Collection* (Edward Le Bas Coll.), Mar. 9 – Apr. 28, 1963 (no. 161).

   Hammer Collection exhibitions: see catalogue reference page. First exhibited: II; not exhibited: XX, XXIII.

   Literature: *L'Esprit nouveau,* May, 1921, repr.; *Impressionist and Modern Drawings, Paintings and Sculpture,* sale catalogue, Christie, Manson & Woods, Geneva, Switz., 1969, no. 165, repr.; Mahonri Sharp Young, "The Hammer Collection: Paintings," *Apollo,* vol. 95 (June, 1972), p. 452.

At the same time that he was painting more clearly Cubist-derived works, Derain was also working in the flatter, heavier style of this picture. One sees the influence of Cubism in the stylization of the shapes, the paint application of the background, and the restricted palette. The particular range of dark hues employed in this picture was favored by Derain throughout his career, and the style of this work is in every way more prophetic of his future than were many of the paintings executed at this time.

C. M.

Oil on canvas: 39¼ x 25⅝" (99.7 x 65.1 cm.)
Signed upper right: Modigliani

Collections: André Léfèvre, Paris; Blair Laing, Toronto; Dr. Armand Hammer, Los Angeles; Los Angeles County Museum of Art, gift of Dr. and Mrs. Armand Hammer.

Exhibited: Brussels, Palais des Beaux-Arts, *Modigliani,* 1933 (no. 53); Paris, Petit Palais, *Les Maîtres de l'Art Indépendants, 1895 – 1937,* June – Oct., 1937 (no. 77); Paris, Musée National d'Art Moderne, *L'Oeuvre du XXe Siècle,* May – June, 1952 (no. 73); London, Arts Council, *XXth Century Masterpieces,* 1952 (no. 67); Paris, Musée National d'Art Moderne, *Collection André Léfèvre,* Mar. – Apr., 1964 (no. 209).

Hammer Collection exhibitions: see catalogue reference page. First exhibited: I; not exhibited: IV, VI, VII, IX, XXI – XXIII.

Literature: Maurice Raynal, *Peintres du XXe siècle,* Geneva, Switz., 1947, repr. plate 38 in color; Claude Roy, *Modigliani* (The Taste of Our Time), Geneva, Switz., 1958, p. 80, repr.; Maurice Raynal, *La Peinture française contemporaine,* Geneva, Switz., c. 1960, repr. plate 37 and on cover in color; *Modigliani* (Skira Color Prints), New York, n.d., plate 1; *Vente Léfèvre,* sale catalogue, Palais Galliéra, Paris, Nov. 25, 1965, repr.; Mahonri Sharp Young, "The Hammer Collection: Paintings," *Apollo,* vol. 95 (June, 1972), p. 452.

This portrait of Germaine Lable, daughter of the concierge of the artist's close friend the poet Max Jacob, was painted in 1918, two years before Modigliani's premature death at the age of thirty-six.

The painting exemplifies Modigliani's distinctive ability to capture the unique character of his sitter through, or one might almost say despite, his personal, elegantly mannered style of portraiture. The elongated oval face, drooping shoulder lines and pursed lips were all favorite devices of the artist. The delicately balanced facial features and the graceful curves of hairline, scarf, and drapery reveal the artist's masterful draftsmanship.

This commonplace woman of the people, seated in a basically static frontal position, is juxtaposed to the diagonal angle of the bed so that the curvilinear pattern of the head rail and pillow complements the curves in the figure and creates a dynamic interplay of compositional forces. The combination of spatial flatness and subtle distortions of linear and shape relationships results in a unified, highly evocative composition; the abstract rhythm of formal elements across the pictorial surface alone carries the weight of the personal content. It is precisely this way of conveying incisive characterization with the most elegant and sparse formal means that makes Modigliani so moving and original an artist.

C. M.

53. CHAIM SOUTINE (1894–1943)
THE VALET, 1929

Oil on canvas: 43 x 25″ (109.2 x 63.5 cm.)

Collections: Pierre Loeb; Marcel Fleischmann, Zurich; Leigh B. Block, Chicago; Paul Rosenberg, New York; Walter P. Chrysler, Jr., New York.

Exhibited: New York, Museum of Modern Art, 1939 – 42; Cleveland Museum of Art, *Soutine,* Apr. – June, 1952 (no. 462); Dayton Art Institute, Dayton, Ohio, *French Painting 1789 – 1929 from The Collection of Walter P. Chrysler, Jr.,* 1960; Provincetown, Mass., Chrysler Museum, *Controversial Century,* June 15 – Sept. 3, 1962; Ottawa, National Gallery of Canada, *Soutine,* Sept. 27 – Nov. 4, 1962.

Hammer Collection exhibitions: see catalogue reference page. First exhibited: XXXVII.

Literature: M. Sachs, "Soutine," *Creative Art,* Dec., 1932, pp. 273 – 78, repr.; M. Wheeler, *Soutine,* New York, 1950, p. 80, repr.

Soutine, the son of a poor tailor from Smilovitch, near Minsk, arrived in Paris in 1911, having studied painting in Wilno. Like his compatriot Chagall, he brought to the cosmopolitan School of Paris a new strain made up of the intense emotional life of a Jewish village and the visionary poetry that grew out of its frustrations and poverty. His tragic sense, which caused him to try to hang himself, is expressed in the distorted and tortured faces of his sitters — valets, bellboys, cooks — whom he portrayed with a mastery of brushwork and pigmentation unsurpassed among modern artists.

In the Hammer picture, painted at the end of the 1920s, this melancholy youth, seated astride a chair, seems ready to spring automatically to attention in spite of his trance-like state. The portrait reveals Soutine's terrible nervous energy, which he has poured into the twisted, elongated face. The pigment is squeezed onto the canvas and brushed with demonic frenzy. After completing a picture like this, Soutine is said to have been physically exhausted.

The Valet has hung on the walls of many museums, where, to the sensitive observer, it has always seemed like a bomb that might explode at any moment. Soutine's pictures are not easy to look at with tranquility!

J. W.

54. GEORGES ROUAULT (1871–1958)
CIRCUS GIRL

Oil on paper: 25¾ x 20¹¹/₁₆″ (65.4 x 52.5 cm.)
Signed lower right: G. Rouault

Collections: Ambroise Vollard, Paris, until 1939; Edwin C. Vogel, New York; Perls Gallery, New York; Vladimir Golschmann, St. Louis; Stephen Hahn Gallery, New York.

Exhibited: New York, Galerie Chalette, 1958; Tokyo, National Museum of Western Art, Oct. 1 – Nov. 10, 1963; Kyoto, National Art Gallery of Kyoto, Nov. 20 – Dec. 10, 1963.

Hammer Collection exhibitions: see catalogue reference page. First exhibited: I; not exhibited: X, XX, XXIII.

Characters from the Bible and from the circus appear frequently in Rouault's paintings and drawings; the circus figures as early as 1915 and as late as 1956. *Circus Girl* was probably painted between 1938 and 1943, when the artist illustrated a book and published a portfolio of paintings with this subject. The first, *Le Cirque de l'étoile filante* (1938), contained seventeen etchings and eighty-two wood engravings. With its companion, *Passion* (1939),

also illustrated by Rouault but composed by his friend the poet André Suarès, these editions represented the two dominant themes of his oeuvre: the church and the cabaret, the sacred and the profane (see Pierre Courthion, *Georges Rouault,* London, 1962, pp. 254 – 55). In 1943 Rouault again depicted the circus in a series of paintings, which, together with his verse, was published as a portfolio called *Divertissements.* In a line from one of his poems, Rouault describes a harlequin as a wasp "golden yellow, and ivory black," a description that equally well applies to the *Circus Girl.* There are several representations by the artist of entertainers similar to the Hammer picture, at least four of which are head-and-shoulder portraits in profile (Courthion, nos. 374, 503, 505, 512). The latter range in date from 1933 to 1948.

The influence of Gustave Moreau, Rouault's teacher, is apparent in the rich pigmentation and dense texture of this painting. However, the use of heavy impasto and thick black line to define the colors is typically Rouault's.

M. E.

55. MAURICE DE VLAMINCK (1876–1958)
SUMMER BOUQUET

Oil on canvas: 25¾ x 21⁹/₁₆″ (65.4 x 54.7 cm.)
Signed lower left: Vlaminck

Collections: James Vigeveno Galleries, Los Angeles; Mr. and Mrs. Henry R. Luce, New York.

Hammer Collection exhibitions: see catalogue reference page. First exhibited: IV; not exhibited: XX, XXIII.

Literature: Mahonri Sharp Young, "The Hammer Collection: Paintings," *Apollo,* vol. 95 (June, 1972), p. 452.

Vlaminck was so prolific as a landscape painter that his vases of flowers are comparatively rare. Yet he did paint flower still lifes sporadically through most of his career. His handling of the thick, juicy paint, which is one of his most attractive talents, is beautifully displayed in this rather late work, especially in the petals of the flowers. De Staël never produced a more brilliant display of palette-knife virtuosity.

J. W.

56. MARIE LAURENCIN (1885–1956)
WOMEN IN THE FOREST, 1920

Oil on canvas: 31⅞ x 39⅝″ (78.5 x 100.7 cm.)
Signed and dated lower right: Marie Laurencin 1920

Collections: Paul Rosenberg, Paris; John Quinn, New York; Forrestal, New York; Martin Horrell, New York; Leo Aarons, New York; Stephen Hahn Gallery, New York.

Exhibited: New York, Art Center, *Memorial Exhibition of the John Quinn Collection,* Jan. 8 – 30, 1926; Washington, D.C., Hirshhorn Museum and Sculpture Garden, *The Noble Buyer: John Quinn, Patron of the Avant-Garde,* May 12 – Sept. 20, 1978.

Hammer Collection exhibitions: see catalogue reference page. First exhibited: II; not exhibited: X, XX, XXIII.

Literature: Roger Allard, *Marie Laurencin (Les Peintres Français Nouveaux,* no. 9), Paris, 1921, repr. p. 49; Forbes Watson, *John Quinn 1870 – 1925, Collection of Paintings, Water Colors, Drawings & Sculpture,* Huntington, N.Y., 1926, p. 11, repr. p. 66; B. L. Reid, *The Man from New York,* New York, 1968, pp. 470 – 71; Mahonri Sharp Young, "The Hammer Collection: Paintings," *Apollo,* vol. 95 (June, 1972), p. 452.

Marie Laurencin was closely associated with the Cubists before World War I and with the artists who formed Cubist splinter movements after the war, but her style was little affected by any of them. Guillaume Apollinaire characterized her painting in *The Cubist Painters* (trans. Lionel Abel, New York, 1944): "Like the dance, it is an infinitely gracious and rhythmical art of enumeration." Her iconography of sylphlike girls and gentle animals in an Arcadian landscape is a personal lyric invention—suggestive rather than literal. This large work, *Women in the Forest,* seems to be a monumental restatement of elements Laurencin had used in numerous small paintings between 1917 and 1920.

J. W.

57. MARC CHAGALL (b. 1887)
BLUE ANGEL

Gouache and pastel: 20 x 26″ (50.8 x 66.1 cm.)

Collections: Frank Crowninshield, New York; Mr. and Mrs. Henry R. Luce, New York.

Exhibited: New York, Galerie Chalette, 1958; Tokyo, National Museum of Western Art, Oct. 1 – Nov. 10, 1963; National Art Gallery of Kyoto, Nov. 20 – Dec. 10, 1963.

Hammer Collection exhibitions: see catalogue reference page. First exhibited: II; not exhibited: X, XX, XXIII.

Literature: Franz Meyer, *Marc Chagall, Life and Work,* New York, 1964, no. 672, repr. p. 757.

The theatrical blue-red color harmony of this work and its juxtaposition of normally unrelated figures, floating and dreamlike, are typical of Chagall. Although the angel may have been particularly in Chagall's mind because of the illustrations for the Bible he had been commissioned by Ambroise Vollard to do in the early 1920s, both it and the bouquet of flowers are common in his scenes of lovers and newlyweds. Franz Meyer suggests that the "new natural sensuousness" of the pictures of 1937 – 39 was the result of the increased security in Chagall's personal affairs during that time.

J. W.

58. GILBERT STUART (1755–1828)
PORTRAIT OF GEORGE WASHINGTON, 1822

Oil on canvas: 44⅛ x 34½" (112 x 87.6 cm.)

Collections: William D. Lewis, Philadelphia; Estate of William D. Lewis (on loan to Pennsylvania Academy of the Fine Arts, Philadelphia, 1881 – 1928); Howard Young Galleries, New York; Mr. and Mrs. Alfred G. Wilson, Detroit (sold Parke-Bernet Galleries, Inc., New York, December 10, 1970 [no. 12]).

Exhibited: Detroit Institute of Arts, *The Eleventh Loan Exhibition, American Colonial and Early Federal Art,* Feb. 4 – Mar. 2, 1930 (no. 81), lent by Mr. and Mrs. Alfred G. Wilson; Detroit Institute of Arts, *Masterpieces of Painting from Detroit Private Collections,* Apr. 23 – May 22, 1949 (no. 30), lent by Mr. and Mrs. Alfred G. Wilson; Los Angeles County Museum of Art, Aug. 6 – Dec. 9, 1974; *Two Hundred Years of American Painting,* traveling exhibition, Bonn, Rheinisches Landesmuseum, Belgrade, Museum of Modern Art, Rome, Galleria D'Arte Moderna e Contemporanea, Warsaw, National Museum of Poland, June 1, 1976 – Jan. 15, 1977.

Hammer Collection exhibitions: see catalogue reference page. First exhibited: VII; not exhibited: X, XX, XXVIII, XXIX.

Literature: Henry T. Tuckerman, *Book of the Artists,* New York, 1867, p. 120; George C. Mason, *Life and Works of Gilbert Stuart,* New York, 1879, p. 113; Elizabeth Bryant Johnston, *Original Portraits of Washington,* Boston, 1882, pp. 81 – 82; Mantle Fielding, *Gilbert Stuart's Portraits of Washington,* Philadelphia, 1923, p. 148, no. 30; Lawrence Park, *Gilbert Stuart: An Illustrated Descriptive List of His Works,* New York, 1926, vol. 2, p. 862, no. 31; John Hill Morgan and Mantle Fielding, *The Life Portraits of Washington and Their Replicas,* Philadelphia, 1931, p. 271, no. 31; G. A. Eisen, *Portraits of Washington,* New York, 1932, p. 126, repr. p. 255; *Important American Paintings, Sculpture and Drawings,* sale catalogue, Parke-Bernet Galleries, Inc., New York, 1970, p. 14, no. 12, repr. in color; Mahonri Sharp Young, "The Hammer Collection: Paintings," *Apollo,* vol. 95 (June, 1972), p. 452.

Whatever Stuart's reasons were for leaving Ireland in 1793, he returned to America expecting to capitalize on the demand for portraits of George Washington. It was an astute and logical move for one of the greatest portrait painters of the period. Such was the stature of Washington, already the personification of the nation, that Stuart and his competitors, the Peales, found it profitable to devote a great part of their energy and time to recording his image.

Sittings in 1795 resulted in the Vaughan type of bust portrait, and in 1796 the president sat for the famous Athenaeum portrait, now in the Boston Museum of Fine Arts. When Senator William Bingham asked for a full-length portrait in 1796, the Athenaeum portrait was used as the model for the head in the composition, which became known as the Lansdowne type. The present half-length, painted for William D. Lewis in 1822, is based on the Lansdowne full-length, specifically on the later version now in the New York Public Library (Lenox Coll.), painted at the request of Peter Jay Munro. The basic composition is that of the Constable-Hamilton half-length of 1797, also in the New York Public Library.

L. C.

59. WILLIAM MICHAEL HARNETT (1848–1892)
STILL LIFE, 1885

Oil on panel: 13¾ x 10⁵/₁₆″ (34.9 x 26.2 cm.)
Signed and dated lower left: WM Harnett 1885

Collections: George Richmond, London (sold Richmond studio sale, Christie, Manson & Woods, London, May 1, 1897 [no. 4]); Lord Justice William Rann Kennedy (sold Christie, Manson & Woods, London, Feb. 19, 1971 [no. 177]).

Exhibited: London, Royal Academy of Arts, May, 1885 (no. 860); St. Helens, Victoria Park, London, *First Summer Exhibition,* 1892 (no. 105); Los Angeles County Museum of Art, Aug. 6 – Dec. 9, 1974.

Hammer Collection exhibitions: see catalogue reference page. First exhibited: IX; not exhibited: XX.

Literature: Algernon Graves, *The Royal Academy of Arts, A Complete Dictionary of Contributors and Their Work from Its Foundation in 1769 to 1904,* London, 1905, p. 395, no. 860; *Magazine of Art,* Feb., 1951, p. 66; Alfred Frankenstein, *After the Hunt: William Harnett and Other American Still Life Painters, 1870 – 1900,* Berkeley and Los Angeles, 1953 (2d ed., 1969), pp. 70 – 71; *Pictures, Drawings, Bronzes and Prints of American, Australian, Canadian, New Zealand and South African Interest,* sale catalogue, Christie, Manson & Woods, London, 1971, p. 49, no. 177, repr. in color; Mahonri Sharp Young, "The Hammer Collection: Paintings," *Apollo,* vol. 95 (June, 1972), pp. 452, 454, repr. plate X in color p. 453.

Though Harnett's *trompe-l'oeil* painting has a counterpart in the history of European art, it stands as a culmination of the long tradition of American realism. Five years abroad had an effect on Harnett's work but did not erase the unique, personal elements of his style nor the stamp of forthright vision that characterizes so much of American painting.

Painted in Paris in 1885, this *Still Life* was sent to the Royal Academy in London, where it was noted in the *Times* as "one of the most miraculous representations that we have ever seen." The writer undoubtedly was referring to the degree of realism of the painting. For, while the arrangement of solid objects in Harnett's *Still Life* does not permit the kind of visual deception typical of the more two-dimensional rack paintings in which flat objects such as cards and envelopes are mounted on a board, it nevertheless achieves an almost tangible extension into space. But Harnett achieves more than an illusion of three-dimensionality. In this work, Harnett displays his particular genius in the highly sophisticated balance of color, form, and texture. Even the subtle shifts in hue among the various faded sheets of music are exploited to the fullest, and the qualities of paper, metal, leather, velvet, and wood are explored and juxtaposed so as to play the full visual scale.

Another almost identical painting at Yale University has been mistaken for this one, which was bought by George Richmond from the Royal Academy in 1885. The only obvious difference between the two, probably introduced to avoid exactly the kind of problem that has arisen, is the reversal of the printed word fragments on the roll of music protruding at the left and again on the top sheet of music at the front edge of the cabinet. Apparently, Harnett himself was a victim of this confusion, for on the back of a photograph — owned by Alfred Frankenstein — of the Yale painting an inscription in the artist's own hand identifies it as the George Richmond still life.

L. C.

60. WILLIAM MICHAEL HARNETT (1848–1892)
CINCINNATI ENQUIRER, 1888

Oil on canvas: 30 x 25⅛" (76 x 64 cm.)
Signed and dated lower left: WMHARNETT./1888
Inscribed on the back: 9/88

Collections: James T. Abbe, Holyoke, Mass.; Mrs. Nina Mathews, Catoosa, Okla., before 1948; Admiral Carl R. Mathews, Monterrey, Mex., in 1953; Hirschl and Adler Galleries, New York, in 1971; J. William Middendorf, II, McLean, Va., by 1977.

Exhibited: Cincinnati Art Museum, May, 1971; New York, Hirschl and Adler Galleries, *American Still Lifes of the Nineteenth Century,* Dec., 1971 (no. 22); The Hague, The American Embassy, 1972 – 73; Washington, D.C., The White House, since 1977.

Literature: Alfred Frankenstein, *After the Hunt: William Harnett and Other American Still Life Painters, 1870 – 1900,* Berkeley and Los Angeles, 1953 (2d ed. 1969), pp. 84, 179, no. 117, plate 76; *Cincinnati Enquirer Magazine,* May 9, 1971, pp. 16 – 18, repr. on cover; *American Still Lifes of the Nineteenth Century,* catalogue, Hirschl and Adler Galleries, New York, 1971, p. 18, no. 22.

A folded-over copy of the *Cincinnati Enquirer* is the focal point of the composition. All the legible headlines were actually printed in the issue of the *Enquirer* of May 8, 1888, but Harnett has made changes in their placement. "Gath," for instance, was part of the extreme righthand column, whereas in the painting it is on the left. As Harnett said, "In painting from still life I do not closely imitate nature. Many points I leave out and many I add. Some models are only suggestions." This is one of the very few pictures by Harnett in which some of the print is legible. Usually, the lettering is simulated with abstract touches.

For years, Harnett's still life disappeared. In 1948 Alfred Frankenstein, the greatest authority on Harnett, gave a radio broadcast devoted to the artist. Mrs. Nina Mathews of Catoosa, Okla., heard it and wrote to him, saying that she owned a number of paintings, mostly bought through Tulsa dealers, and among them was the *Cincinnati Enquirer.* Frankenstein provided the information that Mrs. Mathews's picture was indeed a lost work by Harnett dated 1888 and originally commissioned by James Abbe, a Massachusetts papermaker.

In 1977 J. William Middendorf, II, who had acquired the painting, lent it to President and Mrs. Carter. They chose to hang it in their main sitting room, and the president has said that he considers it one of the finest paintings in the entire White House collection. Dr. Hammer, its present owner, intends that Harnett's masterwork of illusionism remain as a gift to the White House.

J. W.

61. JOHN SINGER SARGENT (1856–1925)
DR. POZZI AT HOME, 1881

Oil on canvas: 80½ x 43⅞″ (204.5 x 111.5 cm.)
Signed and dated upper right: John S. Sargent, 1881

Collection: Estate of the Hon. Jean Pozzi (sold Palais Galliéra, Paris, Dec. 4, 1970 [no. 84]).

Exhibited: Los Angeles County Museum of Art, Aug. 6 – Dec. 9, 1974.

Hammer Collection exhibitions: see catalogue reference page. First exhibited: VIII; not exhibited: XX.

Literature: *L'Art et les artistes,* vol. 4 (1905 – 7), p. 368, repr.; William Howe Downes, *John S. Sargent, His Life and Work,* Boston, 1925, pp. 10 – 11, 113; Hon. Evan Charteris, *John Sargent,* New York, 1927, p. 258; Charles Merrill Mount, *John Singer Sargent,* London, 1957, pp. 61, 65, 67, 69, 116, 153; Richard Ormond, *John Singer Sargent, Paintings, Drawings, Watercolors,* New York, 1970, p. 34; *Tableaux modernes, sculptures,* sale catalogue, Palais Galliéra, Paris, 1970, no. 84, repr., also in color on cover; Mahonri Sharp Young, "The Hammer Collection: Paintings," *Apollo,* vol. 95 (June, 1972), repr. plate XI in color p. 455

While there was still a decidedly youthful quality in Sargent's work in 1881, he was rapidly reaching full stride as an artist. Already honored in the Salon of 1879 for the dramatic portrait of his teacher Carolus-Duran, in 1881 he received a medal second class, making him "*hors concours* and a great swell," as he jokingly put it. The portrait *Dr. Pozzi at Home* was eagerly undertaken by an artist brimming with enthusiasm and confidence.

Innovative from the beginning, Sargent was never content with a formal, straightforward likeness. Even in the early portrait of Carolus, the teacher assumes a special vitality in a dynamic pose conveying force and movement. It was perhaps the influence of Impressionism that led Sargent to ask Mme. Pailleron to pose standing out-of-doors when he painted the full-length standing portrait that appeared in the Salon of 1880. Some of his greatest portraits are the most informal ones, catching the subject engaged in life, as it were; the portrait of Dr. Pozzi is a powerful statement of this kind. Moving beyond the snapshot effect that could so easily result from this approach, the artist brings to the painting much more than the experience of Carolus's studio. Certainly, the solid grasp of form and light, particularly in the head, reflects the method of his teacher, but Sargent's own personal gift, expanded and refined by a close study of the old masters, is affirmed. The drama of the painting is an extension of the artist's responses to the work of Velázquez and Hals, which he had studied so closely in previous months. In gesture and movement, the figure is purely Baroque, and, despite the overt drama of the technically superb glazes, there is a subtlety of light and tone that could have had its source in Velázquez.

L. C.

62. JOHN SINGER SARGENT (1856–1925)
PORTRAIT OF MRS. EDWARD L. DAVIS AND HER SON,
LIVINGSTON DAVIS, 1890

Oil on canvas: 86 x 48″ (218.4 x 121.9 cm.)
Signed lower right: John S. Sargent

Collections: Edward Livingston Davis, Worcester, Mass.; Livingston Davis, Boston, Mass.; Mrs. A. Winsor Weld, Boston, Mass. (sold Parke-Bernet Galleries, Inc., New York, Mar. 19 – 20, 1969 [no. 74]); James Graham & Sons, New York; Los Angeles County Museum of Art (Frances and Armand Hammer Purchase Fund, 1969).

Exhibited: New York, National Academy of Design, 1890; New York, Society of American Artists, 1891; Boston, Mass., Boston Art Museum, 1891; Chicago, *World's Columbian Exposition,* 1893 (no. 875); Boston, Mass., Copley Hall, *Loan Collection of Portraits of Women,* 1895 (no. 257); Philadelphia, Pennsylvania Academy of the Fine Arts, 1896; Boston, Mass., Copley Hall, *Paintings and Sketches by John S. Sargent, R.A.,* Feb. 20 – Mar. 13, 1899 (no. 5); Worcester, Mass., Worcester Art Museum, 1909; Boston, Mass., Museum of Fine Arts, 1913 (no. 757), 1916 (no. 573), 1918 (no. 480), 1920 (no. 340), 1921 (no. 420); New York, Grand Central Art Galleries, *Retrospective Exhibition of Important Works of John Singer Sargent,* Feb. 23 – Apr. 6, 1924 (no. 20), repr. in cat. p. 45; New York, Metropolitan Museum of Art, *Memorial Exhibition of the Works of John Singer Sargent,* Jan. 4 – Feb. 14, 1926 (no. 26), repr. in cat.; Boston, Mass., Museum of Fine Arts, 1928 (no. 168), 1929 (no. 993), 1930 (no. 530); Boston, Mass., Museum of Fine Arts, centennial exhibition, *Sargent's Boston,* Jan. 3 – Feb. 7, 1956 (no. 20); Los Angeles County Museum of Art, Aug. 6 – Dec. 9, 1974.

Hammer Collection exhibitions: see catalogue reference page. First exhibited: II; not exhibited: IV – VII, IX, X, XX, XXIII.

Literature: Leila Mechlin, "The Sargent Exhibition," *American Magazine of Art,* vol. 15, no. 4 (Apr., 1924), pp. 169 – 90, repr. p. 184; Rose V. S. Berry, "John Singer Sargent: Some of His American Work," *Art and Archaeology Throughout the Ages,* vol. 18, no. 3 (Sept., 1924), pp. 83 – 112, repr. p. 100; William Howe Downes, *John S. Sargent, His Life and Work,* Boston, 1925, pp. 33, 157 – 58, repr. p. 128; Hon. Evan Charteris, *John S. Sargent,* New York, 1927, pp. 109, 137, 263; Charles Merrill Mount, *John Singer Sargent,* London, 1957, p. 153; David McKibbin, *Sargent's Boston,* catalogue, Museum of Fine Arts, Boston, Mass., 1956, pp. 43, 68, 91, no. 20, repr. p. 41; *18th – 20th Century American Paintings, etc. —Various Owners,* sale catalogue, Parke-Bernet Galleries, Inc., New York, 1969, no. 74, repr.; Richard Ormond, *John Singer Sargent, Paintings, Drawings, Watercolors,* New York, 1970, pp. 43, 246, repr.

Sargent's portrait of *Mrs. Edward L. Davis and Her Son, Livingston Davis* is not a simple bust portrait but an imposing composition demanding the artist's full powers of invention and execution. For Sargent the inherent challenge becomes inspiration, and the figures of the full-length double portrait spring to life almost spontaneously.

The seemingly casual relationship between the two figures is actually a relationship of considerable formal and psychological complexity. The precarious movement of the boy is played against the monumentally stable form of his mother, who looms forward as she forcefully confronts the viewer. While the broad, loose brushwork continues to reflect Sargent's debt to the Dutch and Spanish masters and even, to an extent, to the Impressionists, the firm modeling and dramatic lighting of the woman's head seem to have something of the quality of the realist John Singleton Copley, whose work Sargent discovered in Boston.

L. C.

63. THOMAS EAKINS (1844–1916)
PORTRAIT OF SEBASTIANO CARDINAL MARTINELLI, 1902

Oil on canvas, mounted on panel: 78⁵/₁₆ x 56¹⁵/₁₆″ (198.9 x 152.3 cm.)

Signed and dated lower right: Eakins 1902

Inscribed on verso (presently covered by panel): EFFI-GIES SEBASTIANI S R E CARDINALIS MARTINELLI QVI ANNOS VI IN STAT FOED AB MDCCCXCVI AD MCMII DELEGATI APOSTOLICI OFFICIO FVNTVS; below: THOS. EAKINS PHILADELPHIEN A.D. MCMII PINXIT

Collection: Catholic University of America, Washington, D.C. (presented by the artist in 1903) (sold Parke-Bernet Galleries, Inc., New York, May 21, 1970 [no. 57]).

Exhibited: Pittsburgh, Museum of Art, Carnegie Institute, *International Exhibition,* 1903; Philadelphia, Pennsylvania Academy of the Fine Arts, *Thomas Eakins Memorial Exhibition,* Dec. 23, 1917 – Jan. 23, 1918 (no. 20); Baltimore Museum of Art, *Thomas Eakins, A Retrospective Exhibition of His Paintings,* Dec. 1, 1936 – Jan. 1, 1937 (no. 34); Philadelphia Museum of Art, *Thomas Eakins Centennial Exhibition,* 1944 (no. 99); Pittsburgh, Museum of Art, Carnegie Institute, *Thomas Eakins Centennial Exhibition,* Apr. 26 – June 1, 1945 (no. 15), repr. in cat.; Washington, D.C., National Gallery of Art, 1969 – 70; Overbrook, Pa., St. Charles Seminary, *Eakins Portraits,* 1970; New York, Whitney Museum of American Art, *Thomas Eakins Retrospective Exhibition,* Sept. 21 – Nov. 29, 1970; Los Angeles County Museum of Art, Aug. 6 – Dec. 9, 1974.

Hammer Collection exhibitions: see catalogue reference page. First exhibited: IV; not exhibited: XX.

Literature: Lloyd Goodrich, *Thomas Eakins—His Life and Work,* New York, 1933, pp. 105 – 6, 194, no. 361; Fairfield Porter, *Thomas Eakins,* New York, 1959, fig. 64; Sylvan Schendler, *Thomas Eakins,* Boston, 1967, pp. 201, 208, 215, 296, plate 102; *Eighteenth, Nineteenth and Twentieth Century American Paintings,* sale catalogue, Parke-Bernet Galleries, Inc., New York, 1970, p. 58, no. 57, repr. in color; Mahonri Sharp Young, "The Hammer Collection:

Paintings," *Apollo,* vol. 95 (June, 1972), p. 454, fig. 5.

As Lloyd Goodrich has pointed out, it seems paradoxical that Thomas Eakins, a Quaker and an uncompromising realist, should have begun in his late years a series of portraits of Catholic prelates. Seen as portraits of friends painted at the artist's own request, however, they begin to take their place very logically within his total oeuvre. Rejected as an artist and rather withdrawn from society, Eakins must have felt a close kinship with these learned men whose mission set them apart from the world.

As is often the case in Eakins's full-length portraits, this figure is placed at some distance from the viewer within a very real space, and the ambience eloquently conveys a feeling of solitary contemplation. This effect is further enhanced by the use of the profile view, which presents the figure as a hieratic image to be beheld without direct involvement of the spectator. From the casually rubbed earth color suggesting wood paneling and parquet floor, to the subtle design of the rug, more or less monochromatic surroundings act as a foil, intensifying the impact of the cardinal's presence.

On September 16, 1903, Eakins wrote from 1729 Mt. Vernon Street, Philadelphia, to the rector of the Catholic University of America:

Dear Sir:

I am the person who painted and presented to the University the full length portrait of Cardinal Martinelli.

I am solicited by the Carnegie Institute to exhibit specimens of my best work, and I should like to send there the Cardinal which has been exhibited in New York, Philadelphia and Chicago....

Please let me know promptly if the picture may be exhibited.

Yours truly,
(signed) Thomas Eakins

L. C.

Oil on canvas: 28⅞ x 39⅜" (73.4 x 100 cm.)
Signed lower right: Mary Cassatt

Collection: Huntington Hartford, New York (sold Parke-Bernet Galleries, Inc., New York, May 10, 1971 [no. 28]).

Exhibited: Baltimore Museum of Art, *Manet, Degas, Berthe Morisot and Mary Cassatt,* Apr. 18 – June 3, 1962 (no. 116), lent by Huntington Hartford; St. Petersburg, Fla., Museum of Fine Arts, *Inaugural Exhibition,* Feb. 7 – Mar. 7, 1965 (no. 28), lent by Huntington Hartford; New York, M. Knoedler & Co., *Mary Cassatt,* Feb. 1 – 26, 1966 (no. 25), lent by Huntington Hartford; Southampton, N.Y., Parrish Art Museum, *Miss Mary Cassatt, Paintings and the Graphic Arts,* July 30 – Aug. 20, 1967 (no. 2), lent by Huntington Hartford; Washington, D.C., National Gallery of Art, *Mary Cassatt,* Sept. 27 – Nov. 8, 1970 (no. 55), lent by Huntington Hartford, p. 28 in cat., repr.; Washington, D.C., National Gallery of Art, May 6 – Aug. 12, 1973, New York, Whitney Museum of American Art, Sept. 18 – Nov. 12, 1973, Cincinnati Museum of Art, Dec. 15, 1973 – Jan. 31, 1974, and Raleigh, North Carolina Museum of Art, Mar. 8 – Apr. 29, 1974, *American Impressionists Exhibition;* Los Angeles County Museum of Art, Aug. 6 – Dec. 9, 1974; Manila, National Museum of Manila, 1976.

Hammer Collection exhibitions: see catalogue reference page. First exhibited: IX; not exhibited: XVII – XX.

Literature: Adelyn Dohme Breeskin, *Mary Cassatt, A Catalogue Raisonné of the Oils, Pastels, Watercolors and Drawings,* Washington, D.C., 1970, p. 116, no. 240, repr.; Meryle Secrest, "The American Impressionist, The Lyrical Mary Cassatt Goes on Exhibit in Washington," *Washington Post,* Sept. 20, 1970 (section K1), repr. in color; *Important Impressionist and Modern Paintings and Drawings,* sale catalogue, Parke-Bernet Galleries, Inc., New York, 1971, p. 50, no. 28, repr. in color; Mahonri Sharp Young, "The Hammer Collection: Paintings," *Apollo,* vol. 95 (June, 1972), p. 454, repr. plate IX in color p. 451.

Though Mary Cassatt's paintings are generally more or less complex figure compositions, she remains essentially a portrait painter, concentrating on the likeness and character of individuals. As a rule, even when she painted figures engaged in some activity out-of-doors, she was as much concerned with portraiture as with the disposition of form and features within a pictorial space. Among the few exceptions are three boating scenes from 1893 – 94 (Breeskin, nos. 230, 233, and 240, the present work). In none of these are the subjects identified, but in the famous *The Boating Party (near Antibes),* 1893, the personalities emerge with great strength. In the other two, which are closely related, the identity of the figures is not an important factor, and the intention seems to be simply the creation of a plein-air view of people in a boat observing or feeding ducks.

A number of important factors entered into the conception of *Summertime.* As early as 1890, Cassatt had resolved to concentrate on strengthening form and drawing, much as Renoir did in mid-career, and the following year a series of prints emulating the Japanese had a profound effect on her style. This is obvious in *The Boating Party,* but while boldness of design is still very important in *Summertime,* it is augmented by a system of slashing, dynamic brushwork verging on abstraction. Interestingly, the large allegory commissioned for the Chicago World's Fair and painted in 1892 also included women and ducks in a landscape.

L. C.

65. MARY CASSATT (1844–1926)
REINE LEFEBVRE AND MARGOT, c. 1902

Pastel on brown paper, mounted on canvas: 32¾ x 26⁹/₁₆″ (83.2 x 67.5 cm.)
Signed lower left: Mary Cassatt

Collections: Felix Doistau, Paris (sold Galerie Georges Petit, Paris, June 18 – 19, 1928 [no. 6]); Galerie Durand-Ruel, Paris and New York, 1929; Mrs. A. L. Adams (sold Parke-Bernet Galleries, Inc., New York, Oct. 15, 1969 [no. 16]).

Exhibited: New York, Galerie Durand-Ruel, *Mary Cassatt,* Apr. 8 – 20, 1929 (no. 1).

Hammer Collection exhibitions: see catalogue reference page. First exhibited: III; not exhibited: VI, XI – XXXIV.

Literature: *Revue de l'art,* Nov., 1928; *Bulletin de l'art ancien et moderne,* vol. 54, Nov., 1928, p. 357, repr.; *Important Impressionist and Modern Paintings and Sculpture,* sale catalogue, Parke-Bernet Galleries, Inc., 1969, no. 16, repr. in color; Adelyn Dohme Breeskin, *Mary Cassatt, A Catalogue Raisonné of the Oils, Pastels, Watercolors and Drawings,* Washington, D.C., 1970, p. 170, no. 430, repr.

Reine Lefebvre, a neighbor living in the village near Mary Cassatt's Château de Beaufresne, posed for the artist, at times along with the child Margot, from 1901 to 1903. Though only sixteen and seventeen years old during this association, she is imbued in this painting with a quiet dignity and conveys a very convincing maternal relationship with the child. Typical of Cassatt's pastels of this period, the present work almost disguises the powerful draftsmanship that won her the admiration of Degas. The free and forceful strokes seem to activate the surface in an almost random way, but ultimately the strength of line emerges in the firm design.

L. C.

66. MAURICE BRAZIL PRENDERGAST (1861–1924)
ON THE BEACH, 1916

Oil on canvas: 26¾ x 39″ (67.9 x 99 cm.)

Collections: Mrs. Charles Prendergast, Westport, Conn.; Lester Avnet, New York; A.C.A. Galleries, New York.

Exhibited: Pittsburgh, Museum of Art, Carnegie Institute, *Twenty-third Annual International Exhibition of Paintings,* Apr. 24 – June 15, 1924 (no. 14); Hartford, Conn., Wadsworth Atheneum, *Connecticut Collections,* Oct., 1957; Stamford, Conn., Stamford Museum and Nature Center, Nov., 1961; New York, A.C.A. Galleries, *Lester Avnet Collection,* Sept. 18 – Oct. 18, 1969; Los Angeles County Museum of Art, Aug. 6 – Dec. 9, 1974.

Hammer Collection exhibitions: see catalogue reference page. First exhibited: VII; not exhibited: XX, XXIII.

Literature: *Catalogue of the Twenty-third Annual International Exhibition of Paintings,* Carnegie Institute, Pittsburgh, 1924, no. 14.

Unlike many of his contemporaries, Prendergast did not embrace the more conservative aspects of Impressionism. Rather, from the beginning, he struck out in a direction close to that of the Post-Impressionists and the Nabis. Later, there were even stylistic parallels with the Fauves.

Typical of Prendergast's later painting in oil, this work exhibits nothing of the realist doctrine generally associated with other members of The Eight group. His subjects were not the crowded streets of the New York slums painted by the Ashcan School but groups of happy people at their leisure on the beach, in the park, thronging the sunny boulevards of Paris or the bridges of Venice. Figures are generally disposed laterally across the foreground against highly simplified forms of sea and land. The ultimate result is a bright, lyrical tapestry of color with shapes loosely defined by a heavy line breaking or fading against shifting planes of color as it approximates contour.

L. C.

Drawings, Watercolors, and Pastels

67. ALBRECHT DÜRER (1471–1528)
TUFT OF COWSLIPS

Gouache on vellum, some tears at left, water stains in upper border, some slight abrasions: 7⁹/₁₆ x 6⅝″ (19.2 x 16.8 cm.)
Inscribed (in a later hand): AD 1526

Collections: priv. coll., England; Hal O'Nians, London.

Exhibited: Washington, D.C., National Gallery of Art, *Recent Acquisitions and Promised Gifts,* June 2 – Sept. 1, 1974 (no. 66); Washington, D.C., National Gallery of Art, *Master Drawings from the Collection of the National Gallery of Art and Promised Gifts,* June, 1978 (no. 23).

Hammer Collection exhibitions: see catalogue reference page. First exhibited: XI; not exhibited: XX, XXIII.

Literature: Otto Benesch, *Master Drawings in the Albertina,* New York, 1967, p. 337; Charles W. Talbot, ed., G. Ravenel, and J. Levenson, *Dürer in America — His Graphic Work,* New York, 1971, p. 110, note 3; *The Armand Hammer Collection,* Los Angeles, 1971, no. 60; Walter Koschatzky and Alice Strobl, *Graphische Sammlung Albertina, die Dürerzeichnungen der Albertina zum 500. Geburtstag,* Vienna, 1971, no. 28; Christopher White, "The Armand Hammer Collection: Drawings," *Apollo,* vol. 95 (June, 1972), pp. 457 – 58, fig. 2; Alan Shestack, "Dürer's Graphic Work in Washington and Boston," *Art Quarterly,* vol. 35 (1972), p. 304; John Rowlands, Review of *Albrecht Dürer: 1471 – 1971* and *Dürer in America, Master Drawings,* vol. 10, 1972, p. 384; Walter L. Strauss, *The Complete Drawings of Albrecht Dürer,* New York, 1974, vol. 2, p. 726, no. 1503/37, repr. p. 727, as Dürer about 1503; *Recent Acquisitions and Promised Gifts,* catalogue, National Gallery of Art, Washington, D.C., 1974, no. 66. Additional literature: Jaro Springer, "Dürers Zeichnungen in neuen Publikationen," *Repertorium für Kunstwissenschaft,* vol. 29 (1906), pp. 555ff.; Joseph Meder, "Die grüne Passion und die Tier- und Pflanzenstudien Albrecht Dürers in der Albertina," *Repertorium für Kunstwissenschaft,* vol. 30 (1907), p. 181; Sebastian Killermann, *A. Dürers Pflanzen und Tierzeichnungen, Studien zur deutschen Kunstgeschichte,* vol. 119, Strasbourg, 1910, pp. 94ff.; Friedrich Winkler, *Die Zeichnungen Albrecht Dürers,* Berlin, 1936, vol. 2, pp. 65ff.; Heinrich Schwartz, "A Water-colour Attributed to Dürer," *Burlington Magazine,* vol. 95 (1953), pp. 149ff.; Hans Kauffmann, "Dürer in der Kunst und im Kunsturteil um 1600," *Anzeiger des Germanischen Nationalmuseums in Nürnberg, 1940 – 53,* Berlin, 1954, p. 29.

The *Tuft of Cowslips* is one of a group of plant studies by Dürer, most of which are now in the Graphische Sammlung Albertina, Vienna, having come there from the collection of Emperor Rudolf II in Prague (see Koschatzky and Strobl, nos. 27 – 32. For the whole group, see the works cited above by Joseph Meder, Sebastian Killermann, Friedrich Winkler, and Charles W. Talbot, ed. [pp. 108 – 10]). The most celebrated of these sheets is the *Large Piece of Turf,* which was drawn on paper in watercolor with some touches of gouache; it bears the date 1503. Other drawings in the group, such as the *Columbine,* the *Celandine,* and the *Three Medicinal Herbs,* are executed on vellum, mostly in a smooth and opaque gouache. The small *Nosegay of Violets,* though also in gouache on vellum, is somewhat freer in style than the works of this latter group.

Although Jaro Springer categorically doubted the authenticity of all the animal and plant studies ascribed to Dürer, the *Large Piece of Turf* has always been accepted as an original, while the drawings on vellum have often been doubted (recently again by Alan Shestack and John Rowlands, who also rejected the Hammer sheet). It has been suggested that they might be by an imitator of Dürer of around 1600, such as Hans Hoffmann, but Professor Hans Kauffmann has correctly repudiated this thesis, explaining clearly the differences between these later imitations and genuine early sixteenth-century works.

The recent catalogue of Dürer's drawings in the Albertina and the latest monograph on Dürer's drawings by Walter Strauss have defended the authenticity of the group of plant studies on vellum, and the Hammer sheet actually helps to support this attribution. (Firm supporters of the Hammer sheet were Otto Benesch and recently Walter Koschatzky and Alice Strobl, all of whom were able to examine the sheet in the Albertina.) The *Tuft of Cowslips* is related to these drawings in general type and tech-

nique; it also bears the inscribed date of 1526 that appears on other sheets in the group, surely the addition of a collector who at one time owned them all. When the Hammer drawing was taken to the Albertina to be studied in 1971, it became clear that the color was much more lively in application and more transparent than it was in the other works on vellum. In fact, the highly differentiated greens corresponded almost exactly to those of the *Large Piece of Turf*, while their loose application resembled that in the leaves of the *Nosegay of Violets*. Although the *Tuft of Cowslips* does not show the linear qualities typical of most of Dürer's plant studies on paper, it does parallel the *Large Piece of Turf* in its spatial depth, in the richness of the observation of light, and in the sense of life that seems to emanate from the plant.

K. O.

68. LEONARDO DA VINCI (1452–1519)
SHEET OF STUDIES

A. (recto): head of an old man in right profile; two detailed studies of the right eye; bust of a woman from three-quarter rear with head in right profile; bust of a girl from three-quarter rear with head turned toward viewer. Pen and brown ink over traces of black chalk
B. (verso): study of a Madonna. Black chalk
Somewhat irregularly cut on right side; upper left corner missing: 6½ x 5½" (16.4 x 13.8 cm.)
Watermark: tulip, close to Charles Moïse Briquet, *Les filigranes: dictionnaire historique des marques du papier,* Geneva, 1907, vol. 2, nos. 6645 – 59

Collection: P. & D. Colnaghi & Co., Ltd., London.

Exhibited: Washington, D.C., National Gallery of Art, *Recent Acquisitions and Promised Gifts,* June 2 – Sept. 1, 1974 (no. 65); Los Angeles County Museum of Art, *Old Master Drawings from American Collections,* Apr. 29 – June 13, 1976; Washington, D.C., National Gallery of Art, *Master Drawings from the Collection of the National Gallery of Art and Promised Gifts,* June, 1978 (no. 32).

Hammer Collection exhibitions: see catalogue reference page. First exhibited: XIII; not exhibited: XX, XXIII.

Literature: *The Armand Hammer Collection,* Los Angeles, 1971, no. 104; *Recent Acquisitions and Promised Gifts,* catalogue, National Gallery of Art, Washington, D.C., no. 65.

This drawing, accepted by Sir Kenneth Clark as an original work of Leonardo, is a fragment of a large sheet once surely the size of the study for a *Virgin, the Christ Child and Saint John* in Windsor Castle. The Hammer drawing is on similar paper in the same color ink and may have been done at the same time in the artist's life, in the 1470s. Typical for Leonardo are the scattered sketches, prominent among them the profile head of the middle-aged man with a large nose and chin and intense gaze, of a type found also on the Windsor sheet, but without the beard (see A. E. Popham, *The Drawings of Leonardo da Vinci,* London, 1946, nos. 22 – 24, 27; Kenneth Clark and Carlo Pedretti, *The Drawings of Leonardo da Vinci in the Collection of Her Majesty the Queen at Windsor Castle,* London, 1968, no. 12276). Close by we find the same face studied from the front, with special emphasis on the eye, and the study of this eye from yet another point of view. Below there are two busts of women. The larger one is definitely connected with another sheet in Windsor Castle where Leonardo used the silverpoint to draw busts of women seen from many different directions (Clark and Pedretti, no. 12513; Popham, no. 22). Both A. E. Popham and Kenneth Clark recognized the relationship between this drawing and the larger Windsor sheet with the study of the Madonna. The smaller bust below on the Hammer sheet with its lively movement and spirited gaze directed at the spectator, drawn with a fresh and fluidly curling stroke that characterizes the puffy sleeve, is extremely close to the study of a maiden with a unicorn in the British Museum (Popham, no. 27), of which there is another version in the Ashmolean Museum in Oxford, both surely drawn at the same time. John Walker had already pointed

out the resemblance of the Oxford drawing to the portrait of *Ginevra de' Benci* in the National Gallery of Art in Washington, D.C. (John Walker, "Ginevra de' Benci by Leonardo da Vinci," *Report and Studies in the History of Art,* National Gallery of Art, Washington, D.C., 1967, p. 20, fig. 19). David Brown very convincingly suggested (in correspondence) that Leonardo may indeed have planned this subject, a symbol of virtue and virginity, for the back of that portrait instead of the more abstract plant symbols that adorn it now. He is also right in proposing that the studies of female busts are indeed drawn in search of the pose of that portrait.

The slight sketches on the back of the sheet are difficult to read. Next to some studies of legs and a torso, the main subject seems to be the Virgin, but no definite relationship to extant studies of works by Leonardo can be found. The drawing style, however, is clearly his and is typical of the slight sketches in metalpoint or black chalk found on many of his sheets.

K. O.

69. MICHELANGELO (1475–1564)
A. (RECTO): MALE NUDE
B. (VERSO): MALE NUDE

Black chalk: 9¼ x 4″ (23.3 x 10 cm.)

Collections: Sir J. C. Robinson, Swanage; John Malcolm, Poltalloch; the Hon. A. E. Gathorne-Hardy, London; Geoffrey Gathorne-Hardy, Newbury, Berkshire; the Hon. Robert Gathorne-Hardy, Stanford Dingley, Berkshire.

Exhibited: London, British Museum, *An Exhibition of Drawings by Michelangelo Belonging to H. M. the Queen, the Ashmolean Museum, the British Museum and Other English Collections,* Apr. 15 – June 28, 1953 (no. 128); Manchester, City Art Gallery, *Between Renaissance and Baroque: European Art 1520 – 1600,* Mar. 10 – Apr. 6, 1965 (no. 338); London, P. & D. Colnaghi & Co., Ltd., Oct. 12 – Nov. 5, 1971, and Oxford, Ashmolean Museum, Nov. 20, 1971 – Jan. 2, 1972, *Loan Exhibition of Drawings by Old Masters from the Collection of Mr. Geoffrey Gathorne-Hardy* (no. 9), plate VII in cat.; London, British Museum, *Drawings by Michelangelo,* 1975 (no. 156); London, Sotheby & Co., *Old Master Drawings from the Gathorne-Hardy Collection,* Apr. 28, 1976 (no. 14), repr. in cat.; Washington, D.C., National Gallery of Art, *Master Drawings from the Collection of the National Gallery of Art and Promised Gifts,* June, 1978 (no. 40).

Hammer Collection exhibitions: see catalogue reference page. First exhibited: XXIX.

Literature: *Descriptive Catalogue of Drawings . . . in the Possession of the Hon. A. E. Gathorne-Hardy,* London, 1902, no. 7; Bernard Berenson, *The Drawings of the Florentine Painters,* New York, 1903, vol. 2, no. 1540; Henry Thode, *Michelangelo; kritische Untersuchungen über seine Werke,* Berlin, 1913, p. 163, no. 368; Bernard Berenson, *The Drawings of the Florentine Painters,* Chicago, 1938, vol. 2, no. 1544b, fig. 717; Johannes Wilde, *Italian Drawings . . . in the British Museum, Michelangelo and His Studio,* London, 1953, p. 116, no. 75; Luitpold Dussler, *Die Zeichnungen des Michelangelo,* Berlin, 1959, no. 338, plate 136; Charles de Tolnay, *Michelangelo, the Final Period,* Princeton, N.J., 1960, p. 206, no. 219, plate 197; Bernard Berenson, *I disegni dei pittori fiorentini,* Milan, 1961, vol. 2, no. 1544b; Frederick Hartt, *The Drawings of Michelangelo,* London, 1971, p. 352, as Michelangelo of 1546, p. 357, no. 509 recto, repr.; John Gere and Nicholas Turner, *Drawings by Michelangelo,* catalogue, British Museum, London, 1975, no. 156, repr.; Paul Joannides, "Review of the Exhibition 'Drawings by Michelangelo' at the British Museum," *Burlington Magazine,* vol. 117 (1975), p. 262.

In his last years, Michelangelo turned to a subject that had occupied him in earlier periods — a synthesis between Christ being carried to the tomb and a presentation of his body. Christ is transported in such a manner that his body is fully and frontally displayed to the beholder. On a sheet in the Ashmolean Museum (Hartt, no. 459), the artist had twice slightly but movingly sketched such a composition: two men are supporting Christ's body on either side with their shoulders and hands. To the left and right of these sketches the artist varied the motif: the body is held by either the Virgin or Joseph of Arimathea alone, as the artist sculpted it in the *Pietà Rondanini* in Milan. The central sketches were therefore regarded by some authors, such as John Gere and Nicholas Turner (*Drawings,* p. 132), as the "germ of the *Pietà.*" Recently, however, Paul Joannides realized that Michelangelo further pursued the idea of showing Christ supported by two men. Testimony to this are several sketches in the Ashmolean Museum (Hartt, nos. 505 – 8) and the Hammer drawing. The somewhat static stance of the figures in the earlier Ashmolean sketch was transformed by Michelangelo in these studies into more emphatic forward movement. He gave a greater flexibility to the legs and a stronger bent and power to the torsos and shoulders.

The two studies on recto and verso of the Hammer sheet are important to this process. The drawing on the verso is lightly traced through from the front and shows that Michelangelo was experimenting here with the placement of this figure at either the left or the right of Christ in an essentially symmetrical composition. The sheets in the Ashmolean show the same preoccupation, presenting the figure with and without drapery. As Joannides pointed out, a drawing by a follower of Michelangelo, once with the Hammer sheet in the Gathorne-Hardy Collection (sold Sotheby, Apr. 28, 1976, no. 15), preserves the results of Michelangelo's studies: here, the figure from the Hammer sheet is employed at the left of Christ, but it shows, in accordance with the Oxford studies, greater forward movement and ecstatic features. Christ no longer rests on the man's shoulders; instead, the man carries the Savior's torso and legs, as does his companion on the right. Two more figures behind support Christ's upper arms.

According to Joannides, architectural sketches on one of the Ashmolean drawings point to a date of about 1560 for these studies.

K. O.

70. RAPHAEL (1483–1520)
STUDY FOR A FRESCO OF THE PROPHETS HOSEA AND JONAH

Pen and brown wash, heightened with white, over preparation in black chalk and stylus, squared with stylus and red chalk: 10⅝ x 7¹³/₁₆″ (27 x 19.8 cm.)

Collections: Jonathan Richardson, Sr. (1665 – 1745), London; Jonathan Richardson, Jr., London (Lugt [Frits Lugt, *Les Marques de collections, de dessins, & d'estampes,* Amsterdam, 1921], no. 2170); P. J. Mariette, Paris (Lugt, no. 2097); H. C. Jennings, London (Lugt, no. 2771); R. Payne Knight, London (Lugt, no. 1577); Baron H. de Triquety, Paris (Lugt, no. 1304); E. Colando, Paris (Lugt, no. 837); Major S. V. Christie-Miller, C.B.E., Salisbury; P. & D. Colnaghi & Co., Ltd., London.

Exhibited: Washington, D.C., National Gallery of Art, *Recent Acquisitions and Promised Gifts,* June 2 – Sept. 1, 1974 (no. 67); Los Angeles County Museum of Art, *Old Master Drawings from American Collections,* Apr. 29 – June 13, 1976, repr. in cat.; Washington, D.C., National Gallery of Art, *Master Drawings from the Collection of the National Gallery of Art and Promised Gifts,* June, 1978 (no. 36).

Hammer Collection exhibitions: see catalogue reference page. First exhibited: XI; not exhibited: XX, XXIII.

Literature: Jonathan Richardson, *An Account of the Statues, Bas-Reliefs, Drawings and Pictures in Italy, France, etc., with Remarks by Mr. Richardson, Sen. and Jun.* (2d ed.), London, 1754, p. 104; C. Metz, *Imitations of Ancient and Modern Drawings,* London, 1798, plate 44; F. A. Gruyer, *Raphaël et l'antiquité,* Paris, 1846, vol. 1, p. 379, no. 1; J. D. Passavant, *Raphaël d'Urbin,* Paris, 1860, vol. 2, p. 142; C. Ruland, *The Works of Raphael Santi da Urbino as Represented in the Raphael Collection in the Royal Library at Windsor Castle,* London, 1876, p. 271, section III; J. A. Crowe and G. B. Cavalcaselle, *Raphael, Life and Works,* London, 1882 – 85, vol. 2, p. 216, note; G. E. Lafenestre and E. Richtenberger, *Rome, le Vatican et les églises,* Paris, 1903, p. 263; Oskar Fischel, "Some Lost Drawings by or near Raphael," *Burlington Magazine,* vol. 20 (1912), p. 299, plate II, fig. 12; Oskar Fischel, "Santi," in Thieme-Becker, *Allgemeines Lexikon der Bildenden Künstler,* vol. 29, Leipzig, 1935, p. 438; Oskar Fischel, *Raphael,* London, 1948, vol. 1, p. 364; Luitpold Dussler, *Raphael, a Critical Catalogue of His Pictures, Wall-Paintings and Tapestries,* London, 1971, p. 94; *The Armand Hammer Collection,* Los Angeles, 1971, no. 61; Christopher White, "The Armand Hammer Collection: Drawings," *Apollo,* vol. 95 (June, 1972), p. 457, fig. 1 p. 456; *Recent Acquisitions and Promised Gifts,* catalogue, National Gallery of Art, Washington, D.C., 1974, no. 67.

This drawing, highly regarded in the eighteenth and nineteenth centuries and possessed by some of the finest collectors of the time, among them the great connoisseur P. J. Mariette, disappeared from view in the beginning of the twentieth century and had since been known only from old photographs. The views expressed by Oskar Fischel and Luitpold Dussler that the sheet could be by a pupil must be regarded in this light. James Byam Shaw, who rediscovered the sheet, clearly recognized its great value. It is a preparatory drawing for the two figures of prophets at the left of the window high above the ground in the Chigi Chapel in Sta. Maria della Pace in Rome, painted by Raphael probably in 1511. As the figures in the fresco have lost much by restoration, the drawing is of special value. Raphael must already have made a number of sketches for these prophets when he drew this sheet. He first squared the sheet with a stylus to have a grid that could facilitate the drawing of the figures to exact scale. Then he drew them in with black chalk and pen. While the ink was still partially wet, he washed in the shadows with large, rapid

touches of the brush and then added the white highlights. The angel between the two was sketched in with the stylus and then with the pen in a much more rapid fashion, after having been placed in a quite different position in an early sketch (see Michael Hirst, "The Chigi Chapel in S. Maria della Pace," *Journal of the Warburg and Courtauld Institutes,* vol. 24 [1961], especially fig. 28c; see also Fischel, *Raphael,* vol. 2, fig. 193). Raphael seems to have reconsidered the angel's pose and place in this sheet, which also explains why it is drawn in the nude; such was Raphael's habit in order to define more clearly a figure's position.

He then covered the sheet with another grid in red chalk, probably to transfer the design directly to the full-scale cartoon for the fresco. Parallels for the drawing style of this sheet, both for the finished and for the rapidly drawn portions, can be found among the studies for the *Parnassus,* painted close in time to the prophets. Parallels for the figure style can be found in the *School of Athens* of about 1510. Influences from Donatello and Michelangelo are clearly discernible, especially in the fierce expression of the seated prophet, Hosea.

K. O.

71. ANDREA DEL SARTO (1486–1530)
FEMALE HEAD

Black chalk: 12⅞ x 8⅞″ (32.7 x 22.5 cm.), the top corners cut

Signed lower left recto, pen and ink: A. Del Sarto

Signed lower left verso, red chalk, twice: Andrea del Sarto

Collections: Jan Pietersz. Zoomer (1641 – 1724), Amsterdam (Lugt [Frits Lugt, *Les Marques de collections, de dessins, & d'estampes,* Amsterdam, 1921], no. 1511); Jonathan Richardson, Sr. (1665 – 1745), London (Lugt, nos. 2183 and 2184); fifth duke of Argyll, by 1784; T. Philipe's Sale, London, May 21 – 23, 1798; Walter Savage Landor, Florence; priv. coll., Zürich.

Hammer Collection exhibitions: see catalogue reference page. First exhibited: XXXIV.

Literature: John Shearman, *Andrea del Sarto,* Oxford, 1965, pp. 385 – 86, p. 289, no. 3, plate 47a.

At one time, John Shearman was not convinced of the authenticity of this drawing; however, after seeing the original he accepted it as an autograph work of the highest quality. Sydney Freedberg and Konrad Oberhuber concur. Shearman believes the Hammer drawing may be a study from life for Andrea's *Borghese Madonna* of about 1516 and could have been used a year earlier by one of his assistants for the *Madonna* at Ottawa. The drawing differs from the Borghese painting only in the eyes and the head-piece and is almost identical in form and expression to the Ottawa *Madonna.* The very unconventional V-shaped composition drawing (Uffizi Gall., no. 304) that was used in its entirety for the Borghese picture lacks a finished study for the head. Another female figure closely resembling the Hammer study and of the same date appears to the left of the preaching Saint John the Baptist in Andrea's fresco at the Chiostro dello Scalzo, Florence, of 1515.

The provenance of the Hammer drawing indicates its importance. By 1690 it had found its way into the hands of J. P. Zoomer, one of the most knowledgeable art dealers of the seventeenth century, and from there it went into the collection of Jonathan Richardson, Sr., a great connoisseur and collector of Italian drawings.

M. E.

72. CORREGGIO (1493–1534)
A. (RECTO): STUDY FOR THE "MADONNA DELLA SCODELLA"
B. (VERSO): STUDY FOR A FRESCO OF SAINT MATTHEW
AND SAINT JEROME

A. (recto): red chalk, pen and brush in brown ink, 7¹⁵/₁₆ x 5″ (20.2 x 12.7 cm.)

B. (verso): red chalk, pen and brush in brown ink, 8¼ x 5½″ (21 x 14 cm.)

Collections: Sir Peter Lely, London (Lugt [Frits Lugt, *Les Marques de collections, de dessins, & d'estampes,* Amsterdam, 1921], no. 2092); P. & D. Colnaghi & Co., Ltd., London; Michael Hirst, London.

Exhibited: Edinburgh, Merchants Hall, Arts Council of Great Britain in association with the Edinburgh Festival Society, *Exhibition of Italian 16th Century Drawings from British Private Collections,* Aug. 23 – Sept. 13, 1969 (no. 30); Washington, D.C., National Gallery of Art, *Recent Acquisitions and Promised Gifts,* June 2 – Sept. 1, 1974 (no. 68).

Hammer Collection exhibitions: see catalogue reference page. First exhibited: VIII; not exhibited: X, XX, XXIII.

Literature: *Italian 16th Century Drawings from British Private Collections,* catalogue, Arts Council of Great Britain in association with the Edinburgh Festival Society, Merchants Hall, Edinburgh, 1969, no. 30; Konrad Oberhuber, "Drawings by Artists Working in Parma in the Sixteenth Century," *Master Drawings,* vol. 8 (1970), pp. 278 – 79, plates 30, 31; *The Armand Hammer Collection,* Los Angeles, 1971, no. 62; Christopher White, "The Armand Hammer Collection: Drawings," *Apollo,* vol. 95 (June, 1972), p. 458, figs. 3, 4; Robert Hodge, "Three Stages in the Genesis of Correggio's Madonna della Scodella," *Burlington Magazine,* vol. 95 (1973), pp. 603 – 6; *Recent Acquisitions and Promised Gifts,* catalogue, National Gallery of Art, Washington, D.C., 1974, no. 68.

In Correggio's drawings, the disposition of light and shade is primarily responsible for creating the shape and volume of the figures. Forms are evoked rather than delineated, and there is a sense of limitless possibility in the figures' movements. The recto of the Hammer Collection drawing contains an unusually complete but still quite free design for the famous *Madonna della Scodella,* painted in 1529 – 30 and now in the Pinacoteca at Parma. This rapid sketch may be earlier, perhaps of 1523 – 24, the date of the earliest surviving documents of the commission for the painting. (See the more extensive discussion of this drawing in Oberhuber, *Master Drawings,* 1970, especially p. 279 and note 8.) Both the figures and the style of drawing correspond more closely to Correggio's works of that time.

There is a copy in Windsor Castle of a lost drawing by Correggio, recently recognized by Robert Hodge, which makes it clear that the artist must have been working intensely on the *Madonna della Scodella* at that earlier date. Like the Hammer drawing, this sheet reflects the style of Correggio's frescoes in S. Giovanni Evangelista in Parma, then in progress, and shows that for this new project he looked back to his own earlier compositions, the *Rest on the Flight into Egypt* in the Uffizi Gallery or the *Mystic Marriage of Saint Catherine* in Naples. The lost drawing of which the Windsor sheet is a copy must have been contemporary with Correggio's *Noli me tangere* in the Prado. Both the Hammer Collection drawing and the lost original of the Windsor drawing seem, therefore, to have been done in the same period. The style of this lost original can be compared to the brush drawings made by Correggio for the frieze in the nave of S. Giovanni Evangelista and for the Del Bono Chapel in the same church (see A. E. Popham, *Correggio's Drawings,* London, 1957, nos. 37 and 44).

On the verso of our drawing, there is actually a study for one of the pendentives of the dome of S. Giovanni Evangelista. It is the earliest known design for the *Saints Matthew and Jerome,* for which other studies are preserved in Munich and London (Popham, *Correggio's Drawings,* nos. 17 and 18; Popham nos. 19 and 20 in the Uffizi and in the Conte Rasini Collection in Milan show a more finished design). Although this is an even freer sketch than the recto drawing, probing for proper positions in space, Correggio still gives his figures a dramatic sense of plasticity.

K. O.

73. REMBRANDT VAN RIJN (1606–1669)
STUDY OF A BEGGAR MAN AND WOMAN IN THE STREET

Pen and brown ink: 5 x 4⅜″ (12.7 x 11.1 cm.)

Collections: Jonathan Richardson, Sr., London (Lugt [Frits Lugt, *Les Marques de collections, de dessins, & d'estampes,* Amsterdam, 1921], no. 2183); Sir Joshua Reynolds, London (Lugt, no. 2364); Sir Thomas Lawrence, London (Lugt, no. 2445); William Esdaile (Lugt, no. 2617; sold Christie's, London, June 17, 1840 [lot 4], bought by Sheath); Sir Archibald Campbell, Bt., Argyllshire; by descent to Sir Ilay Campbell, Bt., Argyllshire.

Hammer Collection exhibitions: see catalogue reference page. First exhibited: XXXII.

Literature: A. M. Hind, *Vasari Society,* 1908 – 9, ser. 1, pt. IV, no. 26; Kurt Bauch, *Die Kunst des jungen Rembrandts,* 1933, pp. 114 – 18, 204 – 5, fig. III; Otto Benesch, *The Drawings of Rembrandt,* London, 1954, vol. 2, no. 206, fig. 223 (2d ed., 1973, fig. 241).

From his earliest days in Leiden, Rembrandt seems to have made a practice of drawing everyday scenes from life. His reliance on nature was commented on by such early biographers as Joachim von Sandrart. It is not, however, entirely clear whether the two figures in this drawing, a beggar man and woman in the street, were studied independently or seen together in a mute dialogue. The man turns away from the woman toward the right, while she veers to the left with arms outstretched. The depiction of shadows on the figures and on the ground from the same light source suggest the manner of the early etching of a *Beggar Man and Woman in Conversation* (Johann Adam Bernhard von Bartsch, *Le Peintre graveur,* no. 164), dated 1630.

There has been some discussion as to exactly when this drawing was made. Whereas Kurt Bauch believed that it was executed about 1630, while Rembrandt was still in Leiden, Otto Benesch was of the opinion that the angular style of drawing indicated a slightly later date, about 1632 – 33, after the artist's move to Amsterdam. Benesch compared the Hammer drawing with *Christ Conversing with Martha and Mary* (Benesch, no. 79), in the Teylers Museum, Haarlem, which one is inclined to think of as a characteristic early Amsterdam study. With the development of his drawing style from such an early study as the *Beggar Couple with a Dog,* c. 1628 – 29, executed in the manner of Jacques Callot's etchings, Rembrandt soon brought more characterization to each head and reduced obvious contrasts of light and shade, both features of the present work. On the other hand, comparison with "late" Leiden etchings, when the artist was much concerned with beggar subjects, suggests that Benesch's dating may be marginally too late. Apart from theme, the Hammer drawing has much in common with the *Beggar Man and Woman in Conversation* of 1630. Perhaps fortuitously, the turned pose of the man, with hands behind his back, recurs in the *Ragged Peasant* (Bartsch, no. 172), of about 1630. The woman reappears, in reverse, in the background of the etching of the *Blind Fiddler* (Bartsch, no. 138), dated 1631.

C. W.

Pen and ink, brown wash, heightened with white: 6¹³/₁₆ x 6¾″ (17.3 x 17.2 cm.)

Watermark: Arms of Amsterdam

Collection: B. F. Nicholson (sold Sotheby & Co., London, Mar. 23, 1971 [no. 90]).

Exhibited: Washington, D.C., National Gallery of Art, *Recent Acquisitions and Promised Gifts,* June 2 – Sept. 1, 1974 (no. 69); Los Angeles County Museum of Art, *Old Master Drawings from American Collections,* Apr. 29 – June 13, 1976.

Hammer Collection exhibitions: see catalogue reference page. First exhibited: IX; not exhibited: X, XX, XXIII.

Literature: Christopher White, "The Hammer Collection: Drawings," *Apollo,* vol. 95 (June, 1972), pp. 458 – 60, fig. 5.

An elderly king, wearing a turban surmounted by a crown, and holding a scepter in his right hand, is seated on a throne beneath a baldachino. On the right, two female figures kneel side by side before him. The woman on the left clasps something on her knee.

The king is similar in type to the artist's representation of biblical kings, as, for example, David in the drawing of *Nathan Admonishing David* of about 1655 in the Metropolitan Museum of Art (see Otto Benesch, *The Drawings of Rembrandt,* London, 1954 – 57, vol. 5, no. 948). He also bears a strong affinity to a number of the figures in the copies Rembrandt made after Moghul miniatures in the mid-1650s (Benesch, nos. 1187 – 1206), suggesting that the artist drew inspiration from these for his representation of an Old Testament figure.

The subject is not easily elucidated. The suggested identification of the Judgment of Solomon, made in the 1971 sale catalogue, is not entirely convincing. In the first place, it is by no means certain that the woman on the left holds a baby. The object could equally well be a jar. Secondly, the position of the second woman suggests that she is an attendant and not a rival. The scene depicted here must represent a woman humbly making some offering to the elderly king.

This sheet, which until its recent appearance in the sale room was unknown, is comparable to a number of late Rembrandt drawings, in particular, *Isaac and Rebecca Spied upon by Abimelach,* in a private collection, New York (Benesch, no. 988), which has been variously dated in the late 1650s or early 1660s (for a discussion of this drawing, which favors the latter dating, see *Rembrandt Drawings from American Collections,* Pierpont Morgan Library, New York, and Fogg Art Museum, Cambridge, Mass., 1960, no. 76). The delineation of the couple in this study is notably similar to that of the two kneeling women in the present sheet.

C. W.

75. GIOVANNI BATTISTA TIEPOLO (1696–1770)
SAINT JEROME IN THE DESERT LISTENING TO THE ANGELS

Pen and brown ink, brown wash, heightened with white, over black chalk: 16¾ x 10⅞″ (42.5 x 27.6 cm.)

Collections: Pietro Monaco, engraved and published by him in 1743 in *Raccolta di centododici stampe di pitture della storia sacra* and then reissued with additional plates in 1763; Ann Payne Robertson (on loan to the Metropolitan Museum of Art, New York, then sold Sotheby & Co., London, Nov. 26, 1970 [no. 71]).

Exhibited: Washington, D.C., National Gallery of Art, Sept. 21 – Nov. 26, 1974, and Fort Worth, Kimbell Art Museum, Dec. 7, 1974 – Feb. 9, 1975, *Venetian Drawings in American Collections;* Los Angeles County Museum of Art, *Old Master Drawings from American Collections,* Apr. 29 – June 13, 1976; Washington, D.C., National Gallery of Art, *Master Drawings from the Collection of the National Gallery of Art and Promised Gifts,* June, 1978 (no. 73).

Hammer Collection exhibitions: see catalogue reference page. First exhibited: VIII; not exhibited: X, XX, XXIII.

Literature: *Important Old Master Drawings,* sale catalogue, Sotheby & Co., London, 1970, p. 113, no. 71, repr.; *Venetian Drawings in American Collections,* catalogue, National Gallery of Art, Washington, D.C., 1974, p. 68, no. 68; Ebria Feinblatt, *Old Master Drawings from American Collections,* catalogue, Los Angeles County Museum of Art, 1976, pp. 50 – 51, no. 58, repr.

This splendid work by Tiepolo belongs to a group of very finished drawings that the artist probably intended for sale. Other drawings of a similar type are in the Museo Civico, Bassano; Civico Museo di Storia ed Arte, Trieste; the Art Institute of Chicago; the Cleveland Museum of Art; the Städelsches Kunstinstitut, Frankfurt; and the Statens Museum for Kunst, Copenhagen.

These drawings have been placed chronologically in the 1730s and were surely executed by the end of the decade since they were engraved by Pietro Monaco by 1740. In pen and rich brown washes, the drawings are heightened with white, a feature Max Goering attributes to the influence upon Tiepolo of the French artist Louis Dorigny (1654 – 1742), who worked for many years in Venice and died in Verona.

Tiepolo, who must be considered one of history's most brilliant draftsmen, began his career as a *tenebroso,* who worked with strong effects of light and shadow to create relief and depth. The present drawing reflects this chiaroscuro treatment as well as the artist's use of continuous binding lines to define the forms, both distinctive of his early style. The free application of the wash and the heavy dark accents create a fluid, dramatic background pattern for a drawing that has the monumental quality of an altarpiece. This solidity of execution, still founded in the Emilian influence upon Tiepolo's earlier work, affords the utmost contrast to the dissolving weightlessness and radiant light of his later drawings.

George Knox has proposed the name of Giovanni Raggi (1712 – 1792), a disciple of Tiepolo, as the author of a copy of this drawing in the Museo Correr, Venice (inv. 4596). It was illustrated by Knox in "A Group of Tiepolo Drawings Owned and Engraved by Pietro Monaco," *Master Drawings,* vol. 3 (Apr., 1966), p. 389, plate 18. Another copy was in the collection of Francis Watson in London; see also Linda Boyer, letter, *Master Drawings,* vol. 4 (Feb., 1966).

E. F.

Pen and brown wash over black chalk: 16¾ x 11¹³/₁₆″ (42.5 x 30 cm.)

Collections: Prince Alexis Orloff (sold Galerie Georges Petit, Paris, Apr. 29 – 30, 1920 [no. 134]); W. W. Crocker, Burlingame, Calif.; Augustus Pollack, Monterey, Calif.; R. M. Light & Co., Inc., Boston, Mass.

Exhibited: San Francisco Museum of Art, *The Opening Exhibition,* Jan. – Mar., 1935; Art Institute of Chicago, *Loan Exhibition of Paintings, Drawings and Prints by the Two Tiepolos: Giambattista and Giandomenico,* Feb. 4 – Mar. 6, 1938 (no. 47); Cambridge, Mass., Fogg Art Museum, Harvard University, *Seventy Master Drawings,* Nov. 27, 1948 – Jan. 6, 1949 (no. 46); Washington, D.C., National Gallery of Art, *Recent Acquisitions and Promised Gifts,* June 2 – Sept. 1, 1974 (no. 70); Washington, D.C., National Gallery of Art, *Master Drawings from the Collection of the National Gallery of Art and Promised Gifts,* June, 1978 (no. 75).

Hammer Collection exhibitions: see catalogue reference page. First exhibited: XI; not exhibited: XX, XXIII.

Literature: Otto Benesch, *Venetian Drawings of the 18th Century in America,* New York, 1947, p. 31, no. 19, plate 19; Agnes Mongan, *One Hundred Master Drawings,* Cambridge, Mass., 1949, pp. 106 – 7, repr.; George Knox, "The Orloff Album of Tiepolo Drawings," *Burlington Magazine,* vol. 103 (June, 1961), p. 275, no. 15; Christopher White, "The Hammer Collection: Drawings," *Apollo,* vol. 95 (June, 1972), p. 460, fig. 8 p. 462; *Recent Acquisitions and Promised Gifts,* catalogue, National Gallery of Art, Washington, D.C., 1974, pp. 115 – 16, no. 70, repr.

The subject of this drawing is not yet fully identified, although the Virgin is obviously showing favor to, recommending, or interceding for the kneeling male figure at the left. The loose long hair and seemingly unclerical attire of this figure do not readily suggest a connection with a religious order or relationship with a familiar saint. The object he holds in his left hand may be a small book.

The drawing comes from the well-known Orloff album, which was sold in Paris in 1920. According to George Knox, the album was assembled by a Russian dilettante, Gregory Vladimirovitch Orloff (1777 – 1826), who published a book on Italian painting. Later the collection was inherited by Prince Alexis Orloff. The ninety-six leaves from the album included several that were highly finished and were often referred to as presentation drawings.

Otto Benesch and Agnes Mongan have ascribed the drawing to Tiepolo's mature period since it is looser in treatment than the preceding work *(Saint Jerome in the Desert),* but the dark wash that serves to accentuate the forms is still distributed in the same highly pictorial manner as in the earlier work. The contouring by means of a firm, continuous line, characteristic of the earlier style, gives way here to the broken, accented strokes and modeling by flat washes that herald the increasingly fugitive means the artist adopted in his later drawings.

In the Hammer work, the figure of Saint John can be compared generally to the larger figure of Saint Sebastian in the Fogg Museum's drawing entitled *The Holy Family Enthroned with Saints Sebastian, Catherine of Alexandria and Francis,* dated by Knox at about 1735. Based on this comparison, the Hammer drawing can probably be assigned the same date rather than Benesch's suggested date of about 1740.

E. F.

77. JEAN-ANTOINE WATTEAU (1684–1721)
YOUNG GIRL

Red and black chalk: 8½ x 5¾″ (21.6 x 14.6 cm.)

Collections: Philippe Wiener, Paris; Albert Meyer (sold Paris, May 24 – June 8, 1935 [no. 100]); Mrs. Jesse I. Straus, New York.

Exhibited: London, Royal Academy of Arts, *The London Exhibition of French Art, 1200 – 1900,* Jan. 4 – Mar. 12, 1932 (no. 713, cat. no. 765), lent by Albert Meyer; Paris, Jean A. Seligmann Gallery, *Collection Albert Meyer,* May 24 – June 8, 1935 (no. 100); Washington, D.C., National Gallery of Art, *Master Drawings from the Collection of the National Gallery of Art and Promised Gifts,* June, 1978 (no. 80).

Hammer Collection exhibitions: see catalogue reference page. First exhibited: VII; not exhibited: XX, XXIII.

Literature: Edmond de Goncourt, *Catalogue raisonné de l'oeuvre peint, dessiné et gravé d'Antoine Watteau,* Paris, 1875, p. 297, no. 652; *The London Exhibition of French Art, 1200 – 1900,* catalogue, Royal Academy of Arts, London, 1932, p. 350, no. 713; *Commemorative Catalogue of the Exhibition of French Art, 1200 – 1900, Royal Academy of Arts, London, January – March, 1932,* Oxford, 1933, p. 163, no. 765; *Dessins de maîtres du XVIIIe siècle, collection Albert Meyer,* catalogue, Jean A. Seligmann Gallery, Paris, 1935, no. 100; K. T. Parker and J. Mathey, *Catalogue de l'oeuvre dessiné d'Antoine Watteau,* Paris, 1957, vol. 2, p. 312, no. 577, plate 577; *The Irma N. Straus Collection of Old Master Drawings,* sale catalogue, Parke-Bernet Galleries, Inc., New York, Oct. 21, 1970, no. 21, repr. in color p. 37.

Watteau had a predilection for a feminine type that appears in nearly all of his drawings of girls and women. The face is a full oval, the nose slightly *retroussé* with large nostrils, the eyes heavy-lidded, long-lashed, oval-shaped, almost slanted, the lips full, the chin plump, and the hair generally drawn up tightly into a knot on the top of the head. In the Hammer portrait—a study that has not been related to a painting—this easily recognized type appears. The modesty and restraint of the model's pose imply that she was drawn from life, a strong likelihood since it is well known that Watteau made hundreds of figure studies that he kept in bound volumes and drew upon as elements for his pictures.

This elegantly dressed young lady looks down, but whether in reverie or shyness it is difficult to determine. Watteau has drawn her face in red chalk, touching her eyebrows lightly with black. The red chalk has taken on the grain of the paper, giving it a porous quality. The hair is only briefly indicated by delicate lines, the paper itself left to convey it. Certain of the deep red accents, such as those on the bow of the necklace and on the lips, suggest that the chalk was moistened. Heavy black shading sets the figure off at the right. Despite her youth, the girl, whom the artist has represented with great sympathy, has an expression of maturity.

Watteau's great friend the Comte de Caylus has been credited with having engraved the girl's head in his *Figures de différentes caractères,* no. 273. On the other hand, Parker and Mathey and E. Dacier and Albert Vuaflart *(Jean de Julienne et les graveurs de Watteau,* Paris, 1922) attribute the engraving to Laurent Cars.

E. F.

78. JEAN-ANTOINE WATTEAU (1684–1721)
COUPLE SEATED ON A BANK

Red, black, and white chalk: 9½ x 13¾" (24.1 x 34.9 cm.)
Inscribed lower right, in ink: Vataux fec.
Inscribed lower left, in crayon: Watteau

Collections: anonymous sale, Paris, 1892 (no. 72); Lallemand (sold Paris, May 2, 1894); Léon Michel-Lévy (sold Galerie Georges Petit, Paris, June 17 – 18, 1925 [no. 106]); George Blumenthal, New York; Mrs. Jesse I. Straus, New York.

Exhibited: Paris, Galerie Georges Petit, *Collection Léon Michel-Lévy,* June 17 – 18, 1925 (no. 106); London, Royal Academy of Arts, *The London Exhibition of French Art, 1200 – 1900,* Jan. 4 – Mar. 12, 1932 (no. 738), lent by George Blumenthal; Washington, D.C., National Gallery of Art, *Recent Acquisitions and Promised Gifts,* June 2 – Sept. 1, 1974 (no. 71); Los Angeles County Museum of Art, *Old Master Drawings from American Collections,* Apr. 29 – June 13, 1976; Washington, D.C., National Gallery of Art, *Master Drawings from the Collection of the National Gallery of Art and Promised Gifts,* June, 1978 (no. 79).

Hammer Collection exhibitions: see catalogue reference page. First exhibited: VII; not exhibited: XX, XXIII.

Literature: *Les Maîtres du dessin,* Paris, 1911, vol. 3, plate 136; K. T. Parker, *The Drawings of Antoine Watteau,* London, 1931, plate 92; *The London Exhibition of French Art, 1200 – 1900,* catalogue, Royal Academy of Arts, London, 1932, p. 359, no. 738; *Commemorative Catalogue of the Exhibition of French Art, 1200 – 1900, Royal Academy of Arts, London, January – March, 1932,* Oxford, 1933, p. 165, no. 780; K. T. Parker and J. Mathey, *Catalogue de l'oeuvre dessiné d'Antoine Watteau,* Paris, 1957, vol. 2, p. 326, no. 665; *The Irma N. Straus Collection of Old Master Drawings,* sale catalogue, Parke-Bernet Galleries, Inc., New York, Oct. 21, 1970, p. 34, no. 20; Christopher White, "The Hammer Collection: Drawings," *Apollo,* vol. 95 (June, 1972), p. 460, fig. 6; *Recent Acquisitions and Promised Gifts,* catalogue, National Gallery of Art, Washington, D.C., 1974, pp. 116 – 17, no. 71, repr.; Ebria Feinblatt, *Old Master Drawings from American Collections,* catalogue, Los Angeles County Museum of Art, 1976, pp. 132 – 33, no. 149, repr.

The great beauty of Watteau's best drawings stems primarily from two factors, the sensitive precision of his line and the enchanting coloristic effects created by his use of three crayons, black, red, and white. These features are brilliantly embodied in this sheet. Although the preliminary figures are not shown in the positions they hold in the paintings for which they served, the artist has drawn them in a remarkable way. The arms of the young man serve as an arc to support the figure of the girl; the index finger of his left hand points directly to the nape of her neck; and the right hands of both figures rest parallel to each other on the ground. The juxtaposition of unrelated yet harmoniously arranged figures gives this drawing a fresh, spontaneous character. In contrast to the extreme foreshortening of the man and the sketchiness of his delineation is the complete, detailed rendering of the girl, which adds to the visual impact of the work.

Although Watteau was never in Italy, he is known to have studied the work of Paolo Veronese in Paris. A measure of the elegance, and indeed the fineness of the features, of his faces is undoubtedly derived from the great Venetian master.

The graceful gentleman in the Hammer study appears in at least two Watteau paintings: *La Famille,* in the Rothschild Collection, engraved by Aveline (E. Dacier and Albert Vuaflart, *Jean de Julienne et les graveurs de Watteau,* Paris, 1922, no. 86); and *Assemblée Galante* (Dacier and Vuaflart, no. 139).

The sitters in *La Famille* have been identified, on the basis of a document of 1777, as members of the family of Jean Le Bouc-Santussan, a master goldsmith who married the daughter of the famed art dealer E. P. Gersaint, with whom Watteau lodged for a while.

E. F.

79. FRANÇOIS BOUCHER (1703–1770)
LANDSCAPE WITH A RUSTIC BRIDGE, c. 1740

Black chalk, heightened with white: 8 x 10¾″ (20.3 x 27.3 cm.)

Collections: Fernand Javel, Paris; Charles E. Slatkin Galleries, Inc., New York; Norton Simon, Los Angeles (sold Parke-Bernet Galleries, Inc., New York, May 7, 1971 [no. 207]).

Hammer Collection exhibitions: see catalogue reference page. First exhibited: IX; not exhibited: XX, XXIII.

Literature: *Great Drawings of All Time, French: 13th Century to 1919* (selected and edited by Ira Moskowitz, text by Agnes Mongan), New York, 1962, vol. 3, no. 696, repr.; *Property of the Norton Simon Foundation and Old Master Drawings and Paintings from the Private Collection of Norton Simon,* sale catalogue, Parke-Bernet Galleries, Inc., New York, 1971, p. 160, no. 207, repr.

Agnes Mongan assigns this drawing to the period about 1740 when Boucher, then designing for tapestries, made frequent trips into the country en route to Beauvais and the Gobelins.

It is noteworthy that in his own time Boucher was roundly criticized by the revolutionists for his pastoral paintings; his countryside was considered romantic and his peasants disguised aristocrats. But a truer note came out in his landscape drawings. Here Boucher took his cue from such Dutch masters as Jacob van Ruisdael, Abraham Bloemaert, and Jan van Goyen, who were among the artists whose work he collected and studied. In consequence, his landscape drawings have a tranquility and restraint that contrast with the energetic sensuousness of his figural works. On the whole, the figures in his landscape drawings are subordinated to the setting, sometimes, as in the present work, appearing as staffage.

Boucher is known to have formed his drawing style upon that of Watteau, whom he copied and engraved. It was this influence that led him to develop his supple contouring and expressive accenting of light and dark. However, the twenty years that separated the two artists can be detected in the change from the older artist's straight, uninterrupted line to the undulant, rococo forms of the younger man. But Boucher's landscape drawings were still marked by a firm lineality in which short flecks of the crayon delineated the foliage and lead white was added to create the shimmer of light in the distance.

E. F.

80. FRANÇOIS BOUCHER (1703–1770)
VENUS RECLINING AGAINST A DOLPHIN

Black chalk, heightened with white: 9 x 13½" (22.8 x 34.3 cm.)

Collections: Charles E. Slatkin Galleries, Inc., New York; Norton Simon, Los Angeles (sold Parke-Bernet Galleries, Inc., New York, May 7, 1971 [no. 206]).

Exhibited: Washington, D.C., National Gallery of Art, Dec. 23, 1973 – Mar. 17, 1974, and Art Institute of Chicago, Apr. 1 – May 20, 1974, *François Boucher in North American Collections: 100 Drawings.*

Hammer Collection exhibitions: see catalogue reference page. First exhibited: IX; not exhibited: XX – XXXIV.

Literature: Marcel Roux, *Inventaire du fonds français, graveurs du XVIIIe siècle,* Paris, 1949, vol. 6, p. 367, no. 88 (engraving by Demarteau); Alexandre Ananoff, *L'Oeuvre dessiné de François Boucher,* Paris, 1966, vol. 1, p. 208, no. 801a; *Property of the Norton Simon Foundation and Old Master Drawings and Paintings from the Private Collection of Norton Simon,* sale catalogue, Parke-Bernet Galleries, Inc., New York, 1971, p. 158, no. 206, repr.; Regina Shoolman Slatkin, "Some Boucher Drawings and Related Prints," *Master Drawings,* vol. 10 (1972), pp. 276 – 77, plate 38; *François Boucher in North American Collections: 100 Drawings,* catalogue, National Gallery of Art, Washington, D.C., 1974.

One of the most productive painters and decorators of the Rococo, François Boucher in his youth studied briefly under François Lemoine before entering the shop of the engraver Jean-François Cars. There he learned the art of etching, which he was to practice all his life. Following the death of Watteau, the latter's patron, Jean de Julienne, engaged Boucher to assist in the engraving of Watteau's work as a monument to the late artist. The more than one hundred etchings Boucher made after Watteau were influential in the formation of his drawing style, a style not always readily datable.

Among his French contemporaries, Boucher was the leader in the revival of mythological subjects and in the depiction of the female nude, which he often endowed with a degree of voluptuousness not present, for example, in the nonsensual, classically inspired nudes of Rubens or the more sensitive, poetically realistic nudes of Watteau.

Boucher executed about fifty drawings on the theme of Venus, "the divinity adored by the courtiers of the age of Louis XV." Several of these studies show the goddess in the familiar reclining position, similar to the present work, but accompanied by different attributes. The motif of the dolphin, for example, the sacred fish of the Greeks, is unusual for this goddess, being much more generally associated with water deities such as Neptune's wife, Amphitrite, or the mother of Achilles, Thetis.

Originally published by Alexandre Ananoff as a counterproof (a proof made by rubbing the backs of both the moistened drawing and a blank sheet placed on it), the Hammer Venus has now been shown by Regina Slatkin to be the artist's original version, serving not only for several copies, both in the same and in reversed direction, but also for a lost painting and for an engraving in the crayon manner by Demarteau. Rhythmically unified in form and execution, the compact, fleshy body of Venus is rendered in a particularly animated way, with flowing lines, rippling curves, and outstretched left arm, while the figure's unabashed sensuality is masterfully counterbalanced by the artist's inherent refinement and *délicatesse.*

E. F.

81. JEAN-BAPTISTE GREUZE (1725–1805)
A TIRED WOMAN WITH TWO CHILDREN

Pen and ink, brown wash, traces of black chalk: 8⅞ x 10⅞" (22.5 x 27.8 cm.)

Collections: John Bryson, Oxford, until 1976; Stephen Somerville, London, until 1977.

Hammer Collection exhibitions: see catalogue reference page. First exhibited: XXXV.

This is an early work, dating from Greuze's first years in Paris (1750 – 61), when he was much influenced by Dutch and Flemish genre painting. With the exception of the two years he spent in Italy (1755 – 57), this is the period when Greuze made his finest studies of everyday life. Stylistically, the Hammer drawing has links with several drawings by Greuze in the Graphische Sammlung Albertina, Vienna. Closest of all are the *Interior with a Woman and a Girl by a Fireplace* and *The Tea*. The technique is the same in all: broad areas of wash, lashed and delineated with frenetic pen line and calligraphic squiggles. (See also *Savoyard with Marionettes,* Albertina, and *Family Begging,* Musée Condé, Chantilly.) The model Greuze used for the old woman, probably grandmother of the children, is the same person who appears in many of his drawings (see *Old Woman with Hands Clasped,* Louvre, of 1756, which is a study for the *Father's Curse,* Louvre). If he had decided to represent the mother in this drawing, Greuze would probably have made the woman young and beautiful.

Greuze never forgot his plebeian beginnings; his concern for the family and the implications of poverty underlies much of his work. The theme of the exhausted woman in charge of lively children is a favorite one (see *The Silence,* Buckingham Palace, of 1759), but Greuze never expressed more eloquently the weariness of a human being than in this masterful drawing.

M. E.

82. JEAN-HONORÉ FRAGONARD (1732–1806)
STUDY FOR "THE EDUCATION OF THE VIRGIN, "c. 1750

Charcoal: 10¹⁵⁄₁₆ x 8⁹⁄₁₆″ (27.8 x 21.7 cm.)

Collections: priv. coll., France; priv. coll., New York; Wildenstein & Co., Inc., New York.

Hammer Collection exhibitions: see catalogue reference page. First exhibited: XXXII.

The Hammer charcoal sketch is the first conception of the black chalk drawing now in the Musée des Beaux-Arts, Rouen. The Rouen drawing is a preparatory study for the painting now in the California Palace of the Legion of Honor, San Francisco (see Georges Wildenstein, *The Paintings of Fragonard,* London, 1960, no. 19; for a reproduction of the Rouen drawing, wrongly described as a study for the unfinished painting [Wildenstein, no. 17, formerly in the collection of M. Bérard, Paris], see Louis Réau, *Fragonard,* Brussels, 1956). The Rouen study is identical to the Hammer sketch except that it is larger (19⅝ x 15¾″ [50 x 40 cm.]) and is more detailed. There is another drawing of this subject that shows the Virgin looking up; this is a preparatory study for the oil sketch that is Plate 8 in the present catalogue (for this second drawing, see sale catalogue, Galerie Charpentier, Paris, June 9 – 10, 1953, no. 6). These are all early works, probably executed about 1750, when Fragonard was still a pupil of Boucher. Biblical subjects were unusual for Fragonard, and this one was probably suggested by his teacher as an exercise. It could not be a more charming scene, representing as it does the young Virgin leaning against her mother's knee, learning to read from the Bible held for her by angels.

M. E.

83. JEAN-HONORÉ FRAGONARD (1732–1806)
THE READING

Brown wash, the corners rounded out: 11 x 8¼" (27.9 x 21 cm.)

Collections: H. Walferdin, Paris (sold Paris, Apr. 12 – 16, 1880 [no. 192]); J. P. Heseltine, London; E. H. Molyneux, Neuilly-sur-Seine; Mrs. Jesse I. Straus, New York.

Exhibited: London, Grafton Galleries, *National Loan Exhibition in Aid of National Gallery Funds,* 1909 – 10 (no. 99); New York, E. Gimpel and Wildenstein & Co., Inc., *Paintings and Drawings by Fragonard,* Jan., 1914 (no. 31); Paris, Musée Carnavalet, *La Vie Parisienne au XVIIIe Siècle,* Mar. 20 – Apr. 30, 1928 (no. 165); Paris, Galerie Jacques Seligmann et Fils, Ancien Hôtel de Sagan, *Exposition de Dessins de Fragonard,* May 9 – 30, 1931 (no. 55), lent by E. H. Molyneux.

Hammer Collection exhibitions: see catalogue reference page. First exhibited: VII; not exhibited: X, XX, XXIII.

Literature: Baron Roger Portalis, *Honoré Fragonard, sa vie et son oeuvre,* Paris, 1889, p. 307; *Drawings by François Boucher, J.-H. Fragonard and Antoine Watteau in the Collection of J. P. H(eseltine),* London, 1900, p. 39, no. 4 (the engraving by Jules de Goncourt was reproduced in place of the drawing); *Dessins de l'école française du XVIIIe siècle, provenant de la Collection Heseltine,* Paris, 1913, no. 32, repr.; *Catalogue of Paintings and Drawings by Fragonard,* E. Gimpel and Wildenstein & Co., Inc., New York, 1914, p. 54, no. 31; Alexandre Ananoff, *L'Oeuvre dessiné de J.-H. Fragonard, catalogue raisonné,* Paris, 1961, vol. 1, p. 55, no. 62, fig. 28; *The Irma N. Straus Collection of Old Master Drawings,* sale catalogue, Parke-Bernet Galleries, Inc., New York, Oct. 21, 1970, p. 58, no. 32, repr.

Traditionally this drawing has been held to represent Mme. Fragonard reading to her younger sister, Marguerite Gérard, who came to live with the Fragonards after their marriage and was not only the pupil of the artist but one of his favorite models. Both women were accomplished miniaturists, and Marguerite left a fine small portrait in oil of her celebrated brother-in-law.

Like *Grandfather's Reprimand* and the *Visit to the Nurse* (Plates 84 and 86), this drawing was originally in the H. Walferdin Collection in Paris. Walferdin (1795 – 1880) was born in the same city as Diderot and shared his admiration for Fragonard. He was a physician and occasional man of politics, but his true pursuits were literature and art, and he was able to acquire an exceptional group of drawings by his favorite artist.

Themes centering on letters or the exchange of confidences and similar *tête-à-tête* situations were popular with Fragonard's audience because they implied human drama or romance. Family scenes were rarer in his work. *The Reading* records such a mood of quiet intimacy. The two sisters sit together, one reading to the other. The younger, drawn in profile, occupies the foreground with the volume of her full skirt, and the older is seen from the rear. The heads of the two women incline toward each other as they share a mutual involvement in the book.

The whole drawing is suffused and unified by the golden tonality of the paper. The dainty, elegant silhouette of Marguerite ranks with the happiest of Fragonard's figures in which the essential is conveyed through a minimum of details. The figures of both women are, in fact, treated more broadly here than in the wash drawing of the same subject and arrangement in the Louvre (Ananoff, vol. 1, no. 61).

E. F.

84. JEAN-HONORÉ FRAGONARD (1732–1806)
GRANDFATHER'S REPRIMAND

Gray-brown wash over black chalk: 13½ x 17¾" (34.3 x 45.1 cm.)

Collections: Louis-Antoine-August Rohan-Chabot, Paris (sold Paris, Dec. 8, 1807 [no. 43]); Baron Vivant-Denon, Paris (sold Paris, Feb. 2, 1846 [no. 269]); H. Walferdin, Paris (sold Paris, Apr. 12 – 16, 1880 [no. 199]); Comte de Jaucourt, Paris; Sigismond Bardas, Paris; Georges and Florence Blumenthal (sold Galerie Georges Petit, Paris, Dec. 1 – 2, 1932 [no. 30]); Jacques Seligmann, Paris; Mrs. Jesse I. Straus, New York.

Exhibited: Paris, Musée des Arts Décoratifs, Pavillon de Marsan, Louvre, *Exposition d'Oeuvres de J.-H. Fragonard,* June 7 – July 10, 1921 (no. 133); Washington, D.C., National Gallery of Art, *Master Drawings from the Collection of the National Gallery of Art and Promised Gifts,* June, 1978 (no. 87).

Hammer Collection exhibitions: see catalogue reference page. First exhibited: VII; not exhibited: XX, XXIII.

Literature: A. N. Pérignon, *Description des objets d'art qui compose le cabinet de feu M. le Baron V. Denon: (II) tableaux, dessins et miniatures,* Paris, 1826, p. 178, no. 732; Baron Roger Portalis, *Honoré Fragonard, sa vie et son oeuvre,* Paris, 1889, p. 311; Georges Wildenstein, *Catalogue de l'Exposition d'Oeuvres de J.-H. Fragonard,* Musée des Arts Décoratifs, Paris, 1921, no. 133; *Catalogue of the Sale of the Georges and Florence Blumenthal Collection,* Galerie Georges Petit, Paris, 1932, p. 28, no. 30, plate 10; Louis Réau, *Fragonard, sa vie et son oeuvre,* Brussels, 1956, p. 206; Alexandre Ananoff, *L'Oeuvre dessiné de J.-H. Fragonard, catalogue raisonné,* Paris, 1961, vol. 1, p. 46, no. 41; *The Irma N. Straus Collection of Master Drawings,* sale catalogue, Parke-Bernet Galleries, Inc., New York, Oct. 21, 1970, p. 62, no. 34, repr.; Christopher White, "The Hammer Collection Drawings," *Apollo,* vol. 95 (June, 1972), p. 460.

Although chalk was the primary drawing medium of Watteau and Boucher, Fragonard, influenced by Tiepolo, revived the technique of drawing with ink and wash. When he visited Italy as a young man, Fragonard was overpowered by Michelangelo and Raphael but was able to make copies of what he in his own words called "second-raters like Pietro da Cortona and Giovanni Battista Tiepolo."

Of the five Hammer Fragonards, the most splendid must be considered the two drawings of children for which the artist's young son, Alexandre-Evariste, called Fanfan, is believed to have been the inspiration. Fragonard married comparatively late, at the age of thirty-seven, and had two children with his eighteen-year-old bride from his native city of Grasse, in Provence. In these two delicious interludes, *The Little Preacher* (Plate 85) and *Grandfather's Reprimand,* the great French artist of *l'amour,* the brilliant portrayer of the frivolous pursuit, turned to familial themes with the same immediacy and verve that made his work so delightful to the Paris of his youth.

The outstanding features of these two drawings are the broad, flowing brushstrokes of the darker wash and the light, which floods the compositions with a vibrating, dissolving intensity. Totally suffused and illuminated, the figures themselves, despite their vigorous, broad execution and volume, seem painted with the same airiness as the palpitating atmosphere that surrounds them. Fragonard's and Tiepolo's graphic techniques are much alike. Both are loose and free, but Tiepolo still remained tied to the tradition of the line, while Fragonard "painted" drawings such as these over nebulous preliminary black chalk indications.

Roger Portalis and Georges Wildenstein indicate that this drawing has had various titles in the course of time: *La Prière au Grand-Père,* 1846; *La Prière,* 1880; *La Réprimande du Grand-Papa,* 1889; and *La Visite chez le Docteur,* 1921 – 1932.

E. F.

85. JEAN-HONORÉ FRAGONARD (1732–1806)
THE LITTLE PREACHER

Brown wash over black chalk: 13¾ x 18¼″ (34.9 x 46.7 cm.)

Collections: anonymous sale, Paris, May 31, 1790 (no. 180); M. Marmontel, Paris (sold Hôtel Drouot, Paris, Jan. 25 – 26, 1883 [no. 100]); Richard Lion, Paris (sold Hôtel Drouot, Paris, Apr. 3, 1886 [no. 40]); M. P. Ledoux, Paris (sold Galerie Georges Petit, Paris, Mar. 5, 1918 [no. 27]); Adrien Fauchier-Magnan, Neuilly-sur-Seine; Arthur Veil-Picard, Paris; Guiraud Brothers, Paris; Jean Straus, New York; Mrs. Jesse I. Straus, New York.

Hammer Collection exhibitions: see catalogue reference page. First exhibited: VII; not exhibited: XX, XXIII.

Literature: Baron Roger Portalis, *Honoré Fragonard, sa vie et son oeuvre,* Paris, 1889, pp. 200, 310; Edmond and Jules de Goncourt, *L'Art du XVIIIe siècle, troisième série, Fragonard,* Paris, 1882, pp. 300 – 301; *Catalogue des tableaux anciens et modernes, aquarelles et dessins de la vente M. P. Ledoux,* sale catalogue, Galerie Georges Petit, Paris, 1918, p. 20, no. 27; *Connaissance des arts,* Aug., 1956, repr. p. 42; Louis Réau, *Fragonard, sa vie et son oeuvre,* Brussels, 1956, p. 205, fig. 79; Alexandre Ananoff, *L'Oeuvre dessiné de J.-H. Fragonard, catalogue raisonné,* Paris, 1961, vol. 1, p. 45, no. 40, fig. 18; *The Irma N. Straus Collection of Old Master Drawings,* sale catalogue, Parke-Bernet Galleries, Inc., New York, Oct. 21, 1970, p. 56, no. 31, repr.; Christopher White, "The Hammer Collection: Drawings," *Apollo,* vol. 95 (June, 1972), p. 460.

Alexandre Ananoff describes *The Little Preacher* as Fanfan, the son of Fragonard. The subject was engraved with variations by N. de Launay in 1781 as a pendant to *L'Education Fait Tout,* a drawing now in the collection of Baron E. de Rothschild (Ananoff, vol. 1, no. 11, fig. 6). The engraving may, however, have been made from the painting of the same subject formerly in the Veil-Picard Collection (G. Wildenstein, *The Paintings of Fragonard,* London, 1960, no. 471, fig. 104) rather than from this drawing.

E. F.

86. JEAN-HONORÉ FRAGONARD (1732–1806)
VISIT TO THE NURSE

Chinese ink wash, heightened with watercolor: 12 x 15″ (30.5 x 38.1 cm.)

Collections: Frédéric Villot, Paris (sold Hôtel Drouot, Paris, May 16 – 18, 1859 [no. 122]); E. H. Molyneux, Neuilly-sur-Seine; H. Walferdin, Paris (sold Paris, Apr. 12 – 16, 1880 [no. 200]); Prince A. d'Arenberg, Paris; Jacques Seligmann, Paris; Mrs. Jesse I. Straus, New York.

Exhibited: Berlin, *Königliche Akademie der Künste, Ausstellung von Werken französischer Kunst des XVIII. Jahrhunderts,* Jan. – Mar., 1910 (no. 178); Paris, Musée Carnavalet, *La Vie Parisienne au XVIIIe Siècle,* Mar. 20 – Apr. 30, 1928 (no. 166); Paris, Galerie Jacques Seligmann et Fils, Ancien Hôtel de Sagan, *Exposition de Dessins de Fragonard,* May 9 – 30, 1931 (no. 22).

Hammer Collection exhibitions: see catalogue reference page. First exhibited: VII; not exhibited: X, XX, XXIII.

Literature: *Catalogue de la vente M. F. Villot, dessins, miniatures et estampes,* sale catalogue, Hôtel Drouot, Paris, 1859, p. 20, no. 122; Baron Roger Portalis, "Le Collection Walferdin et ses Fragonards," *Gazette des beaux-arts,* vol. 21 (1880), p. 313; Louis Réau, *Fragonard, sa vie et son oeuvre,* Brussels, 1956, pp. 81, 206; *The Irma N. Straus Collection of Old Master Drawings,* sale catalogue, Parke-Bernet Galleries, Inc., New York, Oct. 21, 1970, p. 54, no. 30, repr.

Fragonard frequently depicted the same subject in a drawing and in a painting. In some instances, the drawings were studies for the later painted work; for example, preparatory drawings are known for *The Education of the Virgin,* the oil on panel now in the Hammer Collection (Plate 8).

Baron Roger Portalis (*Honoré Fragonard,* Paris, 1889, p. 291) lists a painting, the subject of which, like the Hammer drawing of the *Visit to the Nurse,* was taken from *Miss Sara,* an English novel that had been translated into French. The *Visit to the Nurse* portrays the theme of parental affection and pride. The treatment of the subject almost suggests, or parallels, an Adoration of the Child in religious art. All the figures are assembled on the foreground plane, with the light from the upper left trained on the *paterfamilias,* who holds his infant. The graded layers of the gray washes throw the illuminated figures into brilliant relief, as though the scene were taking place on a stage.

Presenting a polar contrast to his celebrated works on the theme of love, the familial themes in Fragonard's oeuvre reflected eighteenth-century French society's pleasure in intimate home-life episodes. Such episodes were most popularly portrayed in the work of Fragonard's contemporary J.-B. Greuze. But whereas the latter, strongly reflecting the ideas of Rousseau and Diderot, frequently infused moralistic and didactic precepts into his art, Fragonard, although partaking of the "sentimentality" of his era, was free of the social propaganda advanced by the revolutionists. As is well known, Fragonard did not fit into the new order after the French Revolution. Rather, he quickly declined in status, eventually dying in poverty and obscurity in his native city of Grasse.

E. F.

87. JEAN-AUGUSTE-DOMINIQUE INGRES (1780–1867)
MRS. CHARLES BADHAM, 1816

Pencil: 10¼ x 8¼″ (26 x 21 cm.)

Signed and dated lower left: J. Ingres, Del Roma 1816

Collections: Charles Badham, Rome; Badham Family; C. Badham Jackson, London (sold Sotheby & Co., London, Dec. 12, 1928 [no. 145], repr. in cat.); Dr. Tancred Borenius, London; Wildenstein and Co., Inc., New York, sold 1929; Mrs. Jesse I. Straus, New York.

Exhibited: New York, Paul Rosenberg Gallery, *Loan Exhibition of Ingres in American Collections,* Apr. 7 – May 6, 1961 (no. 22), p. 32, repr.; Cambridge, Mass., Fogg Art Museum, Harvard University, *Ingres Centennial Exhibition, 1867 – 1967, Drawings, Watercolors and Oil Sketches from American Collections,* Feb. 12 – Apr. 9, 1967 (no. 37); Washington, D.C., National Gallery of Art, Jan. 23 – Feb. 21, 1971, Philadelphia Museum of Art, Mar. 16 – Apr. 11, 1971, and New York, Wildenstein & Co., Inc., Apr. 24 – May 23, 1971, *Ingres in Rome;* Washington, D.C., National Gallery of Art, *Recent Acquisitions and Promised Gifts,* June 2 – Sept. 1, 1974 (no. 72); Washington, D.C., National Gallery of Art, *Master Drawings from the Collection of the National Gallery of Art and Promised Gifts,* June, 1978 (no. 93).

Hammer Collection exhibitions: see catalogue reference page. First exhibited: VII; not exhibited: XX, XXIII.

Literature: Morton D. Zabel, "Ingres in America," *The Arts,* vol. 16 (Feb., 1930), p. 378, repr.; Jean Cassou, "Ingres et ses contradictions," *Gazette des beaux-arts,* vol. 11 (Mar., 1934), p. 157, fig. 15; Brinsley Ford, "Ingres' Portrait Drawings of English People at Rome, 1806 – 1820," *Burlington Magazine,* vol. 75 (July, 1939), pp. 8ff., plate III, c; Hans Naef, *Rome vue par Ingres,* Lausanne, 1960, p. 27, fig. 52; Agnes Mongan and Hans Naef, *Ingres Centennial Exhibition, 1867 – 1967, Drawings, Watercolors and Oil Sketches from American Collections,* catalogue, Fogg Art Museum, Harvard University, Cambridge, Mass., no. 37, repr.; *Ingres,* catalogue, Petit Palais, Paris, 1967, p. 130 (portrait of Dorothea Mackie); *Apollo,* vol. 92 (Oct., 1970), p. 128, repr.; *The Irma N. Straus Collection of Old Master Drawings,* sale catalogue, Parke-Bernet Galleries, Inc., New York, Oct. 21, 1970, p. 92, no. 49, repr.; *Apollo,* vol. 93 (Jan., 1971), p. 78, repr.; Christopher White, "The Hammer Collection: Drawings," *Apollo,* vol. 95 (June, 1972), p. 460, fig. 7 p. 461; *Recent Acquisitions and Promised Gifts,* catalogue, National Gallery of Art, Washington, D.C., 1974, pp. 117 – 18, no. 72, repr.

This drawing ranks among the most enchanting made by Ingres of English visitors to Rome in the second decade of the nineteenth century.

As in the Fogg Art Museum's double portrait of *Mrs. Vesey and Her Daughter* (Mongan and Naef, no. 36), Ingres here obviously took great delight in the details of his subject's attire, from the frills of her bonnet to her conspicuously draped Roman-striped scarf. All of these details are drawn with blunt and shaded strokes that heighten the contrast with the extremely delicate stippling of the soft face and long, slender neck — a contrast further emphasized by the dark accents of the profuse curls. In depicting all of these decorations of Mrs. Badham's person, Ingres has drawn a beguiling image of the charming feminine overdress of the early nineteenth century.

In addition to the fascinating appeal of the sitter, the off-center contraposto position she occupies further heightens the visual interest of the composition. The artist placed her so as to provide a view of the Villa Medici and the obelisk at the top of the Spanish Steps in the background.

J. Fred Cain, Jr., has drawn a comparison between this portrait and that of another English lady, Dorothea Mackie. "Although the subjects face in opposite directions, both sheets display startlingly similar compositions. In each drawing the sitter has been positioned, in what appears to be the same chair, at the head of Via Gregoriana. . . . Ingres indicated on the drawing of Dorothea Mackie that he made the work in April of 1816. That the portrait of Dorothea Mackie may have preceded that of Margaret Badham can be supported by the fact that the latter is shown wearing summer attire: an untied bonnet and a light Roman scarf" (*Recent Acquisitions and Promised Gifts,* p. 118).

E. F.

Watercolor, ink, and gouache: 6¼ x 8½″ (15.9 x 21.6 cm.)
Signed lower left: h. Daumier

Collections: Bellino (sold Paris, 1892 [no. 32]); H. P. (sold Paris, 1901 [no. 5]); Paul Gallimard, Paris; Paul Cassirer, Berlin; Jakob Goldschmidt, Berlin and New York; Alfred E. Goldschmidt, Stamford, Conn.

Exhibited: Paris, Louvre, *Exposition de Tableaux, Statues et Objets d'Art, au profit de l'oeuvre des orphelins d'Alsace Lorraine,* 1885 (no. 101), lent by Bellino; Paris, Ecole Nationale des Beaux-Arts, *Exposition des Peintures, Aquarelles, Dessins et Lithographies des Maîtres Français de la Caricature et de la peinture de moeurs au XIXe siècle,* 1888 (no. 392), lent by Bellino; Paris, *Exposition Universelle, Exposition Centennale de l'Art Français,* 1889 (no. 135), lent by Bellino; Paris, Galerie L. and P. Rosenberg, *Exposition de Dessins, Aquarelles et Lithographies de Honoré Daumier,* Apr. 15 – May 6, 1907, lent by Paul Gallimard; St. Petersburg (now Leningrad), *L'Art Français, Exposition Centennale,* Jan. 15 – 28, 1912 (no. 3), lent by Jakob Goldschmidt; Berlin, Galerie Paul Cassirer, *Ein Jahrhundert Französischer Zeichnung,* Dec., 1929 – Jan., 1930 (no. 17); London, Matthiesen Gallery, *A Century of French Drawings,* May 3 – 21, 1938 (no. 39); London, Tate Gallery, Arts Council of Great Britain, *Daumier — Paintings and Drawings,* June 14 – July 30, 1961 (no. 223), lent by Mr. and Mrs. A. E. Goldschmidt.

Hammer Collection exhibitions: see catalogue reference page. First exhibited: VII; not exhibited: XXIII.

Literature: *Catalogue de l'Exposition des Peintures, Aquarelles, Dessins et Lithographies des Maîtres Français de la Caricature et de la peinture de moeurs au XIXe siècle* (preface Paul Mantz), Ecole Nationale des Beaux-Arts, Paris, 1888, p. 85, no. 392; Armand Dayot, *Un Siècle d'art, notes sur la peinture française à l'Exposition Centennale des Beaux-Arts, catalogue complet des oeuvres exposées,* Paris, 1890, p. 150; René Jean, *Catalogue commemoratif: L'Art Français à Saint-Petersbourg, Exposition Centennale,* Paris, 1912, p. 34, no. 3; Erich Klossowski, *Honoré Daumier,* Munich, 1923, p. 102, no. 177b; Eduard Fuchs, *Der Maler Daumier,* Munich, 1927 (and 2d ed., 1930, with suppl.), p. 54, no. 198a, plate 198; K. E. Maison, *Daumier Drawings,* New York and London, 1960, p. 29, no. 134, plate 134; Arts Council of Great Britain, *Catalogue of an Exhibition of Daumier Paintings and Drawings at the Tate Gallery,* London, 1961, p. 67, no. 223; K. E. Maison, *Honoré Daumier, Catalogue Raisonné of the Paintings,*

Watercolours and Drawings, London, 1968, vol. 2, no. 675, plate 259; *Important Impressionist and Modern Paintings and Drawings,* sale catalogue, Parke-Bernet Galleries, Inc., New York, Oct. 28, 1970, p. 24, no. 13, repr.; Christopher White, "The Hammer Collection: Drawings," *Apollo,* vol. 95 (June, 1972), p. 463, fig. 9.

The legal profession was one that allowed Daumier the full vent of his piercing satire. At the same time, his devastating interpretations were cushioned by the artist's overriding comic sense. The Hammer watercolor is unusual in that it is not a risible but, on the contrary, almost a sympathetic interpretation. The subject is an old, buck-toothed pleader, who is shown in an intense, impassioned moment that seems to embody a lifetime of courtroom behavior and to capture the timelessness of ingrained custom. Light illuminates the intent, even earnest, wrinkled face—its expression molded by constant harangue—silhouettes the semaphoric right hand, and falls sensitively on the knuckles of the other, in which the brief is clasped. The head, so intensely realistic that one can almost hear the lawyer's words, is drawn with Daumier's unique lineality. Daumier fully signed the work, which, although relatively small, is a highly finished masterpiece among his legal subjects.

The difficulty of arriving at an exact chronology for many of Daumier's drawings and watercolors has been pointed out repeatedly. K. E. Maison suggested that the time span between "early" and "late" works in Daumier's oeuvre may be as much as twenty-five years. A systematic or consistent evolution in the artist's drawings appears improbable, and his studies and sketches defy definite dating.

Although the Hammer Collection drawing has not been dated by Maison, a reasonable or justifiable chronology for Daumier's large group of drawings of legal subjects may be suggested by their apparent relationship to the thirty-nine lithographs *Les Gens de Justice,* which were printed in *Le Charivari* from 1845 to 1848. Jean Adhémar (*Honoré Daumier,* Paris, 1954) has placed many paintings, drawings, and watercolors of legal subjects in the period of 1843 – 46, although he dates a spirited drawing, *Lawyer,* in the Museum Boymans van Beuningen, Rotterdam, as late as about 1865. Maison places a drawing, *Two Lawyers,* in 1860.

E. F.

89. HONORÉ DAUMIER (1808–1879)
THIRD-CLASS CARRIAGE

Red chalk: 10⁹/₁₆ x 13″ (26.7 x 33 cm.)

Collections: Roger Marx, Paris, until 1914; Alfred Strölin, Paris; Franz Hirschland, Harrison, N.Y.; Myrtil Frank, New York.

Hammer Collection exhibitions: see catalogue reference page. First exhibited: XXXII.

Literature: *Catalogue de la vente Roger Marx,* sale catalogue, Hôtel Drouot, Paris, Apr. 27 – May 2, 1914 (included in either lot 388 or lot 1456); Erich Klossowski, *Honoré Daumier,* Munich, 1923 (2d ed.), no. 258C; K. E. Maison, *Honoré Daumier, Catalogue Raisonné of the Paintings, Watercolours and Drawings,* London, 1968, vol. 2, no. 287, plate 74.

This drawing is close to, though the reverse of, the painting *Third-Class Carriage* (9¼ x 12⅝″ [23.5 x 32 cm.]) in the collection of Sidney L. Bernstein, London (Maison, *Honoré Daumier,* 1968, vol. 1, no. 178, plate 63). The drawing shows the traveler's hands resting on the head of his stick, whereas the painting shows them resting on his knees. The Hammer Collection drawing and the painting are the only studies by Daumier of a solitary traveler. Similar in size, the Hammer Collection drawing could be either the original chalk drawing for the Bernstein painting, which Daumier reversed when he painted it, or a counterproof of a lost preparatory chalk drawing for the painting. The rigidity and evenness of the line, reminiscent of a tracing, point to the latter possibility. A counterproof is made by dampening a chalk drawing and pressing it against a blank piece of paper, thus leaving a reverse image, or counterproof, of the drawing. Maison notes that Daumier made use of the counterproof and inverse-tracing methods (tracing from the back of a drawing held against the light) presumably in order to print from them or to see if he preferred the reversed representation of the composition. It was also a good way to make a record of a given composition. (See K. E. Maison, "Daumier's Preparatory Drawings," *Burlington Magazine,* vol. 96 [Jan., 1954], p. 14, and Maison, *Honoré Daumier,* vol. 2, nos. 75, 76, and 77 for the traveling showmen series, which includes a drawing, a counterproof, and a lithograph.)

It has been pointed out that the intensity of the orange-red chalk in contrast to the electric-blue paper seems to charge the drawing with light and life, as if it were etched by the sun. Only two other red chalk drawings by Daumier are known, the artist preferring to use ink with black chalk for shading or white chalk for heightening.

Daumier started using the railroads as subject matter about 1855, when trains, then reaching speeds of up to 50 m.p.h., had become a popular means of transport (see Robert Rey, *Honoré Daumier,* London, 1966, p. 130). Daumier's sympathetic rendering of the faces of the travelers, weary or bored, impatient or resigned, makes the omnibus and railway studies one of his most beautiful and popular series.

M. E.

90. HONORÉ DAUMIER (1808–1879)
THE VIRGIN HOLDING THE INFANT CHRIST, WITH SAINT ANNE

Pen, brown and black wash, heightened with white chalk: 8¼ x 7¹/₁₆″ (21 x 18 cm.)
Signed lower right near center: h D.

Collections: Mme. Bureau, Paris, by 1878; Paul Bureau, Paris (sold Galerie Georges Petit, Paris, May 20, 1927 [no. 60]).

Exhibited: Paris, Galerie Durand-Ruel, 1878 (no. 123); Paris, Ecole Nationale des Beaux-Arts, 1901 (no. 160).

Hammer Collection exhibitions: see catalogue reference page. First exhibited: XXXIV.

Literature: Arsène Alexandre, *Honoré Daumier, l'homme et l'oeuvre,* Paris, 1888, p. 377; Erich Klossowski, *Honoré Daumier,* Munich, 1923 (2d ed.), no. 304; *Catalogue de la vente P. Bureau,* sale catalogue, Galerie Georges Petit, Paris, 1927, no. 60; Eduard Fuchs, *Der Maler Daumier,* Munich, 1927 (and 2d ed., 1930, with suppl.), p. 56, no. 232a, plate 232; Jean Adhémar, *Honoré Daumier: Drawings and Watercolours,* New York and Basel, 1954, p. 18, no. 3, plate 3; K. E. Maison, *Honoré Daumier, Catalogue Raisonné of the Paintings, Watercolors and Drawings,* London, 1968, vol. 2, no. 691, plate 268.

At the Durand-Ruel exhibition of 1878 in Paris, the only important showing of Daumier's work during his lifetime, this pen and wash drawing was labeled *Two Women and a Child.* Despite its clear representation of the Holy Child, the Virgin, and Saint Anne, the original title has persisted. K. E. Maison's catalogue raisonné (1968) has brought together other works by Daumier treating religious subjects, which until recently have received little critical attention. We know the artist did such pictures between 1849 and 1852, when, encouraged by a commission from the Direction des Beaux-Arts (1849) to paint a Saint Madeleine for a provincial church, he depicted eleven different sacred scenes. Characteristically, the stories that particularly appealed to him involved human frailty: the Prodigal Son, the Magdalene, Christ and the Adulteress, the Drunkenness of Noah, and Adam and Eve in the Garden.

A drawing in the Lessing J. Rosenwald Collection at the National Gallery of Art, Washington, D.C., shows the same use of white chalk (Maison, vol. 2, no. 759), and in the painting *Jesus and His Disciples* in the Rijksmuseum, Amsterdam, deposited with the Stedelijk Museum, Amsterdam (Maison, vol. 1, no. 30), white paint is used to give the effect of a radiant halo in exactly the way the white chalk is used in the Hammer Collection drawing.

The provenance of *The Virgin Holding the Infant Christ, with Saint Anne* is distinguished. It was probably bought from the artist by Mme. Bureau, whose collection of Daumier drawings was the finest assembled in the nineteenth century.

M. E.

91. JEAN-FRANÇOIS MILLET (1814–1875)
PEASANTS RESTING

Pastel: 16¾ x 20¼" (42.5 x 51.4 cm.)
Signed lower right: J. F. Millet

Collections: Boussod, Valadon & Co., Paris; Leonard Gow, Scotland; Barbizon House, London; L. M. Flesh, Piqua, Ohio (sold Sotheby & Co., London, July 9, 1958 [no. 101], p. 21 in cat., repr.); Thomas Agnew & Sons, Ltd., London; Norton Simon, Los Angeles (sold Parke-Bernet Galleries, Inc., New York, May 5, 1971 [no. 23]).

Exhibited: Paris, Ecole Nationale des Beaux-Arts, *Exposition Millet,* 1887 (no. 96).

Hammer Collection exhibitions: see catalogue reference page. First exhibited: IX; not exhibited: X, XXIII.

Literature: *Catalogue descriptif des peintures, aquarelles, pastels, dessins, rehaussés, croquis et eaux-fortes de J. F. Millet, au profit de la souscription pour élever un monument à la memoire du maître* (intro. Paul Mantz), Ecole Nationale des Beaux-Arts, Paris, 1887, no. 96, p. 70; *Barbizon House 1937, an Illustrated Record,* London, 1937, no. 41, repr.; *Highly Important 19th and 20th Century Paintings, Drawings & Sculpture from the Private Collection of Norton Simon,* sale catalogue, Parke-Bernet Galleries, Inc., New York, 1971, p. 38, no. 23, repr. in color.

The subject is a typical one for Millet — peasants resting from their labors. In this case, the man uses a tinderbox to light his pipe, while the woman, seated on the ground, watches him. Etienne Moreau-Nélaton (*Millet, raconté par lui-même,* Paris, 1921, vol. 3) reproduces a variant (fig. 223), which he dates 1866, and two pencil sketches (figs. 341 and 342), one of which (341) is clearly for this pastel. The work is known in French as *Le Briquet,* the tinderbox.

E. F.

92. EUGÈNE BOUDIN (1824–1898)
BEACH SCENE, 1869

Pencil and watercolor: 4⅝ x 9⁷/₁₆″ (11.7 x 24 cm.)
Signed and dated lower right: Boudin 69
Inscribed lower left: Trouville

   Hammer Collection exhibitions: see catalogue reference page. First exhibited: II; not exhibited: XX, XXIII.

Boudin favored watercolor to give transparency to his compositions and to capture the evanescent light effects of the beaches at which he worked. The dark range of figures defining a lateral middleground against a light foreground and background (beach and sky) is typical of him. The horizontal format helps in the diffusion of focus. This scene, like the *Beach at Trouville* (Plate 21), shows fashionable figures taking their ease at a popular resort.

E. F.

93. CAMILLE PISSARRO (1830–1903)
A. (RECTO): PEA HARVEST, c. 1880
B. (VERSO): PORTRAIT OF GEORGES, c. 1880

A. (recto): watercolor and charcoal, 9 x 11″ (22.8 x 27.9 cm.)
Signed lower right: C. P.
B. (verso): pencil and watercolor, 8½ x 11⅝″ (21.6 x 29.5 cm.)

Collections: M. Knoedler & Co., Inc., New York; Mrs. Henry Gerstle, New York.

Hammer Collection exhibitions: see catalogue reference page. First exhibited: II; not exhibited: IX, XX, XXIII.

Literature: *Important Drawings and Watercolors of the 19th and 20th Centuries,* sale catalogue, Parke-Bernet Galleries, Inc., New York, May 15, 1969, no. 40A, repr.

There are several drawings and aquatints by Pissarro of laborers in the pea and bean fields dating from between 1880 and 1896 that are close to the Hammer Collection drawing in style and content: *A Kneeling Woman,* Louvre, of 1878 – 81; *Two Peasant Women in a Field of Beans,* of 1891, and *Two Peasant Women Talking,* of 1896, both in the Bibliothèque Nationale, Paris. The large woman on the right in the Hammer Collection drawing may well have been a study for a painting of 1880 entitled *La Mère Larcheveque* (Ludovic-Rodo Pissarro and Lionello Venturi, *Camille Pissarro, son art – son oeuvre,* Paris, 1939, no. 513). They are identical in expression and attitude; only the clothes are different.

The outlines of the figures in the *Pea Harvest* have been drawn loosely and quickly, but not effortlessly. Pissarro, unlike Degas, whom he greatly admired, was not a profi-

cient draftsman. His method of obtaining mastery over a subject was to draw it again and again and to reuse it in engravings and paintings. In a letter to his son Lucien of July, 1883, he wrote, "For preference choose simple objects . . . figures seated or standing. . . . Lots of drawings, lots and lots, remember Degas."

It was not until 1880, well on in Pissarro's career, that figures appeared at all prominently in his work. Until then, apart from a few portraits of himself and members of his family, his predilection for landscape dominated his paintings and drawings. As there are affinities with Corot in Pissarro's early landscapes, there are connections with Millet in his studies of peasants and workmen. Unlike Millet, however, Pissarro had no moralizing vision of rural life. And if the viewer thought he saw Christian overtones in Pissarro's work, the artist liked to remind him, "It is I who am a Hebrew and it is Millet who is biblical." Pissarro continued to make figure studies such as this one until the mid-1890s, when his subject matter again changed completely and he began what was to be the last series of his life: cityscapes of Rouen, Dieppe, and Paris.

The small, vivid sketch of a child on the verso of the sheet is a portrait of the artist's third child, Georges-Henri, painted when the boy was nine years old. It was probably the first study for the oil of about 1880 *Georges* (Pissarro and Venturi, no. 528) and reveals the artist's capacity for characterization, particularly evident when the sitter was well known to him.

M. E.

94. CAMILLE PISSARRO (1830–1903)
MONTMORENCY ROAD

Pencil: 9¼ x 12⅜″ (23.5 x 31.4 cm.)
Estate stamp lower left: C. P.
Inscribed lower right: Montmorency Enghien
    Collection: Hall Establishment.
    Hammer Collection exhibitions: see catalogue reference page. First exhibited: II; not exhibited: X, XX, XXIII.

After studying in Paris between 1842 and 1847, Pissarro settled there permanently in 1855 at the age of twenty-five. Greatly impressed by the landscape paintings of Corot and Courbet, he soon took a studio in the suburbs and painted at such places as Montmorency, La Roche-Guyon, Pontoise, and Louveciennes. In 1856 he made a first attempt at entering the Salon and was successful with a landscape of Montmorency (Ludovic-Rodo Pissarro and Lionello Venturi, *Camille Pissarro, son art – son oeuvre,* Paris, 1939, no. 10). The Hammer Collection drawing, like much of Pissarro's early work, reveals the influence of Corot in the feathery trees, silvery light, and subtle shading. Corot had advised Pissarro to study values—the prop-

erty of light that renders a color dark or pale. He said, "We don't see in the same way; you see green and I see gray and 'blond' but this is no reason for you not to work at values; for that is the basis of everything." This pencil drawing is a study in black and white of the variations or values of light about which Corot spoke.

The composition is a typical one for Pissarro. The motifs contained here appear again and again in his early paintings and engravings. Such devices as the winding road that leads the eye to a distant view, and the object, in this case the thicket at the right, that anchors the foreground of the composition are favorite ones. The notes on color and atmosphere scattered over this sheet were intended to help the artist remember the scene when he came to paint or engrave it. In technique this drawing is extremely close to one of Pissarro's first etchings, *Field near Asnières* (L. Delteil, *Le Peintre-graveur illustré,* Paris, 1923, vol. 17, no. 3), but there is no known etching or painting after this composition.

M. E.

95. EDOUARD MANET (1832–1883)
A. (RECTO): MAN WEARING A CLOAK, 1852–58
B. (VERSO): MAN WEARING A CAPE, 1852–58

A. (recto): charcoal, 16 x 8¾″ (40.6 x 22.5 cm.)
Signed lower left: ed m
B. (verso): charcoal, 16 x 8¾″ (40.6 x 22.5 cm.)

Collections: Hector Brown, London; Arcade Gallery, London; Francis Cooke, Esq., London; Matthiesen Gallery, London; Hugh Chisholm, New York.

Exhibited: Washington, D.C., National Gallery of Art, *Master Drawings from the Collection of the National Gallery of Art and Promised Gifts,* June, 1978 (no. 97).

Hammer Collection exhibitions: see catalogue reference page. First exhibited: VI; not exhibited: X, XX, XXIII.

Literature: Alain de Leiris, *The Drawings of Edouard Manet,* Berkeley and Los Angeles, 1969, no. 135 (recto), no. 136 (verso), figs. 186, 187; *Impressionist and Modern Drawings, Paintings and Sculpture,* sale catalogue, Christie, Manson & Woods, London, June 30, 1970, no. 1, repr.

These monumental studies of mantled figures were drawn under the influence of Manet's teacher Thomas Couture, who encouraged a broad style of modeling, with large masses of light blocked out by straight and simplified lineal contouring. This approach was based on the bold technique used by the Italian masters of the Renaissance in fresco painting. Manet made many drawings after Renaissance artists in order to master the elements of design and composition. However, in the present drawings the glancing surfaces of light created from the reserved parts of the paper bespeak Manet's early interest in a flattening and generalizing of the form rather than in its strict structural volume.

E. F.

96. EDGAR DEGAS (1834–1917)
LAUNDRESSES CARRYING LINEN

Charcoal: 17 x 23″ (43.2 x 58.4 cm.)

Collections: Atelier Degas (sold Galerie Georges Petit, Paris, fourth sale, July 2 – 4, 1919 [no. 357], repr. in cat.); Monsieur S —.

Hammer Collection exhibitions: see catalogue reference page. First exhibited: V; not exhibited: X, XX, XXIII.

Literature: *Collections de Monsieur S —,* sale catalogue, Hôtel Drouot, Paris, Nov. 13, 1969, no. 20, plate III.

The composition of *Laundresses Carrying Linen* is a masterpiece of balanced tensions, one of the most beautiful designs that Degas ever achieved. The thrust and counter-thrust of the two women, joined in the center by their overlapping burdens, convey an effect of forces in perfect equilibrium. Note also how effectively the figures are placed on the sheet. As Ebria Feinblatt has noted in other catalogues of the Hammer Collection, "The softness of much of this drawing suggests that it may be a reworked counterproof, probably executed rather late in Degas's career. The figure at the right is almost identical to that in the Hammer *Laundress Carrying Linen* [Plate 97], but in reverse." The astute supposition that the drawing may be a counterproof suggests that Degas, having created a design of such brilliant originality, wished to preserve it in more than one example and that he also wanted to see how his composition would look in reverse, which the counterproof would show. However, if there was a counterpart, which this drawing reproduces, it has disappeared.

J. W.

97. EDGAR DEGAS (1834–1917)
LAUNDRESS CARRYING LINEN, c. 1888–92

Pastel: 24 x 36½" (61 x 92.7 cm.)

Collections: Atelier Degas (sold Galerie Georges Petit, Paris, first sale, May 6 – 8, 1918 [no. 170]); Galerie Durand-Ruel, Paris; Henri Fèvre, Monte Carlo; Mrs. Charles R. Henschel, New York; Lilli Wulf, New York; Irving Vogel, Philadelphia; Benjamin D. Gilbert, Stamford, Conn.

Exhibited: Paris, Galerie André Weil, *Degas, Peintre du Mouvement,* June 9 – 30, 1939 (no. 37), repr. p. 22 in cat.

Hammer Collection exhibitions: see catalogue reference page. First exhibited: I; not exhibited: XX, XXIII.

Literature: *Catalogue des tableaux, pastels et dessins par Edgar Degas,* catalogue of first atelier sale, Galerie Georges Petit, Paris, 1918, p. 95, no. 170, repr.; P. A. Lemoisne, *Degas et son oeuvre,* Paris, 1947, vol. 3, p. 559, no. 961, repr.

Degas returned to laundresses as a theme intermittently throughout his career. They offered him not the social overtones one senses in Daumier's use of the same subject, but a habitual and balanced movement. His first use of the pose appearing in this pastel, which also occurs in a charcoal drawing in the Hammer Collection (Plate 96), was in a painting of about 1877 (Lemoisne, no. 410), in which it was paired with a similar figure seen from the front.

This double pose was repeated at least three times about 1902, once with horses in the background (Lemoisne, nos. 1418, 1420, 1420 bis); at the same time, the single figure was also repeated against a background of horses (Lemoisne, no. 1419). There is, finally, an almost identical pastel probably close in date to this one (Lemoisne, no. 960). In this pastel, one sees how Degas could use a figure simultaneously to render volume and to create a flat pattern activating the entire surface of the composition.

E. F.

98. EDGAR DEGAS (1834–1917)
JACQUET, c. 1878

Pastel: 10¼ x 8⅛″ (26 x 20.6 cm.)
Signed center right: Degas

Collections: Professor Hermann Heilbuth, Copenhagen; Bachstitz Galleries; Mrs. Jesse I. Straus, New York.

Hammer Collection exhibitions: see catalogue reference page. First exhibited: VII; not exhibited: XX, XXIII.

Literature: *Art News,* Mar. 7, 1931, p. 5, repr.; Jean Sutherland Boggs, *Portraits by Degas,* Berkeley and Los Angeles, 1962, p. 120, as c. 1878; *The Irma N. Straus Collection of Old Master Drawings,* sale catalogue, Parke-Bernet Galleries, Inc., New York, Oct. 21, 1970, p. 94, no. 50; Christopher White, "The Hammer Collection: Drawings," *Apollo,* vol. 95 (June, 1972), p. 463, fig. 10.

Degas was a master at establishing three-dimensional volume without sacrificing a sense of the surface on which he was working, in this case the bare paper. Of the subject of his drawing Jean Sutherland Boggs notes laconically, "Know nothing of him." At the time the work entered the Straus Collection, however, *Art News* identified Jacquet as Degas's framemaker. Ms. Boggs dates the portrait at about 1878.

E. F.

99. EDGAR DEGAS (1834–1917)
THEATER BOX, 1885

Pastel: 22 x 16½″ (56 x 41 cm.)

Collections: Atelier Degas (sold Galerie Georges Petit, Paris, second sale, Dec. 11 – 13, 1918 [no. 162]); Mlle. Jeanne Fèvre (the artist's niece), Nice (sold Galerie Charpentier, Paris, June 12, 1934 [no. 94]); Mrs. Kay, Berkshire; Reid and Léfèvre Galleries, Glasgow and London; James Archdale, London.

Hammer Collection exhibitions: see catalogue reference page. First exhibited: XI; not exhibited: XXIII.

Literature: *Catalogue des tableaux, pastels et dessins par Edgar Degas,* catalogue of second sale, Galerie Georges Petit, Paris, 1918, p. 87, no. 162, repr.; *Catalogue des tableaux, aquarelles, pastels, dessins, estampes et monotypes par Edgar Degas,* sale catalogue, Galerie Charpentier, Paris, 1934, no. 94, plate VII, repr.; P. A. Lemoisne, *Degas et son oeuvre,* Paris, 1947, vol. 3, p. 480, no. 829, repr.; Lillian Browse, *Degas Dancers,* New York, 1949, p. 347, no. 110, plate 110 and frontis., repr. in color; *Impressionist and Modern Drawings, Paintings and Sculpture,* sale catalogue, Christie, Manson & Woods, London, July 6, 1971, p. 49, no. 48, repr. in color.

Degas began fairly early in his career to use foreground audience figures as foils for more or less distant figures on stage. These foreground figures seldom functioned as traditional *repoussoirs,* but were used as silhouettes to establish the plane of the composition. Inevitably, the middleground was dropped away and the background brought forward by the use of intense colors, obvious paint or pastel application, and complex compositional arrangements, as in this picture. Lemoisne dates this and a related composition (Lemoisne, no. 828) to 1885 although he assigns other similar compositions to 1878 – 80 (Lemoisne, nos. 476, 577). In 1879 – 80 Mary Cassatt, who was close to Degas at the time, executed several similar pictures with the auditorium rather than the stage as a background (see Adelyn Dohme Breeskin, *Mary Cassatt,* Washington, D.C., 1970, nos. 61, 62, 64, 73). There is a related Degas lithograph.

E. F.

100. PIERRE-AUGUSTE RENOIR (1841–1919)
GIRLHOOD

Pencil: 13⅜ x 11⅜″ (34 x 28.9 cm.)
Signed lower right: Renoir

Collection: Mrs. William Wilson, New York.

Exhibited: Paris, Galerie Charpentier, *L'Exposition au Profit des Pauvres de la Fédération Nationale des Fils des Morts pour La France,* 1949 (no. 282 bis).

Hammer Collection exhibitions: see catalogue reference page. First exhibited: II; not exhibited: X, XX, XXIII.

Literature: *L'Exposition au Profit des Pauvres de la Fédération Nationale des Fils des Morts pour La France,* catalogue, Galerie Charpentier, Paris, 1949, no. 282 bis.

This drawing served Renoir as the model for his drypoint *On the Beach at Berneval* (1892?), which Loys Delteil also used as the frontispiece for his catalogue of the artist's prints in volume sixteen of *Le Peintre-graveur illustré.* According to Delteil, there are three states of the print. It is the last state, after the beveling of the plate, that is reproduced in his catalogue.

The placement of the two girls is reversed in the print: they face toward the middle right. Figures of bathers have been added in the background.

When the third state of the print was sold at the G. Pochet sale in 1902, it was entitled *Aux Bains de Mer.*

E. F.

101. PAUL CÉZANNE (1839–1906)
A. (RECTO): STUDY OF THE "ECORCHÉ"
B. (VERSO): PAGE OF STUDIES: THE FATHER OF THE ARTIST

A. (recto): pencil, 6¼ x 7″ (15.9 x 17.8 cm.)

B. (verso): pencil, 10¾ x 7″ (27.3 x 17.8 cm.)

Collections: Sir Michael Sadler, Oxford; Leicester Galleries, London; Edward Le Bas, Brighton (sold Christie, Manson & Woods, Geneva, Switz., Nov. 6, 1969 [no. 154]).

Exhibited: London, Leicester Galleries, *Selection of Works from the Collection of Sir Michael Sadler,* Jan., 1944 (no. 9); London, Royal Academy of Arts, *From a Painter's Collection* (Edward Le Bas Coll.), Mar. 19 – Apr. 28, 1963 (no. 233).

Hammer Collection exhibitions: see catalogue reference page. First exhibited: II; not exhibited: X, XX, XXIII.

Literature: *Impressionist and Modern Drawings, Paintings and Sculpture,* sale catalogue, Christie, Manson & Woods, Geneva, Switz., 1969, no. 154, repr.; Adrien Chappuis, *The Drawings of Paul Cézanne; a Catalogue Raisonné by A. C.,* London, 1973, vol. 1, p. 249, no. 1087 bis (recto), p. 180, no. 662 bis (verso), vol. 2, nos. 1087 bis, 662 bis, repr.

Cézanne did a series of drawings (see Lionello Venturi, *Cézanne, son art – son oeuvre,* Paris, 1936, nos. 1317, 1453, 1586) and a painting (Venturi, no. 709) of a plaster cast. The cast was mistakenly attributed to Michelangelo in the nineteenth century and is called the *Ecorché.* The recto of this sheet is one of the drawings of this series.

The verso is still more interesting. In 1866 the young Cézanne decided to paint a portrait of his father, now in the National Gallery of Art, Washington, D.C. They were never on affectionate terms. The father disapproved of Paul's profession; and after the elder Cézanne died, his only son paid him an ironic compliment: "My father was a man of genius; he left me twenty-five thousand francs." In the drawing it is perhaps significant that the face is left blank.

E. F. and J.W.

102. PAUL CÉZANNE (1839–1906)
MONT STE. VICTOIRE, c. 1895

Watercolor: 6⁷/₁₆ x 10⅝″ (16.4 x 27 cm.)

Collections: Leicester Galleries, London; Edward Le Bas, Brighton (sold Christie, Manson & Woods, Geneva, Switz., Nov. 6, 1969 [no. 155]).

Exhibited: London, Royal Academy of Arts, and Edinburgh, Scottish National Gallery of Modern Art, *From a Painter's Collection* (Edward Le Bas Coll.), 1968 (no. 231).

Hammer Collection exhibitions: see catalogue reference page. First exhibited: II; not exhibited: XX, XXIII.

Literature: *Impressionist and Modern Drawings, Paintings and Sculpture,* sale catalogue, Christie, Manson & Woods, Geneva, Switz., 1969, no. 155, repr.

The characteristic profile of one of Cézanne's favorite motifs is not easily discernible in this watercolor, which emphasizes the horizontal line of trees in the middleground. Cézanne has used wash tones close to that of the paper to increase the all-over effect of the composition, an effect further enhanced by the dispersion of his accustomed broken contour.

On the verso of the sheet there is a pencil and watercolor sketch of a bedpost (7¼ x 10¼″ [18.4 x 26 cm.]).

E. F.

103. ODILON REDON (1840–1916)
VASE OF FLOWERS

Pastel: 15¾ x 12⅜″ (40 x 31.4 cm.)
Signed lower right: Odilon Redon

Collection: Ruth V. McVitty, Princeton, N.J.

Hammer Collection exhibitions: see catalogue reference page. First exhibited: II; not exhibited: XX, XXIII.

Literature: François Daulte, "Hammer en dix chefs-d'oeuvre," *Connaissance des arts,* Sept., 1970, p. 80, repr.; Christopher White, "The Hammer Collection: Drawings," *Apollo,* vol. 95 (June, 1972), p. 463.

Redon's flower pieces are at once dreamlike in their disembodiment and surreal in their clarity. With no background other than the intermediate tonality of the bare paper, the colors in this work stand out with unusual sharpness from each other and from the ground. Although the ground tends to be so infinitely atmospheric as to overwhelm the vase of flowers, the composition is wholly convincing. One hardly notices, for example, that the poppies or anemones are an impossible blue.

E. F.

104. PAUL GAUGUIN (1848–1903)
LANDSCAPE AT PONT-AVEN, c. 1888

Brush and ink: 12½ x 17¼″ (31.8 x 43.8 cm.)
Inscription lower right: 181
  Collection: Hall Establishment.
  Hammer Collection exhibitions: see catalogue reference page. First exhibited: II; not exhibited: XX, XXIII.

This outstanding drawing was executed during Gauguin's stay in Pont-Aven, an artists' colony on the coast of Brittany, "a land which had been little touched by Roman civilization."

According to André Schoeller, the number that appears in pencil at the lower right is an indication that the drawing was once in the possession of Emile Schuffenecker (1851 – 1934), an artist who was Gauguin's close friend for a time at Pont-Aven. He owned several of Gauguin's drawings, which were numbered in this fashion.

It was in his Brittany period, from 1886 to 1890, that Gauguin developed his style of Synthetism, in which he sought to extract from the forces of nature what they inherently communicated to him rather than to represent the forms of nature's outward appearance. To accomplish this end he eschewed the traditional "sciences" of painting in favor of his own subjective response and interpretation. This led to a flattening out of forms, an overriding of optical perspective, and a use of non-naturalistic color. During these years he was also influenced by the Art Nouveau movement, as is evident from the use of the curvilinear border that divides the central motif of the drawing from the one at the extreme left and gives the composition an intriguing inner ornamental frame.

It seems possible to ascribe the drawing to the period of about 1888, based on the similarity of the house and trees with those in the painting of the same name, dated 1888, now in a private collection.

E. F.

105. PAUL GAUGUIN (1848–1903)
A. (LEFT): PARAU NO TE VARAU INO
B. (RIGHT): TAHITIAN LEGEND

Pen, brush and india ink; two drawings on one sheet, side by side: 6 x 3½" (15.2 x 8.9 cm.)

Collections: Galerie Druet, Paris; Sotheby & Co., London (sold Apr. 16, 1970 [no. 49]).

Hammer Collection exhibitions: see catalogue reference page. First exhibited: IV; not exhibited: X, XX, XXIII.

Literature: *Impressionist and Modern Drawings and Watercolors,* sale catalogue, Sotheby & Co., London, 1970, p. 39, no. 49, repr.

The drawing on the left is the reverse of the woodcut *Eve* by Gauguin (Marcel Guérin, *L'Oeuvre gravé de Gauguin,* Paris, 1927, vol. 2, no. 57, repr.), and it is not improbable that it is a preliminary model for the print. The woodcut was printed in an edition of thirty. Guérin states that in the original manuscript of *Noa Noa,* Gauguin attached a photograph of a drawing representing the same figures that appear in the woodcut, but in reversed positions. The Hammer sketch may have been the one described. *Parau No Te Varau Ino* is a study for the painting of the same title, meaning "words of the devil," in the collection of the National Gallery of Art, Washington, D.C. (Georges Wildenstein, *Gauguin,* Paris, 1964, no. 458).

The support of the two Hammer studies is heavy wove J. Whatman paper. Their borders indicate that they were undoubtedly intended for prints.

E. F.

106. PAUL GAUGUIN (1848–1903)
TAHITIAN HEADS

Page from the Tahiti sketchbook
Pencil: 6¾ x 4″ (17.2 x 10.2 cm.)

Collections: Dr. Warner Muensterberger, New York; Robert Q. Lewis, Los Angeles.

Hammer Collection exhibitions: see catalogue reference page. First exhibited: II; not exhibited: X, XX, XXIII.

Literature: Bernard Dorival, ed., *Paul Gauguin, carnet de Tahiti,* Paris, 1954, no. 85; Ronald Pickvance, *Drawings of Gauguin,* London, 1970, pp. 10, 19, references to the Tahiti sketchbook; Daniel Wildenstein and Raymond Cogniat, *Paul Gauguin,* Milan, 1972, p. 88.

Gauguin's first sojourn in Tahiti lasted from April, 1891, until 1893. This sheet of studies of Maori women's heads comes from the artist's Tahiti sketchbook of this period; it originally contained 130 pages, but is now broken up. Stylistically, the Hammer drawing is remarkably close to the strong, simple, almost schematic rendering of the Gauguin self-portrait (Tahiti sketchbook, p. 5 verso) and of the head of a boy (Pickvance, *Drawings,* plate 57). The studies in the sketchbook, mostly figures and faces in silhouette, were Gauguin's way of familiarizing himself with a race of people new to him. He planned to use the sketches in his paintings when he went home. In a letter of 1892 to his wife, he wrote, "I believe that when I return, I will have in my pocket enough original material to enable me to paint for a long time." Bernard Dorival notes that nowhere in Gauguin's painting do we find faces of such intense ethnic characterization as those in this sketchbook.

M. E.

107. PAUL GAUGUIN (1848–1903)
PAGES FROM BRETON SKETCHBOOK
NO. 16, 1884–88

Page size: 6¼ x 4¼" (16.5 x 10.8 cm.)

Collections: Henri Mahaut, purchased in Cherbourg before World War I; priv. coll., U.S.A.

Hammer Collection exhibitions: see catalogue reference page. First exhibited: II; not exhibited: X, XX, XXIII.

Literature: Henri Mahaut, "Notes synthétiques par Gauguin," *Vers et prose,* July – Sept., 1910; John Rewald, *Gauguin,* Paris, 1938, boy with a pail repr. p. 8, boy with a goose repr. p. 9; *Paul Gauguin: A Sketchbook,* facsimile ed., texts by Raymond Cogniat and John Rewald, New York (Hammer Galleries), 1962; Merete Bodelsen, *Gauguin's Ceramics,* Copenhagen, 1964, pp. 23, 38, 42, 46, 50, 87, 170, 190 – 91, 199 – 200 (Appendix A), 204, figs. 12, 13, 17, 23 – 25, 28 – 30, 40a, 110, 143 a – h, 145; Georges Boudaille, *Gauguin,* London, 1964, p. 54; Georges Wildenstein, *Gauguin,* Paris, 1964, references to the Breton sketchbook in nos. 136, 138, 139, 144, 193, 196, 201, 203, 206, 215, 216, 245, 250, 255, 256, 258, 264, 269, 282, 305; Ronald Pickvance, *Drawings of Gauguin,* London, 1970, pp. 9, 11; Mark Roskill, *Van Gogh, Gauguin, and French Painting of the 1880s: A Catalogue Raisonné of Key Works,* Ann Arbor, Mich., 1970, pp. 121, 127, 140 – 41; Daniel Wildenstein and Raymond Cogniat, *Paul Gauguin,* Milan, 1972, p. 84, illustrating eight pages of the sketchbook; Christopher White, "The Hammer Collection: Drawings," *Apollo,* vol. 95 (June, 1972), pp. 460, 463; Pierre Leprohon, *Paul Gauguin,* Paris, 1975, pp. 348 – 49.

With the exception of a sketchbook filled for the most part with portraits, now dispersed, and an unpublished sketchbook of 1870 – 80 in the Nationalmuseum, Stockholm, Gauguin's Breton sketchbook of 1884 – 88, in the Hammer Collection, contains the earliest of Gauguin's drawings. Using the figure and animal studies etched on Gauguin's ceramics as evidence, Merete Bodelsen has recently shown that all the Breton sketches in the notebook date from 1886 (the year of Gauguin's first stay in Brittany). Many of them were used, however, in paintings of 1888 (see Cogniat and Rewald, *Paul Gauguin).* During the four years the sketchbook spans, Gauguin also went to Copenhagen, Arles, and Martinique, but only a few sketches remain from those visits and none from the artist's sojourn in the Caribbean. Like most sketches, these drawings give an opportunity to see the artist's initial reaction to and first rendering of a subject. They are intimate, quick, and random impressions showing the origin of ideas that would later be developed in paintings and ceramics.

Brittany was the earliest source of Gauguin's artistic inspiration. In a letter of February, 1888, from Pont-Aven, to his old friend Emile Schuffenecker, he wrote: "I love Brittany, I find a primitive savagery here. When my wooden shoes echo on this stony ground, I hear the sound of dull, muffled power, and it is that for which I search in my painting." As one of the first expressions of Gauguin's artistic genius, the importance of this sketchbook can hardly be exaggerated.

M. E.

107 – A. *Breton Peasant*
Pencil and crayon
Page 18 of sketchbook

This could be a study for *The Washerwomen at Pont-Aven* of 1886 (Wildenstein, *Gauguin,* no. 196). (See also Bodelsen, *Gauguin's Ceramics,* 1964, p. 199.)

107 – B. *Little Breton Boy*
Pencil and crayon
Page 20 of sketchbook

This sketch and 107 – F were part of a series of studies of the little Breton boy who appears in paintings of 1888 (Wildenstein, *Gauguin,* nos. 255 and 256) and in *The Little Breton with a Goose,* painted in 1889 (Wildenstein, no. 367).

107 – C. *The Bridge at Pont-Aven (?)*
Pencil and crayon
Page 26 of sketchbook

107 – D. *Two Breton Women*
Pencil and crayon
Page 29 of sketchbook

107 – E. *Head and Hand of a Monkey*
Pencil and crayon
Page 36 of sketchbook

107 – F. *Little Breton Boy with a Pail*
Pencil and crayon
Page 39 of sketchbook

See 107 – B.

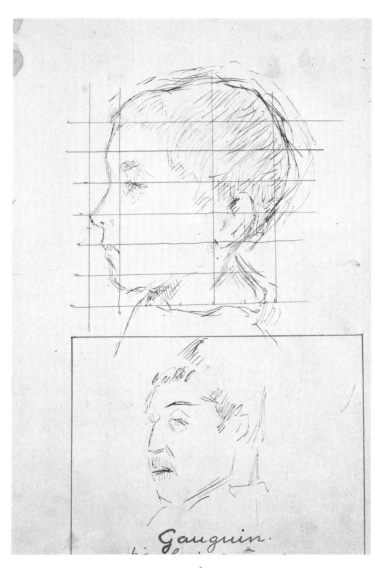

107 – G. *Landscape*
Ink
Page 81 of sketchbook

107 – H. *Head of a Child and Self-Portrait*
Ink
Page 86 of sketchbook

The head of the child has been squared for transfer to a canvas or larger paper. There is no known painting of this subject. The self-portrait is inscribed: gauguin par lui-même.

107 – I. *Head of a Child and Head of a Man* (probably a self-portrait)
Ink
Page 87 of sketchbook

107 – J. *Profile of a Woman and Profile of a Boy*
Ink
Page 95 of sketchbook

108. VINCENT VAN GOGH (1853–1890)
THE MAGROT HOUSE, CUESMES, c. 1879–80

Charcoal: 9 x 11¾" (22.9 x 29.8 cm.)
Signed lower left: V. G.

Collections: Charles Decrucq, Cuesmes; M. G. Delsaut, Cuesmes; Samuel Delsaut, Cuesmes (sold Christie, Manson & Woods, London, Apr. 14, 1970 [no. 41]).

Exhibited: Paris, Musée Jacquemart-André, *Vincent van Gogh,* Feb. – Mar., 1960 (no. 199), p. 56 in cat.; Cuesmes (Borinage), Belgium, *Vincent van Gogh,* Oct. 1 – 20, 1960 (no. 9).

Hammer Collection exhibitions: see catalogue reference page. First exhibited: IV; not exhibited: X, XX, XXIII.

Literature: *The Letters of Vincent van Gogh to His Brother, 1872 – 1886,* London, Boston, and New York, 1927, vol. 1, Letter 136, pp. 220 – 25; *Museum Journaal* (Stedelijk Museum, Amsterdam), ser. 5, no. 4, Oct., 1959, pp. 80 – 81, repr.; M. E. Tralbaut, *Le Mal Aimé,* Lausanne, 1969, p. 63; J. B. de la Faille, *The Works of Vincent van Gogh: His Paintings and Drawings,* Amsterdam, London, and New York, 1970, p. 609, no. 32, repr.; *Impressionist and Modern Drawings, Paintings and Sculpture,* sale catalogue, Christie, Manson & Woods, London, 1970, p. 34, no. 41, repr.

When Van Gogh's desire to be an evangelist was frustrated by the refusal of the Committee of Evangelization to give him a permanent post, he decided to stay in the Borinage, the mining district of Belgium, at his own expense. He lived during the summer of 1880 in the home of a miner, Charles Decrucq, at Cuesmes. The drawings of the Magrot House and the Zandemennik House were once owned by Decrucq and were probably given to him as part payment for lodgings.

Van Gogh was always desperately poor. He shared a small room with two of the Decrucq offspring, and, as he wrote his brother Theo, there were two beds, "one for the children and one for me." He continued in the same letter of September 24, 1880, "I do not want to upset the people in their household arrangement, and they have told me already that I could by no means have the other room in the house, even if I paid more, for the woman needs it for her washing, which in the house of a miner has to be done almost every day. So I would just like to take a little miner's house that costs about fr. 9 a month."

In spite of his discomfort he was hard at work. His letter to Theo was encouraging: "Though every day difficulties come up, and new ones will present themselves, I cannot tell you how happy I am to have taken up drawing again. I have been thinking of it for a long time, but I have always considered the thing impossible and beyond my reach. But now though I feel my weakness and my painful dependency in many things, I have recovered my mental balance, and day by day my energy increases. . . . The thing for me is to learn to draw well, to be master of my pencil or my crayon or my brush; this gained, I will make good things anywhere, and the Borinage is just as picturesque as old Venice, as Arabia, as Brittany, Normandy, Picardy or Brie."

J. W.

Charcoal: 9 x 11¾" (22.9 x 29.8 cm.)
Signed lower right: V. G.

Collections: Charles Decrucq, Cuesmes; M. G. Delsaut, Cuesmes; Samuel Delsaut, Cuesmes (sold Christie, Manson & Woods, London, Apr. 14, 1970 [no. 42]).

Exhibited: Paris, Musée Jacquemart-André, *Vincent van Gogh,* Feb. – Mar., 1960 (no. 200), p. 56 in cat.; Cuesmes (Borinage), Belgium, *Vincent van Gogh,* Oct. 1 – 20, 1960 (no. 8).

Hammer Collection exhibitions: see catalogue reference page. First exhibited: IV; not exhibited: X, XX, XXIII.

Literature: *The Letters of Vincent van Gogh to His Brother, 1872 – 1886,* London, Boston, and New York, 1927, vol. 1, Letter 137, pp. 225 – 28; *Museum Journaal* (Stedelijk Museum, Amsterdam), ser. 5, no. 4, Oct., 1959, pp. 80 – 81, repr.; M. E. Tralbaut, *Le Mal Aimé,* Lausanne, 1969, p. 63; J. B. de la Faille, *The Works of Vincent van Gogh: His Paintings and Drawings,* Amsterdam, London, and New York, 1970, p. 609, no. 33, repr.; *Impressionist and Modern Drawings, Paintings and Sculpture,* sale catalogue, Christie, Manson & Woods, London, 1970, p. 34, no. 42, repr.

The drawings Van Gogh made in 1879 – 80 of the humble houses of the Borinage mining district of Belgium (see also Plate 108) show the type of dwelling he hoped to rent or at least to board in. It is startling to realize that these little sheets of paper, rapidly drawn on in charcoal by the young painter and handed down from one generation to another in the Decrucq family, brought at auction, ninety years later, enough to buy all the houses in the village of Cuesmes. Yet Vincent was unable to find even nine francs a month to live in one of them!

When nothing came of his plan to find a suitable place in Cuesmes, he left the Borinage and went to Brussels. In a letter to his brother Theo of October 15, 1880, he explained, "I thought it better to change my domicile for the present. And that for more than one reason. In the first place it was urgently necessary, because the little room where I was lodged, and which you saw last year, was so narrow, and the light there was so bad, that it was very inconvenient to draw. . . . It is true that nevertheless I drew there 'Les Exercices au Fusain' and 'Les Modèles d'après la bosse de Bargue,' either in the little room or outside in the garden, but now that I am as far as the portraits after Holbein in the third part of the 'Cours de Dessin,' it became impossible."

While Vincent was staying with Decrucq, Theo had written him asking his opinion of Charles Meryon. He replied, "I know his etchings a little. Would you like to see a curious thing? Put one of his correct and masterly drawings side by side with some print by Viollet-le-Duc, or some other architect. Then you will see Meryon in his full strength, because the other etching will serve to set off his work or to form a contrast. Well, what do you see then? This Meryon, even when he draws bricks, or granite, or iron bars, or a railing of a bridge, puts in his etchings something of the human soul, moved by I do not know what inward sorrow." Van Gogh's sketches of miners' houses are likewise endowed with a soul, and there is also something in their stark bleakness that suggests Van Gogh's own inward sorrow.

J. W.

110. VINCENT VAN GOGH (1853–1890)
OLD MAN CARRYING A BUCKET, 1882

Pencil, heightened with gray and black wash: 18¾ x 8¼″ (47.6 x 21 cm.)

Collections: Ubbergen, the Netherlands; H. C. Stork, Vienna; W. P. Maclaine Pont, Bilthoven; Mrs. A. W. Maclaine Pont-Stork, Zwolle; J. Donna, The Hague.

Hammer Collection exhibitions: see catalogue reference page. First exhibited: VI; not exhibited: X, XX, XXIII.

Literature: *The Letters of Vincent van Gogh to His Brother, 1872 – 1886,* London, Boston, and New York, 1927, vol. 2, Letter 251, pp. 40 – 46; J. B. de la Faille, *L'Oeuvre de Vincent van Gogh, catalogue raisonné,* Paris and Brussels, 1928, vol. 3, p. 33, no. 964, vol. 4, plate XXXV; Dr. Walther Vanbeselaere, *De Hollandsche Periode (1880 – 1885) in Het Werk van Vincent van Gogh,* Antwerp, 1937, pp. 97, 170, 208, 409; *The Complete Letters of Vincent van Gogh* (ed. Mrs. J. van Gogh-Bonger, preface Vincent W. van Gogh), London, 1958, vol. 1, Letter 251, pp. 504 – 8; J. B. de la Faille, *The Works of Vincent van Gogh: His Paintings and Drawings,* Amsterdam, London, and New York, 1970, pp. 360, 648, no. F964, repr.; *Impressionist and Modern Watercolours, Drawings and Bronzes,* sale catalogue, Sotheby & Co., London, July 2, 1970, p. 35, no. 20, repr., and on cat. cover.

In 1881 Van Gogh fell in love with a cousin, a widow. His passions were always violent, and, when she rejected him, he was in despair. It seemed no longer possible to remain with his parents at the vicarage at Etten, and he moved to The Hague. There, in January, 1882, he met a poor, neglected prostitute, the mother of two children and again pregnant. He took her to live with him, partly from pity and partly from loneliness. The ménage was a disaster, and the painter passed through two of the most unhappy years of his life.

Art, however, was a solace, and he drew constantly. In an undated letter to his brother Theo (no. 251), he wrote, "You have received my letter in which I wrote you how during my work the idea developed itself of making figures *from the people for the people.* How it seemed to me that it would be a good thing, not commercially but of charity and duty if a few persons combined to do it. . . . I have said to myself that the duty that comes first to me is to try my very best on the drawings. So that since my last letter on the subject I have now made a few new ones. In the first place, a Sower. . . . Then one of those little old fellows in short jacket and high old top-hat, which one meets sometimes in the dunes. He carries home a basketful of peat. . . . These fellows are all in action and that fact especially must be kept in mind in the choice of subjects, I think. You know yourself how beautiful are the numerous figures in rest which are made so very, very often. They are made more often than figures in action. It is always very tempting to draw a figure at rest; to express action is very difficult, and the former effect is in many people's eyes more 'pleasant' than anything else. But this 'pleasant' aspect may not take from the truth, and the truth is that there is more drudgery than rest in life. So you see my idea about it all is especially this, that I for my part try to work for the truth."

J. W.

111. VINCENT VAN GOGH (1853–1890)
MAN POLISHING A BOOT, 1882

Black chalk, pencil, heightened with white and gray wash: 19 x 10½" (48.3 x 26.7 cm.)

Collections: H. P. Bremmer, The Hague; Heirs of H. P. Bremmer, The Hague; E. J. van Wisselingh & Co., Amsterdam; Mrs. J. G. ter Kuile-ter Kuile, Switzerland (sold Christie, Manson & Woods [New York], Houston, Apr. 6, 1970 [no. 61]).

Exhibited: Amsterdam, E. J. van Wisselingh & Co., *Vincent van Gogh, Aquarelles et Dessins de l'Epoque 1881 – 1885, provenant de collections particulières néerlandaises,* Apr. 19 – May 18, 1961 (no. 19), repr. in cat.

Hammer Collection exhibitions: see catalogue reference page. First exhibited: IV; not exhibited: X, XXIII.

Literature: *The Letters of Vincent van Gogh to His Brother, 1872 – 1886,* London, Boston, and New York, 1927, vol. 1, Letter 235, pp. 530 – 33, Letter 236, pp. 533 – 35, Letter 238, pp. 539 – 43; J. B. de la Faille, *L'Oeuvre de Vincent van Gogh, catalogue raisonné,* Paris and Brussels, 1928, vol. 3, no. 969, vol. 4, plate XXXVII; Dr. Walther Vanbeselaere, *Der Hollandsche Periode (1880 – 1885) in Het Werk van Vincent van Gogh,* Antwerp, 1937, pp. 88, 91, 170, 190, 409; *Letters to an Artist: From Vincent van Gogh to Anton Ridder van Rappard, 1881 – 1885* (trans. Rela van Messel, intro. Walter Pach), New York, 1937, p. 48; *The Complete Letters of Vincent van Gogh* (ed. Mrs. J. van Gogh-Bonger, preface Vincent W. van Gogh), London, 1958, vol. 1, Letter 235, pp. 463 – 66, Letter 236, pp. 466 – 67, Letter 238, pp. 470 – 73; J. B. de la Faille, *The Works of Vincent van Gogh: His Paintings and Drawings,* Amsterdam, London, and New York, 1970, pp. 361, 648, no. F969, repr. p. 361; *Impressionist, American and Modern Paintings and Watercolors,* sale catalogue, Christie, Manson & Woods (New York), Houston, 1970, no. 61, p. 46, repr.

Van Gogh wrote his brother Theo in an undated letter (no. 235), "Once again being engrossed in drawing, I sometimes think there is nothing so delightful as drawing. . . . I was interrupted in writing this letter by the arrival of my model. And I worked with him until dark. He wears a large old overcoat, which gives him a curious broad figure."

Perhaps the reference in this letter was to the model in the Hammer drawing, who patiently brushes a worn-out boot. Van Gogh's studies of old men are drawn with compassion and understanding. As he remarked to his brother (Letter no. 239), "I believe that if one wants to make figures one must have a warm feeling, what *Punch* calls in his Christmas pictures: Goodwill to all — that means one must have real love for one's fellow creatures. I for one hope to try my best to be in such a mood as much as possible."

Love for one's fellow creatures imbues every line of the Hammer drawing. There is an innate dignity in the old veteran who humbly cleans a shoe. He was probably once a soldier, since in his lapel there is a medal in the form of a Maltese cross. He is now apparently poor and earns a pittance posing for a still poorer artist, an artist who must cadge a little money from his brother to whom he wrote (Letter no. 238), "Drawing much after the model . . . is rather expensive, but it fills my portfolios in proportion as it empties my purse."

Vincent's portfolios were bursting with drawings. In another letter (no. 239), he told Theo, "When I happened to arrange my drawings this morning, namely the studies after the model made since your last visit (not counting the older studies or those I drew in my sketchbook), I counted about a hundred. . . . I do not know whether all painters, even those who look down on my work to such a degree that they think it below themselves to take the least notice of it, work more than I do. Neither do I know if they know a better way than to work from the model, though, in my opinion they do it too little; as I wrote you before I cannot understand why they do not take more models."

It was this painstaking apprenticeship that gave Van Gogh mastery and made him one of the greatest draftsmen of the nineteenth century. He was indefatigable, and the long hours with pencil and pad, with brush and canvas, exhausted his frail health and caused his ultimate collapse.

J. W.

112. VINCENT VAN GOGH (1853–1890)
THE WEAVER, c. 1884

Watercolor: 12½ x 17¾" (31.8 x 45.1 cm.)

Collections: Galerie Druet, Paris; Georges Gérard, Limoges; Galerie Druet, Paris; Mrs. G. Guibert, Limoges; Heirs of Mrs. Guibert (sold Palais Galliéra, Paris, June 20, 1968 [no. 225]); Drs. Fritz and Peter Nathan, Zurich; Dr. Armand Hammer, Los Angeles; Musée du Louvre, gift of Dr. Armand Hammer, 1977.

Hammer Collection exhibitions: see catalogue reference page. First exhibited: III; not exhibited: X, XXIII, XXIV – XXXVIII.

Literature: *The Letters of Vincent van Gogh to His Brother, 1872 – 1886,* London, Boston, and New York, 1927, vol. 2, Letter 351, pp. 376 – 78; J. B. de la Faille, *L'Oeuvre de Vincent van Gogh, catalogue raisonné,* Paris and Brussels, 1928, vol. 3, no. 1108, vol. 4, plate LXX; Dr. Walther Vanbeselaere, *De Hollandsche Periode (1880 – 1885) in Het Werk van Vincent van Gogh,* Antwerp, 1937, pp. 257, 317, 410; *The Complete Letters of Vincent van Gogh* (ed. Mrs. J. van Gogh-Bonger, preface Vincent W. van Gogh), London, 1958, vol. 2, Letter 351, p. 249; J. B. de la Faille, *The Works of Vincent van Gogh: His Paintings and Drawings,* Amsterdam, London, and New York, 1970, no. F1108, pp. 406, 652, repr.

In 1883 Van Gogh's father was transferred from his church at Etten to a village called Nuenen in the Brabant. In December of that year, the painter rejoined his family. He was in a melancholy state of mind and a most difficult guest. His parents were wonderfully gentle and understanding, although his father wrote his son Theo that Vincent never "feels any self-reproach, only soreness against others. . . . We must be very careful with him, for he seems to be in a fit of contrariness."

A fellow artist and one of Van Gogh's few friends, Anton Rappard, came to stay at the rectory. It was a very happy visit. In 1890, after Vincent's suicide, Rappard wrote a touching letter to the artist's mother: "How often do I think of the studies of the weavers which he made in Nuenen; with what intensity of feeling did he depict their lives, what deep melancholy pervaded them, however clumsy the execution of his work may have been then" (quoted in *The Letters,* vol. 1, p. XLII).

During Van Gogh's sojourn with his parents, an unlucky romance caused the villagers to shun him. He expressed his reaction to this ostracism in a letter to Theo (no. 351) of 1884: "I for my part prefer to be with people who do *not even know* the world, for instance, peasants, the weavers, etc., rather than with those from the more civilized world. That's lucky for me. So for instance since I am here, I have been absorbed in the weavers. Do you know many drawings of weavers? I know only very few. I began by making three watercolors of them. Those people are very hard to draw, because in those small rooms one cannot take enough distance to draw the loom. I think that is the reason why so many drawings become failures. But I have found a room here where two looms are, and where it can be done. Rappard has painted in Drenthe a study of it, which I like very much. It is very gloomy — they are but poor creatures, those weavers."

The Hammer watercolor is perhaps one of the three paintings Van Gogh mentions. Ebria Feinblatt has pointed out in previous catalogues of the Hammer Collection that, "The tonality and application of the watercolor in this work show what Vincent owed to Anton Mauve and the Hague School." And she mentions a closely related painting (de la Faille, no. 162).

J. W.

Pen and ink: 10¹/₁₆ x 6⅜″ (26 x 16.5 cm.)
Signed lower left: Seurat

Collections: Emile Seurat, Paris; Alexandre Natanson, Paris; Galerie Bolette Natanson, Paris; Jean-Charles Moreux, Paris; Mme. Jean-Charles Moreux, Paris; Wildenstein & Co., Inc., New York; Norton Simon, Los Angeles (sold Parke-Bernet Galleries, Inc., New York, May 5, 1971 [no. 46]).

Exhibited: Paris, La Revue Blanche, *Seurat,* Mar. 19 – Apr. 5, 1900 (hors cat.); Paris, Galerie Bernheim-Jeune, *Rétrospective Georges Seurat,* Dec. 14, 1908 – Jan. 9, 1909 (no. 197); Paris, Galerie Bernheim-Jeune, *Les Dessins de Seurat,* Nov. 29 – Dec. 24, 1926 (no. 114); London, Galerie Syrie Maugham, Bolette Natanson, *Seurat,* May 21 – June 7, 1935; Paris, Galerie Paul Rosenberg, *Georges Seurat,* Feb. 3 – 29, 1936 (no. 130), suppl.; Paris, Galerie Bolette Natanson, "Les Cadres," *Peintres de la Revue Blanche,* 1936 (no. 50), suppl.; Paris, Musée Jacquemart-André, *Seurat,* Nov. – Dec., 1957 (no. 55); Washington, D.C., National Gallery of Art, *Recent Acquisitions and Promised Gifts,* June 2 – Sept. 1, 1974 (no. 73).

Hammer Collection exhibitions: see catalogue reference page. First exhibited: IX; not exhibited: X, XX, XXIII.

Literature: Paul Adam, "Les Impressionistes à l'Exposition des Indépendants," *La Vie moderne,* Apr. 15, 1888, p. 229, repr.; André Lhote, *Georges Seurat,* Rome, 1922, p. II, repr.; Florent Fels, "Les Dessins de Georges Seurat," *L'Amour de l'art,* no. 1, Jan., 1927, p. 43, repr.; Gustave Kahn, *Les Dessins de Georges Seurat,* Paris, 1928, vol. 2, plate 98; Waldemar George, *Seurat et le divisionnisme,* Paris, 1928, p. 15, repr.; Thadée Natanson, "Sur une exposition des peintres de la Revue Blanche," *Arts et métiers graphiques,* no. 54, Aug. 15, 1936, p. 16, repr.; Robert J. Goldwater, "Some Aspects of the Development of Seurat's Style," *Art Bulletin,* vol. 23, no. 2 (June, 1941), pp. 117 – 30, fig. 4; Henri Dorra and John Rewald, *Seurat, l'oeuvre peint, biographie et catalogue critique,* Paris, 1959, p. 222, no. 179a, repr.; C. M. de Hauke, *Seurat et son oeuvre,* Paris, 1961, vol. 2, p. 254, no. 665, repr.; *Highly Important 19th and 20th Century Paintings, Drawings & Sculpture from the Private Collection of Norton Simon,* sale catalogue, Parke-Bernet Galleries, Inc., New York, 1971, p. 88, no. 46, repr.; A. Chastel, *Seurat,* Milan, 1972, pp. 105 – 6, no. D47, repr.; L. Hautecoeur, *Georges Seurat,* Milan, 1972, pp. 42 – 43, plate 2; *Recent Acquisitions and Promised Gifts,* catalogue, National Gallery of Art, Washington, D.C., 1974, pp. 118 – 19, no. 73, repr.

Despite the brevity of Seurat's career, a prodigious body of drawings celebrates his genius as a draftsman. Curiously, among the several hundred drawings assigned to his hand, only two were intended by the artist to be graphically reproduced. The present drawing derives from one of Seurat's major canvases, *The Models,* and was used for an illustration in the April 15, 1888, issue of *La Vie moderne* (see Dorra and Rewald, *Seurat*). In the following year, Seurat designed a cover for *L'Homme à femme,* a novel by the Polish writer Victor Joze. Both of these studies were in pen and ink, a technique Seurat rarely used for his drawings. Another atypical feature common to both is the undisguised use of outline.

J. F. C.

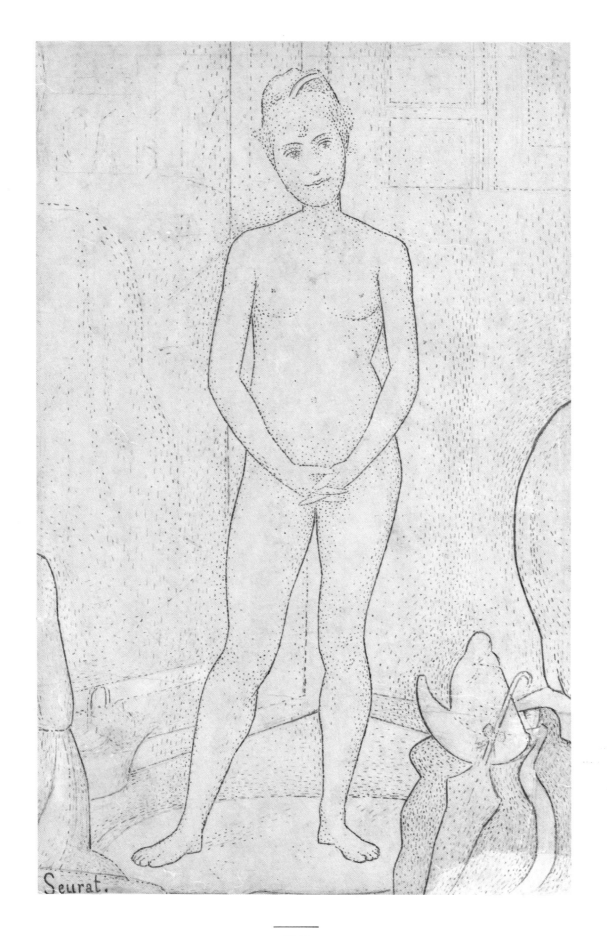

114. HENRI-EDMOND CROSS (1856–1910)
CYPRESSES, 1896

Gouache: 9½ x 13¼" (24.1 x 33.7 cm.)

Collections: William J. Holliday, Indianapolis; Modern Art Foundation, Geneva, Ill.; Pierre Matisse Gallery, New York.

Exhibited: Cleveland Museum of Art, *Tenth Exhibition of Watercolors and Pastels,* Jan. 10 – Feb. 12, 1933.

Hammer Collection exhibitions: see catalogue reference page. First exhibited: II; not exhibited: X, XX, XXIII.

Literature: Isabelle Compin, *H. E. Cross,* Paris, 1964, repr. pp. 146, 338.

Isabelle Compin *(H. E. Cross)* reproduces an oil, 25½ x 36¼", of the identical image, entitled *Nocturne,* painted in 1896. She also reproduces a four-color lithograph, 11⅛ x 16⅛", published by Ambroise Vollard in 1896 as *La Promenade.* Compin believes she may have found the source of the subject in a play of 1892 by Edouard Dujardin. In the play, *Le Chevalier Passé,* Act III, Scene I, night is falling, and the four Floramyes, preparing to leave the isle of Antonia, lament: "Adieu, les rives où nous avons vécu! Adieu, les charmants bords où nos songes longtemps ne sont plus!"

E. F.

115. PIERRE BONNARD (1867–1947)
GIRL PUTTING ON HER STOCKING

Pencil: 13 x 9½″ (33 x 24.1 cm.)
Signed lower right: Bonnard

Collection: Norton Simon, Los Angeles (sold Parke-Bernet Galleries, Inc., New York, May 5, 1971).

Hammer Collection exhibitions: see catalogue reference page. First exhibited: II; not exhibited: X, XX, XXIII.

Bonnard was fascinated by the ancient theme of the bath, a subject he first painted in 1895, and which he continued to depict until 1938. Like most artists, he wished to paint from the nude. The privacy of the bathroom and the boudoir made a relaxed and natural setting in which to portray this figure. Bonnard met his wife, Maria Boursin, known as Marthe de Méligny, in 1894. Apparently, she had a passion for bathing, and it is she who figures in most of Bonnard's paintings and drawings of this subject. As early as 1886, Bonnard had been impressed by the nude studies he had seen exhibited by Degas at the Durand-Ruel gallery. Though he did not treat the nude figure in the same sculptural way as Degas, Bonnard did study Degas's treatment of the effect of atmosphere and light on the naked body. The figure in the Hammer drawing is placed in an empty space, with the surroundings indicated by the curtain and the outline of the bathtub. This simplification of the background occurs in Bonnard's work after 1900 (see Denys Sutton, *Catalogue of the Bonnard Exhibition,* Royal Academy of Arts, winter exhibition, London, 1966). The Hammer drawing has been executed in a quick, repetitious hatching technique characteristic of Bonnard's drawings of the 1920s. A pencil study, called *La Toilette,* of nearly the same size (13 x 8⅜″) was probably made at the same time as the present drawing. It is handled in the same way, though with a heavier pencil, and the pose differs slightly (see André Fermigier, *Bonnard,* London, 1970, repr. p. 33, as Bonnard about 1920, whereabouts unknown). Four paintings of a young woman after the bath are related to the Hammer sketch and all date from between 1924 and 1927 (see Jean and Henry Dauberville, *Bonnard — catalogue raisonné,* Paris, 1973, nos. 1277, 1278, 1283, and 1388).

M. E.

116. PABLO PICASSO (1881–1973)
A. (RECTO): FEMALE NUDE, c. 1906
B. (VERSO): YOUNG MAN, c. 1906

A. (recto): pencil, 6½ x 4″ (16.5 x 10.2 cm.)
Signed upper right: Picasso
B. (verso): pen and ink, 6½ x 4″ (16.5 x 10.2 cm.)
Signed lower right: Picasso

Collections: Saidenberg Gallery, New York; George Axelrod, New York.

Hammer Collection exhibitions: see catalogue reference page. First exhibited: IV; not exhibited: X, XX, XXIII.

Literature: *Impressionist and Modern Drawings and Watercolors,* sale catalogue, Sotheby & Co., London, Apr. 16, 1970, pp. 118 – 19, no. 92, repr.

This double-sided drawing belongs to the period of 1906, and the female nude incorporates many of the "classicizing" features Picasso adopted at that time. His work became simplified, more abstract and sculptural. The face with its far-off gaze is delineated with a minimum of lines and accords with various other "masklike" portraits of the period. But the relatively broad, squat body, treated in summary fashion, has some of the quality of the late Iberian sculpture that was another factor in Picasso's earlier work.

That the verso sketch is so close to a caricature suggests that it may have been drawn of a friend, perhaps at a cafe. An earlier sketch of roughly the same type, in which the man leans his arm on a cafe table, was formerly in the Galerie Rosengart in Lucerne, Switzerland.

C. M.

117. ANDREW WYETH (b. 1917)
BRANDYWINE VALLEY, 1940

Watercolor: 21 x 29″ (53.3 x 73.7 cm.)
Signed and dated lower right: Andrew Wyeth 1940
   Hammer Collection exhibitions: see catalogue reference page. First exhibited: III; not exhibited: X, XX, XXIII.

In contrast to the structure and design of Wyeth's more recent works in drybrush, which have much in common with his tempera paintings, the freely flowing washes of this early example take every advantage of the inherent qualities of transparent watercolor.

The lessons found in the work of such artists as Winslow Homer and the rigorous tutelage of his father helped Wyeth to develop absolute mastery of the medium at an early age. This watercolor, painted more than thirty years ago at the John Chad house in Chadds Ford, Pa., reveals his deep involvement with the Brandywine Valley, where he still lives and works without regard for contemporary trends in the United States or abroad.

L. C.

*118. HONORÉ DAUMIER (1808–1879)
DON QUIXOTE AND SANCHO PANZA, 1866–68

Oil on canvas: 15¾ x 13″ (40.2 x 33 cm.)
Signed lower left: h.D.

Collections: Ferdinand Roybet, Paris; Paul Selignon, Paris, gift of Roybet, 1880; Maurice Goldblatt, New York, 1924; Julius Weitzner, New York, 1927; Dr. Franz H. Hirschland, Harrison, N.Y., 1927 – 78; Eugene Thaw, New York, 1978; Artemis (David Carritt, London), 1980.

Exhibited: New York, Museum of Modern Art, *Corot-Daumier,* Oct. 16 – Nov. 23, 1930 (no. 52), repr. in cat.; Chicago, Art Institute, *A Century of Progress, Exhibition of Paintings and Sculpture,* June 1 – Nov. 1, 1934 (no. 181 in cat.); Springfield, Mass., Museum of Fine Arts, extended loan prior to 1940.

Literature: Eduard Fuchs, *Der Maler Daumier,* Munich, 1927, no. 303, repr.; K. E. Maison, *Honoré Daumier, Catalogue Raisonné of the Paintings, Watercolors and Drawings,* Greenwich, Conn., 1967 – 68, vol. 1, p. 164, no. 1-206, repr. pl. 162; L. Barzini and G. Mandel, *L'opera Pittorica Completa di Daumier,* Milan, 1971, p. 111, no. 265, repr.

To the Romantic artists of the nineteenth century, Don Quixote, knight-errant in fantasy, was not a ridiculous mock hero but a tragic, real one, who like themselves was misunderstood and rejected by society. He thus became the sympathetic subject of painters from Delacroix to Daubigny and Corot. For the literary critics of the 1860s the tall, emaciated Knight of La Mancha on his skeletal steed, ready to make every sacrifice for his dreams and illusions, and his rotund squire, Sancho Panza, for whom human comforts were aspirations enough, embodied the antithesis of idealism and realism. Daumier's paintings and drawings of Don Quixote and Sancho Panza incorporate both these interpretations, but are not restricted to them, for Daumier's images are so free of limiting narrative and descriptive detail that they permit interpretations as boundless as those of Cervantes's novel.

The Hammer *Don Quixote and Sancho Panza* is the most classic of Daumier's paintings of the Knight and his squire riding into the canvas from the darkness of the mountain night to the brilliance of the new day. The rocky landscape in the foreground opens upon a broad, sunny valley toward which the protagonists descend. The bulky figure of Sancho, giving weight to the foreground, sleeps astride the donkey, incapable of understanding or sharing in his master's lofty dedication. Don Quixote, high in the saddle like a St. George with lance raised, calmly looks out over the valley, ready for whatever unknown perils it may hold, whatever noble deeds it may require of him—a heroic figure in a heroic landscape.

No other literary figures so fascinated Daumier as did Don Quixote and Sancho Panza. He painted and drew them a few times separately but much more frequently as a pair, sharing one of their recorded adventures or resting or riding together. Maison reproduces thirty-five drawings (vol. II, pls. 139 – 51), without dating, and twenty-nine paintings (vol. I, pls. 146 – 69 and pl. 198), which he dates between 1847 – 48 and 1870 – 73, twenty of them between 1864 – 65 and 1868 – 70. Among the latter are the five typologically related paintings of Don Quixote and Sancho Panza in the mountains. Two, dated by Maison 1864 – 65, are earlier than the Hammer version; two are a bit later. In the earlier paintings — Burrell Collection, Glasgow City Corporation; and heirs of Herman Schulman, Israel—the mountain that occupies three-quarters of the painting is a barrier to be overcome, and what lies beyond is unknown. In the Glasgow painting, the contrasts are somewhat intensified by the darkening of the pigments over the century; the earthly Sancho is almost absorbed into the landscape, while the ethereal Knight, high above his squire, ascends as in a Baroque apotheosis to the glory of the sunrise. Maison's proposed date for the Hammer picture is 1866 – 68. The two slightly later pictures, one in the collection of Dr. Oskar Reinhart, Winterthur, the other in the Nationalgalerie, Berlin, are both unfinished; in the latter, only Don Quixote and his horse are by Daumier's hand. They are quite different from the Hammer picture in conception, being concerned with the movement of forms and colors.

Daumier's lack of technical knowledge of painting often resulted in repeated restoration, beginning in the artist's lifetime. The excellent condition of the Hammer painting is thus quite exceptional.

Since the first owner of the picture, Ferdinand Roybet, is recorded as having given the painting to Paul Selignon in 1880, the year following Daumier's death, he must have acquired it directly from the artist or from his estate.

K. D.

*Recent acquisition

I. NEW YORK CITY, New York, Hammer Galleries, 40th Anniversary Loan Exhibition, 1928 – 1968, November 7 – December 7, 1968

II. MEMPHIS, Tennessee, Brooks Memorial Art Gallery, October 2 – December 30, 1969

III. WASHINGTON, D.C., Smithsonian Institution, The Armand Hammer Collection, March 20 – May 17, 1970

IV. KANSAS CITY, Missouri, William Rockhill Nelson Gallery of Art, June 30 – August 2, 1970

V. NEW ORLEANS, Louisiana, Isaac Delgado Museum, August 15 – September 20, 1970

VI. COLUMBUS, Ohio, Columbus Gallery of Fine Arts, October 9 – November 1, 1970

VII. LITTLE ROCK, Arkansas, Arkansas Art Center, November 21, 1970 – January 12, 1971

VIII. SAN FRANCISCO, California, California Palace of the Legion of Honor, February 11 – March 14, 1971

IX. OKLAHOMA CITY, Oklahoma, Oklahoma Art Center, June 15 – July 11, 1971

X. SAN DIEGO, California, Fine Arts Gallery of San Diego, July 23 – September 5, 1971

XI. LOS ANGELES, California, Los Angeles County Museum of Art, December 21, 1971 – February 27, 1972

XII. LONDON, England, Royal Academy of Arts, June 24 – July 24, 1972

XIII. DUBLIN, Ireland, The National Gallery of Ireland, August 9 – October 1, 1972

XIV. LENINGRAD, U.S.S.R., The Hermitage Museum, October 23 – December 2, 1972

XV. MOSCOW, U.S.S.R., The Pushkin Museum, December 8, 1972 – February 11, 1973

XVI. KIEV, U.S.S.R., State Museum of Fine Art of the Ukraine Soviet Socialist Republic, March 6 – March 31, 1973

XVII. MINSK, U.S.S.R., State Fine Art Museum, April 27 – May 26, 1973

XVIII. RIGA, U.S.S.R., State Museum of Foreign Fine Arts, June 8 – July 8, 1973

XIX. ODESSA, U.S.S.R., Fine Arts Museum, July 25 – August 25, 1973

XX. LOS ANGELES, California, Los Angeles County Museum of Art, June 22 – December 9, 1974

XXI. CARACAS, Venezuela, Fine Arts Museum, January 9 – February 2, 1975

XXII. LIMA, Peru, Italian Art Museum, February 15 – March 9, 1975

XXIII. LOS ANGELES, California, Los Angeles County Museum of Art, 10th Anniversary Show, April 9 – June 29, 1975

XXIV. TOKYO, Japan, Ikebukuro-Seibu Museum, September 20 – November 3, 1975

XXV. KYOTO, Japan, Municipal Museum of Art, November 10 – December 20, 1975

XXVI. FUKUOKA, Japan, Fukuoka Prefectural Culture Center Museum, January 4 – February 1, 1976

XXVII. NAGOYA, Japan, Aichi Prefectural Museum, February 11 – March 20, 1976

XXVIII. NASHVILLE, Tennessee, Tennessee Fine Arts Center at Cheekwood, June 12 – August 15, 1976

XXIX. NASHVILLE, Tennessee, Cheekwood Extension, August 15 – September 12, 1976

XXX. MEXICO CITY, Mexico, Palace of Fine Arts, February 21 – March 15, 1977

XXXI. PARIS, France, Jacquemart-André Museum, March 29 – July 25, 1977

XXXII. PARIS, France, Louvre Museum, Department of Drawings, March 29 – May 25, 1977

XXXIII. PARIS, France, Louvre Museum, Department of Drawings, and Jacquemart-André Museum, March 29 – July 25, 1977

XXXIV. MALIBU, California, The J. Paul Getty Museum, September 13 – October 29, 1977

XXXV. ATLANTA, Georgia, The High Museum of Art, November 20, 1977 – January 15, 1978

XXXVI. DENVER, Colorado, The Denver Art Museum, February 18 – April 9, 1978

XXXVII. BUFFALO, New York, Albright-Knox Art Gallery, April 20 – June 19, 1978

XXXVIII. EDINBURGH, Scotland, The National Gallery of Scotland and The Royal Scottish Academy, August 17 – September 17, 1978

XXXIX. OSLO, Norway, National Gallery of Norway, December 8, 1978 – January 28, 1979

XL. STOCKHOLM, Sweden, Nationalmuseum, February 20 – April 22, 1979

XLI. HOUSTON, Texas, The Museum of Fine Arts, October 26, 1979 – January 20, 1980

XLII. MOULTRIE, Georgia, The Moultrie-Colquitt County Library, February 1 – February 14, 1980

XLIII. LOS ANGELES, California, Los Angeles County Museum of Art, April 24 – August 31, 1980

XLIV. WASHINGTON, D.C., Corcoran Gallery of Art, October 4 – November 30, 1980

INDEX OF ARTISTS

INDEX OF ARTISTS